God's Tapestry

God's Tapestry

Understanding and Celebrating Differences

William M. Kondrath

Herndon, Virginia
www.alban.org

The Alban Institute
2121 Cooperative Way, Suite 100
Herndon, VA 20171

Scripture quotations, unless otherwise noted, are from the New Revised Standard Version of the Bible, © 1989, Division of Christian Education of the National Council of Churches of Christ in the United States of America, and are used by permission.

Scripture quotations noted as KJV are from The Holy Bible, King James Version.

Cover design by Tobias Becker, BirdBox Designs.

Cover art by Jan Smiley.

Library of Congress Cataloging-in-Publication Data

Kondrath, William M.
God's tapestry : understanding and celebrating differences / William M. Kondrath.
p. cm.
Includes bibliographical references.
ISBN 978-1-56699-363-0
1. Church and minorities. 2. Social integration—Religious aspects—Christianity. 3. Marginality, Social—Religious aspects—Christianity. 4. Multiculturalism—Religious aspects—Christianity. 5. Religious pluralism—Christianity. I. Title.

BV639.M56K66 2008
250—dc22

2008004477

12 11 10 09 08 VG 1 2 3 4 5

To George Lewis Blackman

Priest, scholar, mentor, host of Fezziwig's Ball;
he celebrates differences while remaining steadfastly authentic.

Contents

Foreword

Together on the Journey of Transformation

God's Tapestry is, like all good Christian literature, an invitation—an invitation not only to show up for the journey but to become fully engaged in the work.

Coming, as I did, from a South Africa convulsed by the agony of apartheid to what I thought to be the land of the free, I was surprised by how vexed the issues of race, gender, and power were in the United States in the 1980s. I was struck by the anger and bitterness that seemed to attend every conversation about race and power and the absence of genuine dialogue across the divides; each group seemed to hunker down in its monocultural silo and talk about those on the outside, those on the other side: People divided by a common language.

More than a quarter of a century later the issues are no less vexed. There is, it seems, no safe place to have genuine dialogue about matters of race, gender, and power. This situation prevails despite a desire for something different. In communities of faith throughout the United States there is a genuine yearning to become a living vision of God's peaceable kingdom. The road to God's dream for humanity is marked by missteps. It so quickly becomes a road to hell, paved with good intentions and faulty understanding, and, too often, with hurtful words and wrong actions. Time and again people of good will bump into the limits of their understanding in encounters across the divides. Time and again people of good will turn away from one another in frustration, with no ken of the stumbling block that upset their bright hopes and their optimistic plans. "We don't get what we don't get and yet we so deeply long to get it and hold the door open for genuine community and for deep relationship." Those on the privileged side of the divide throw up their hands: "We tried, but there is no satisfying you people. . . ." Those on the other side of the divide cannot afford to throw up their hands; they study the powerful and stay in relationship muttering their resentment.

But the God who created the rainbow created us, too. God created us in all our diverse expressions of humanity. We yearn to recruit the richness of that diversity to form flourishing communities in which God's people can thrive. We endure impoverished relationships while praying for a road map to the abundance promised by a life in Christ.

This book is not a "how-to. . ." manual. It is a guidebook, a companion for the journey. We spend lifetimes negotiating difference. Sometimes we are more skilled in the encounters than others. Sometimes we get it right in spite of ourselves. Sometimes we get it wrong in spite of our own best selves. Often we cannot pinpoint what we did right in order to repeat it, or what we did wrong in order to avoid making the same mistake. We can read our encounters in light of this book and elucidate where things fell apart. We can interrogate our behavior in light of this book and see some of our graces and some of our shortcomings.

Like the sacred texts of the Christian tradition, this book abounds with stories. These narrative illustrations make the book all the more accessible because we are able to see ourselves at various points along the way.

During my undergraduate years at Howard University, my half-joking, self-description had been, "I am black and oppressed." My experience at Episcopal Divinity School, and the language of target and non-target introduced in the VISIONS curriculum, helped me to more fully explore my social location. In this country, in that I am black, female, and a foreigner I am target; in that I am an English speaker, married, educated, a clergyperson and a home owner I am non-target. Black and oppressed is not, after all, a complete description of me or my power. The language of target and non-target helped me to see that I am not always and only located on one side of the power divide. That awareness has allowed me to recruit the insights garnered from powerlessness to understand and serve the powerless where I am powerful—and to recognize and interrogate my own assumptions and behaviors where I am, or feel myself to be, relatively powerless.

There are people for whom some of this material may not be new. Perhaps the contours of this book have been described in antiracism work in educational institutions, businesses, or congregations of which the reader has been a member. The stories and exercises invite the reader to renew their acquaintance information and to come along for the roadtest of this way of working.

The journey of transformation is not an abstract journey, a journey of the imagination. The journey of transformation has real lived consequences for each of us and all of us. In a country that is becoming increasingly pluralistic in terms of race, gender identity, expressed sexual orientation, language, and economic status we will be repeatedly confronted with boundaries of difference. We who are Christian are called to be transformed into the likeness of Christ—called to be those who offer to others the experience of God's shalom. Often we travel blind—with a consummate lack of the self-awareness that discipleship requires.

We have some tools for the journey. This book offers us a common language to negotiate difference. So we are on a journey towards being united by a common language, united by the language of faith.

The Rev. Mpho A. Tutu
The Tutu Institute for Prayer and Pilgrimage
Alexandria, Virginia

Preface

Tapestry is an obvious image for the inclusiveness of God's reign. Who can take issue with the beauty and the rich textures of a finely woven tapestry? It seems such a fit analogy for God's dream of an inclusive people of faith. And what is a tapestry before the weaving commences and the strands are skillfully interlaced? Individual fibers of various textures, some coarse, some smooth. Threads of many hues and tones, bright and drab; colors that complement and clash. And yet the weaver sees in these differences the possibility of a new creation—a coming together in which the uniqueness of each strand is valued precisely for what it brings out in its neighbors. A tapestry depends on differences, thrives on multiplicity. Were all the fibers the same, the lavish beauty would be lost. Historically, tapestries were more than art. In the days before central heating, tapestries had functional value. They were hung on the walls of castles and houses to serve as insulation. They improved the odds of survival in a hostile atmosphere.

I believe congregations are tapestries in the making—potentially beautiful communities that provide warmth and protection in difficult environments. And the warmth is not simply for the sake of each separate congregation—but for the rest of the world, too. These tapestries are about the identity and purpose of God's people as a worldwide community.

People of faith are the threads, fibers, cords, yarn, filaments, twine, and cables that God weaves together into magnificent mutually protective and supportive art that reflects to the world the wonder of the Artist and provides warmth and security in what might otherwise be a cold and dangerous environment. The problem is we often only see ourselves and others as separate threads. Lacking the Artist's view, we are unable to imagine the woven whole we are part of or could become part of. Sometimes, as individual strands, we judge ourselves to be better than the other fibers—more useful, more beautiful, more significant. Or perhaps we see ourselves to be poorer, duller, weaker by comparison. Sometimes the problem is temporal perspective—we cannot imagine the whole because it does not yet exist. Other times the problem is attitude—we see differences and judge them as more than or less than.

For more than thirty years I have worked with congregations and agencies on issues of differences, power, imagination, and community. I frequently begin these training or consulting sessions with an icebreaker activity in which participants (not-yet-woven threads, if you will) are invited to see themselves as either kite strings or clotheslines—claiming their unique gifts and noticing the special contributions of others who are different.

"Kite Strings and Clotheslines" is a wonderful exercise for bringing about greater multicultural awareness within a congregation.[1] The facilitator begins by asking people gathered in the middle of a room: "How do you see yourself? Are you more like a kite string or a clothesline? Kite strings to one end of the room. Clotheslines to the other end of the room." Then the participants are invited to notice, without speaking, which people are on their end of the room and which are on the other end. After a moment, the facilitator asks the individuals in the kite-string group to tell why the see themselves that way. The kite-string folks usually give several different reasons, such as "I like to move about freely," "I'd rather play than work," or "I'm a child at heart." Sometimes the reason is simply "I don't know why I am with these folks, but I know I am not a clothesline." In a similar way, the folks on the clothesline end are given the opportunity to explain why they see themselves as clotheslines.

As I continue the exercise, I offer another pair of images (for example, picture window or screened porch, automobile or carousel), out of a total set of five pairs. Individuals again choose between the pairs, move to one side of the room or the other, then discuss their decision. Several things become clear very quickly. The ways individuals describe their decisions to belong to a particular group vary considerably. Reasons given by people in the same group even seem to contradict one another. A few people volunteer that they could see themselves equally in either group—as automobiles or as carousels. At times these ambivalent people begin to feel loyal or defensive once *their* group members begin to speak. A few people find themselves grouped together with the same people repeatedly, though rarely for every decision. Sometimes I hear explanations that assume one group is *better than* another group as distinct from being *different from* the other group. Competition easily arises.

On occasion an individual or two will balk at the necessity of making forced choices and will withdraw inward. But most often people are surprised about how emotionally engaged they become in justifying why they are where they are—why they have chosen one side. Some folks clearly identify their very being with one image. "I *am* a kite string." Or, "No doubt about it, I've been a clothesline all my life. Everyone is always hanging their stuff on me and depending on me to hold it all up." Others see their choices as having less to do with personal identity and more to do with current life choices that could change given different circumstances. A few people change sides when they hear the other side's explanation or when someone on *their* side gives a rationale they find repugnant.

When the group is given many opportunities to choose between different images, nuances appear. Folks might say, "Had you asked me a year ago, I would have been in the other group." Or, "I was with John, Judy, and Jane for all the previous questions, but now I find myself in a different place from them." Inevitably someone says, "I have always been on the opposite side from Kate. Now we are together. I never expected that to happen."

Kite Strings in Real Life

The icebreaker activity is meant to allow people to notice the dynamic of difference and the ways we construct and reinforce our identities individually and as communities. It also shows how we sometimes construct the "other" as not only *different from* but also as *less than*. It seems to me that church folks are forever playing a real-life version of "Kite Strings and Clotheslines." Unfortunately, the game is often not very friendly.

Sometimes in real life we divide ourselves along lines of race or cultural identity. Sometimes we distinguish ourselves by how we read the Bible—literally or critically. At other times our understandings of human sexuality and marriage separate us. Or our theologies of baptism or Eucharist divide us. Expanding beyond the Christian community, religious people differ in how we name God, how we understand salvation, how or whether we pray, and on what days our faith communities gather. No matter what separates us, we share the tendency to see our differences as the basis for judging "others" as less than us or as unworthy of our love or our consideration. The tendency to judge others can make it hard to deeply understand our differences and to imagine that they might actually make our human or church communities richer and more vibrant. At other times, individuals and congregations attempt to celebrate differences without really understanding the differences in any significant way.

Power and Privilege

One of the most important and most difficult areas to consider in understanding differences is the role of power. Power and privilege often influence how we see other people and ourselves as more than or less than. Therefore, we need to talk concretely about the mutually reinforcing dance of oppression and internalized oppression that prevent us from valuing and celebrating our differences and similarities. One way to do this is by looking at the groups we belong to in order to notice where we have privilege and power and where we are members of a group that is historically or statistically in a one-down position. We need to take seriously the ways we can be unwitting agents in our own oppression. Problematic patterns of behavior apply to race, gender, age, health, religious affiliation, and other dimensions of difference. Because we all have varying degrees of privilege and power or lack it in different dimensions of our lives, we can use what we know of racial privilege or gender discrimination, for example, to learn how similar dynamics operate in other areas where we may be powerful or disadvantaged socially. Looking at the role power plays in relation to the roles of lay people and clergy is essential for understanding what often prevents communities of faith from being transformed. The open and ongoing discussion of how power is exercised by laity and clergy can in itself begin the transformation of congregations into more multicultural communities. (Throughout this book I distinguish between *diversity,* which I understand to mean primarily the demographic and statistical fact of differences, and *multiculturalism,* by which I mean the process of seeing, understanding, and appreciating differences so that they transform individuals and communities.) Conversely, the avoidance of discussing power—who has it and how they use it—can effectively block congregational change.

Reflecting on Change and Resistance

While I have studied and taught organization change for years, I am increasingly convinced that the best way to introduce corporate change in a congregation is to begin by helping individuals reflect on change and resistance to change within themselves. When we begin with what we know of change on an individual level, such as getting or losing a job, having a child, getting married or divorced, experiencing the death of a loved one, or moving to a new town, we can learn a great deal about the rhythms of change and equilibrium. When I work with leadership groups and even larger congregational gatherings, I begin by asking people to recall and reflect on a personal experience of significant change so that we can become more aware of the resources we possess that enable us to cope with and sometimes even become excited about transformation. From what we know as individuals, we can more easily understand the resources for and obstacles to change on a community level. Because change affects different members of an organization to greater or lesser degrees, I discuss the impact and rate of change. I trace the movement from equilibrium through disequilibrium to a new equilibrium and I focus on the emotional impact of change. At the heart of my faith, I understand the church as a community coping with twenty centuries of change and therefore as a wellspring of resources for transformation.

And I have my own experience of change and my own personal social location. I am a white, heterosexual, partnered man with children. I am wealthy relative to the vast majority of people in the world. As I have become less scared of differences and less frightened about what I do not know, I have realized how lush life can be when I notice, deeply understand, and appreciate the multitude of differences I encounter in people. The more I have been able to embrace people of different cultures, political views, religious persuasions, and lifestyles, the more I have become at home with myself and the more I have understood how inclusive God's love is.

This may seem backwards to you. You may think that conversion to openness happens because you believe in a God who loves all people and invites everyone into that way of loving. If that is how you frame it, I have no quarrel with you. We are likely allies in the struggle to live without oppressing others with attitudes of superiority and behaviors that belittle or dismiss others. However, I will take a different approach in this book. My experience has been that the personal conversion to embracing others and the communal transformation to becoming a radically welcoming and multicultural community begin with paying attention to our feelings and our behaviors as much as they do with working out our ways of thinking or our theologies. As long as I can remember, I have espoused a theology of God's all-inclusive love while at the same time struggling to deal the realities of sin, abuse, violence, and evil.[2] The difficulties I continued to encounter in my own life and in leading communities of faith were not, however, so much on the rational level. My difficulties were more in how to make my beliefs operational or incarnate, how to walk the talk. And what I have discovered is that, for me and for many others, the stumbling block has been in my emotional or affective being—in my heart, not in my head.

Often the leaders of congregations and agencies, both lay and clergy, try to bring about transformation by relying only on cognitive analysis and changing the ways people think. Such an approach leaves out the *affective* dimension of transformation. Seminaries and business schools emphasize intellectual skills of leadership. Few of us have been trained or have learned on our own to become affectively competent. Furthermore, gender and cultural factors contribute to learning affective skills and validating their use. I have found that becoming affectively competent is a way of acknowledging my internal multicultural dimensions. It is a way of seeing, understanding, and valuing difference within me. My experience has also been that most conflicts begin (and sometimes end) with people arguing about theories, beliefs, and ideas on a cognitive level. When we fail to connect or when we disconnect, we frequently muster further or more nuanced ideas to support our positions. Becoming affectively competent means we have another repertoire of skills to employ that will help us and those whom we are trying to engage get connected or reconnected. Put another way, when you find yourself and the other person traipsing over the same intellectual ground for the third time, the issue is likely not intellectual but affective. Change happens only if we are emotionally ready. All the right thinking in the world will not bring about conversion from racism or heterosexism if we are overwhelmed by anger, fear, or sadness.

My Story

Three communities—Episcopal Divinity School, VISIONS, and Ecclesia Ministries—have most deeply influenced my transformation and have given me the tools, support, and inspiration for working with others who are much different from me to discover and foster creative, sustainable multicultural communities. I became a member of these three communities at nearly the same time, though with varying levels of commitment and differing trajectories of growth.

In July 1995, I left my position as rector of a suburban Episcopal congregation for a position as director of Theological Field Education and assistant professor of Pastoral Theology at Episcopal Divinity School (EDS). Nearly twenty years of direct service ministry in congregational, university, and hospital settings—some in very diverse settings—prepared me well to assist students and supervisors with many of the traditional skills of ministry, such as preaching, pastoral care, and collaborative leadership. What I was not prepared for was the profound change that the faculty of EDS was about to undergo and the consequences of this change for students, staff, and trustees. Having been proactive in the civil rights era,[3] EDS became an advocate for women's rights and advocated the full inclusion of gay men and lesbians in the life and ministry of the church. Rev. Carter Heyward and Rev. Suzanne Hiatt—two of the Philadelphia Eleven, the first women ordained to priesthood in the Episcopal Church—were hired to join the nearly all-male faculty of the Episcopal Divinity School in 1974. When I joined the faculty twenty-one years later, half of the sixteen members, including the academic dean, were women and five members were lesbian or gay. Yet, in spite of this outstanding accomplishment, the school and faculty were predominately white. An ordained Presbyterian African American woman ethicist and a lay Anglican woman theologian from Hong Kong were the only faculty of color. In October 1995, seventy members of the EDS community (faculty, students, trustees, graduates, and friends) met for three days to develop a vision and goals for the school—including achieving thirty percent faculty of color. Today, half the members of a somewhat smaller faculty are people of color, including our president, who is a member of the Choctaw nation.

It would be easy to think that the transformation of the school came about because we set a goal and moved toward it in some primarily rational way. The truth is more complicated, with starts and stops, two steps forward and one back. And movement took place with a significant amount of training for administrators, faculty, staff, and students in the area of affective competence. The theory and tools that brought about our transformation represent the many of the core ideas of this book.

VISIONS, Inc.—the multicultural consulting and training organization that was the leaven for our growth at EDS—has also been a major influence on my growth in understanding and celebrating differences.[4] Within two years after we started working with VISIONS, all EDS faculty members, key administrators, and numerous staff members including building and grounds and kitchen staff had attended four-day VISIONS training sessions. A multicultural, antiracism course became the only *required* course for EDS masters degrees. The application process changed to include two questions, one for applicants of color and one for white applicants, that focused on how racism affected them. The questions differed because the impact of racism is different for people of color and for white people. Syllabi changed to include attention to multicultural issues and power. Valerie Batts, the executive director of VISIONS who is black, and Emily Schatzow, a white, Jewish VISIONS consultant, became adjunct faculty members with whom I taught an antiracism course. They also provided ongoing training and consultation for faculty, administrators, staff members, the chapel staff, and the student executive committee. A transformation was underway for the school.

And on a personal level, I engaged in several years of additional training with VISIONS to become a consultant in the organization. That training included monthly day-long peer supervision that transformed how I taught lay and clergy leaders to supervise students and how I supported supervisors in their ongoing growth. In addition, VISIONS reintroduced me to transactional analysis (TA), which is a key psychological theory underlying much of their transformative training and consulting. Looking at the role of feelings and what TA theorists refer to as "the Free Child" has given me new insights into setting goals for individual and corporate change. Put most simply, I used to spend a lot of time "shoulding on myself." Revisiting TA theory and combining it with lessons from appreciative inquiry have helped me envision the reign of God as if it were actually happening. And with that vision comes the energy to invite others into the work and the joy of sustaining equitable, compassionate, and life-giving relationships.

The third transforming community that has affected how I understand the radical embrace of multicultural hospitality is Ecclesia Ministries.[5] Within a month of beginning work at EDS, I met with Debbie Little, then a deacon in the Episcopal Church, to talk about the possibility of students doing field education or an internship with *common cathedral*, a community of homeless and housed people who worship year-round outdoors on Boston Common and then share a nourishing meal served by suburban church members and university chaplaincy groups on the very altar from which communion was served.[6] Many members also participate in a weekly art program on Wednesdays, *common cinema* on Fridays, Bible study, and 12-step programs. As a founding member of the board of directors and a frequent worship leader and preacher within this community, I have been challenged to make everything I teach in the seminary classroom real to people who live and die on the margins of society. Though I will not often refer to this community (that is another whole book), the way in which the homeless and housed members of this community form connections and strive to understand and value their differences and their similarities gives me reasons to keep believing in a new creation.

I strongly believe that significant, ongoing transformation can only happen in community. The work is hard, and support and challenge from allies are essential. These three communities—EDS, VISIONS, and Ecclesia Ministries—have formed me, continue to affirm me, and dare me to risk moving forward even when I don't know the way. Recognizing, understanding, and valuing their differences has transformed my life.

Perhaps the single greatest impact on how I understand personal and organization change has come through my relationship with my wife, Christina Robb, and her commitment to relational theory. In the last thirty years there has been a revolution in the way many psychologists look at human development. Relational theorists such as Jean Baker Miller, Carol Gilligan, Joyce Fletcher and their colleagues have advocated seeing relationship, rather than self, as the primary category for understanding human development. Their work echoes the *ubuntu* theology of Archbishop Desmond Tutu, which posits, "Because we are, I am."[7] Being immersed in this different way of viewing human development has led me to understand how true transformation is always a mutual, collaborative effort. Congregations are transformed into more just, more compassionate communities of reconciliation not by individuals acting on their own, but in and through mutual, vibrant, growth-inspiring relationships. As relational theory was breaking onto the horizon, Chris was interviewing the courageous pioneers and writing about their lives and their theory, first for the *Boston Globe*, and then in a book. At the same time, our relationship was beginning and "test drove" the theory down the road of courtship, marriage, and parenting. I met the women and men she wrote about and we talked about the ways in which we were socially conditioned to value relationships differently—as men and as women. We spoke about gender as a factor in how we perceive power, change, and resistance to change. And most significantly, Chris modeled staying in connection as the way to plumb the depths of differences and similarities in order to celebrate all of who we are.

Our Journey in This Book

I assume some of you who read this book are ahead of me on the journey of personal transformation. Others are walking alongside. Some may have been traveling what seems like a lonely road and are looking for company and assurance that the journey is worth taking. Wherever we are, I invite us to begin the journey of transformation with some behavioral guidelines for noticing, understanding, and celebrating differences. The guidelines I present in the first chapter are meant to function as signposts or rules of the road. At times when our differences seem overwhelming, they ensure that we can speak and act in ways that will honor who we are in all our uniqueness. I believe these guidelines are both simple and profound: simple in that they seem obvious to nearly everyone who hears them, and profound in that if we ever truly lived them out in all their implications, little other regulation would be necessary. Every conflict I have been part of, small or large, can be traced to the violation of one of these guidelines. Most often the violation includes denying that significant differences exist or seeing differences as *greater than* or *less than.*

But these practices are simply guidelines—this book is not a blueprint for individual change or community transformation. Most definitely it is not a magician's manual to trick congregations into the appearance of change or to wow them with abstract theories. I think of this book as a road map for transformation. Be assured the map and the landscape are different. While this roadmap offers many useful tools, they all need to be adapted for specific situations. What this book may represent for groups that choose to read it together is a common language, or the beginnings of a language, that allows the differences within a group to surface in a manner that serves ongoing growth for individuals and for groups as they discover new insights for themselves. This language allows some safety in encountering differences and some commonality so that, I hope, the arguments can be about how to be more fully present to one another with all our differences.

Finally, you are invited to embrace all the parts of you—the parts that are like a kite string *and* the parts that are like a clothesline, as well as those parts that are more like bailing wire, ski tow ropes, and fiber-optic cables. Once you begin to notice and value the differences, the possibilities are endless. Once we all embrace who we are and celebrate those who are similar to and different from us, we may catch a glimpse of the multicultural tapestry that God would have us become!

Acknowledgments

I have been blessed with many wonderful companions and teachers on my journey toward becoming a more multicultural person. Pat Dunn, Jim Gorman, and Bernie Swain first invited me to join them in offering consultation and congregational renewal programs to parishes and training in theology and ministry for laity. Their ideas on congregational transformation and their practical tools for implementing and evaluating change are the backbone of my teaching about how organizations overcome resistance and embrace change.

I joined the faculty of Episcopal Divinity School, Cambridge, Massachusetts, as it was beginning to seriously engage in examining the ways racism and classism affected what it was and everything it taught. Over twelve years, I have had the honor to be supported and challenged by teaching courses with Karen Montagno, Suzanne Ehly, Cyndi Morse, Dee Woodward, Gale Yee, Angela Bauer-Levesque, Fredrica Harris Thompsett, Ed Rodman, Ian Douglas, and Julie Lytle. From day one, these colleagues had the grace and good sense to confront my white, heterosexual, male, clerical privilege and to help me see and hear what I could not perceive on my own. They taught me the joy of discovering diverse assumptions and working through differing pedagogies. In a truly excellent academic environment, they welcomed my on-the-ground experience in congregations, hospitals, and campus ministry. They helped me to value and integrate into my learning and teaching what I had been taught by people in the pews, by university students and faculty, and by residents in health care settings. My current academic dean, Sheryl Kujawa-Holbrook, encouraged me as a writer and invited me to find a way to lighten my teaching load. Frank Fornaro took up that challenge and offered to teach the Pastoral Offices course to great acclamation. Penny Kohn assumed increasing field education managerial responsibilities during my writing project and calmly addressed urgent as well as mundane requests when I was nowhere to be found. Alden Flanders oversaw the field education office during my sabbatical as I did research in preparation for writing. Knowing that no backlog would await my return to administration was a relief. For a delightful year, I lunched and taught a weekly seminar for entering students with Mpho Tutu, whose wit, laughter, and penetrating insights made Mondays a day to look forward to. She offered direct, fresh perspectives on all our conversations from prayer to power and from vocation to social location.

Colleagues from VISIONS, Inc., have taught me how to be gentle with the parts of myself that are still learning and struggling to overcome oppressive behaviors and internalized oppression which prevent me from seeing and celebrating differences. They have also challenged me to learn the history of racism in the United States and the political, economic, and psychological consequences of ongoing racism and other oppressions. They have given me tools to help others actively engage in personal and institutional anti-oppressive transformations. More important, they have taught me what it means to be an ally and a member of a multicultural community. In particular, I am grateful to Valerie Batts and Emily Schatzow, with whom I have taught antiracism courses at EDS and who, along with Joe Steele, read portions of the manuscript and offered valuable suggestions.

Colleagues from parish ministry and academia offered support and feedback. Ted Rice, Kate Ekrem, Jim Gorman, and Cyndi Morse, who know the rigors of day-to-day ministry in congregations, read early versions of chapters improving their accuracy and cogency. Emily Click, Scott Cormode, Joe Tortorici, and Dudley Rose made it possible for me to join other researchers and writers to discuss our budding ideas and initial drafts. Jenny Te Paa and Hone Kaa invited me to Aotearoa (New Zealand). Ian Ernest hosted me in Mauritius. I am still learning from the opportunities I had to be surrounded by people speaking languages I did not understand and operating from cultural assumptions that were both foreign and refreshing. Perhaps more than anything, I learned from them how true hospitality enables the celebration of multicultural differences.

Debbie Little, Joan Murray, and Kathy McAdams have been my pastors and teachers at Ecclesia Ministries, a community of faith and hope, where homeless and housed people of vastly different economic and health resources gather weekly to share their reflections on daily life and the Gospels, to partake in the Eucharist, and to share a weekly meal. Their ministry to me has provided balance to my academic life and sustenance for the struggle to incarnate God's reign more fully even as they have provided a vision of that new creation where all people are valued and celebrated.

Janet Surrey, Steve Bergman, and Chuck Walker have encouraged me to write what I know even as they have helped me see what I have yet to learn. I will be ever indebted to Abigail Johnson for introducing me to my editor at Alban. Beth Ann Gaede has been everything a rookie author could hope for in an editor: critic, cheerleader, dialogue partner, skeptic, and teacher. Our differences in experience and outlook led to conversations in cyberspace and by phone that brought precision and clarity to what might otherwise have been half-baked expressions on my part. This book is better for her diligence, wisdom, humor, and interrogation. Andrea Lee tackled the tedious task of copyediting the manuscript and checking references. She also improved the text significantly through careful attention to voice and style as well as to what could be omitted without losing meaning or nuance. Rachel Robb Kondrath was a wizard at tracking down the original sources for quotations.

Finally and foremost, this book benefits from the relationship that is most central to my life and work. I am blessed to live with a partner, Christina Robb, whose integrity and creativity as a writer and an editor have encouraged me to strive for honest, clear, and straightforward communication. More important, with Chris and our daughters, Susannah and Rachel, I have learned the true meaning of connection and transformation and the truth

1

Guidelines for Recognizing and Valuing Differences

The tough-minded . . . respect difference. Their goal is a world made safe for differences.

—*Ruth Fulton Benedict*[1]

[There are] two sorts of truth: trivialities, where opposites are obviously absurd, and profound truths, recognized by the fact that the opposite is also a profound truth.

—*Niels Bohr*[2]

Do not judge, and you will not be judged; do not condemn, and you will not be condemned. Forgive, and you will be forgiven; give, and it will be given to you. A good measure, pressed down, shaken together, running over, will be put into your lap; for the measure you give will be the measure you get back.

—*Luke 6:37-38*

"You won't believe the meeting I just came from. It was a train wreck," sighed the mother of one of the congregation's teenagers.

"Everything started off okay. The pastor opened the meeting with a prayer and said she thought it would be a good idea for people to introduce themselves and say what their hopes for the future of the youth group were. She said she couldn't stay, because she had just received a call that a parishioner had been in an automobile accident and she had to leave for the hospital. So, after we all prayed for the parishioner, she left.

"People were polite at first and started to list the things they hoped would happen for their children. Some folks wanted their children to continue to receive some sort of religious education. Others thought the children should be involved in a service project. Some said their children wouldn't be interested in either of those ideas. Their children just wanted to get together with their friends, and what was the harm in that? That led to the suggestion that maybe the youth themselves should be involved in the decision.

"Then a few people, who seemed like they had axes to grind, began to criticize what had happened last year. They sounded really angry and began to dominate the conversation. Before long, a number of people—including me—stopped participating. Last year's youth leader got defensive, and in a short time, people were shouting at one another. Someone tried to call the meeting back to order, but by then it was too late. Some people had already left. Someone suggested that the group meet again when people had cooled down, but only if the pastor could be present. There was arguing about that as well. Then more people just started walking out."

Wouldn't you just love to be the pastor or the lay leader who facilitates the next meeting of this group? Or maybe you have been there, done that, and earned the T-shirt—the one with the bull's-eye on the front.

I am not sure why nice, intelligent people often seem to lose their civility in church settings. Perhaps they have to exercise a lot of self-control in other settings and they feel that they can let it all out at church. Or maybe they work in a tightly controlled environment where they have little opportunity to speak out, and they feel that they have license to say whatever they want at church. Often congregations have a history of people behaving in inappropriate ways. Maybe past abuse of some kind by an ordained or lay leader has occurred, has left its mark, and has not been adequately healed. Other times, I think church people naively believe that because they are Christian or religious, they do not need any structure or explicitly stated rules of conduct. Whatever the reason, most of us have been in situations where by the time someone tried to bring about order, it *seemed* too late.

As a person of faith, I want to believe that it is never really too late to recover from a messy conflictual situation.

Throughout this book, we will be exploring ways for people to transform their communities of faith through recognizing and valuing differences. We will be talking about behavioral guidelines that enhance the ability to see and value differences. We will talk about how power shapes the ways people see and respond to others who are different from them. We will discuss the role of feelings, especially during times of significant change. We will talk briefly about how imagination opens the door to new possibilities of transformation. We will speak specifically about how cultural conditioning as women and as men affects how people interact. Finally, we will look at institutional level change and see how these other factors (power, feelings, imagination, and gender) influence the resistance to or acceptance of change. Many of the theories and tools you will read about are crucial for understanding and intervening in situations that become messy, like the one above. But why wait until then?

Leaders *and members* of groups can think about their life together before something horrible happens. They can work together from their first encounter to ensure something wonderful will happen. They can prepare their hearts and minds as fertile ground for the planting of God's seed, which will flourish (Mark 4:20). I am reminded of the old saw, "Pray as if everything depended on God; work as if everything depended on you." Throughout this book, the "you" will most often be plural and diverse—lay and clergy, women and men, people of all races and cultures, volunteers and paid staff, young and old, newcomers and long-time members. So where do we start? How do we begin to do our part, so that we are as fully receptive as possible to who God would have us be and what God would have us do?

Guidelines Enable Healthy, Diverse Communities

At the first meeting of a group, I have found it best to lay out some ground rules or guidelines that the group can agree to abide by and that will govern the group's interaction. Guidelines for acceptable behavior can be the ounce of prevention that makes a pound of healing unnecessary.

Especially if their interaction is likely to become heated or highly conflictual, when group members come to an early agreement about how they will treat one another, they realize that they have *already* agreed upon something, and thus they gain confidence that they *might* be able to agree on some other things. In other situations where conflict is not as likely, commonly agreed-upon guidelines make it safer for people to engage one another when they exhibit significant differences in race, culture, theology, politics, or other variables. Guidelines also enable people in a group to go to deeper levels of trust more easily and more readily. Sometimes groups are scared of their differences or fear that if the status quo is disrupted, conflict will occur. And so they only engage one another superficially. An agreed-upon set of guidelines can be the first step in encouraging and enabling such groups to take some initial risks. Guidelines can release energy for self-discovery and the discovery of the other. With basic guidelines in place to ensure their safety, more people are willing to open the door and let the transforming Spirit of God enter.

The "Guidelines for Recognizing and Valuing Differences" presented here serve one other specific purpose. They invite the Spirit's movement in a particular way by challenging us to be radically inclusive. They call us to transform ourselves and our institutions by recognizing and valuing differences. In my experience, the sincere exercise of these guidelines over time transforms communities of faith into more welcoming and diverse gatherings.

The first seven guidelines are ones developed and used by consultants and trainers at VISIONS, Inc.[3] I have added my own examples and theological reflections to the VISIONS guidelines as well as two additional guidelines.

Guidelines for Recognizing and Valuing Differences

1. Try on.
2. It's okay to disagree. It's not okay to shame, blame, or attack oneself or others.

3. Practice self-focus.
4. Practice "both/and" thinking.
5. Be aware of intent and impact.
6. Take 100 percent responsibility for one's own learning.
7. Maintain confidentiality.
8. It's okay to be messy.
9. Say ouch.

Try On

The try on guideline invites us to be creative, to open ourselves to new learning. It invites us to suspend judgment for a moment and look at something from a different perspective. Try on new ideas. Try on new processes. Try on new relationships.

The simplest example of trying on something new is the process of buying a pair of shoes. When I need a new pair of shoes, I may go to a store where I have shopped before or I may go to a new store or I may sometimes do both. When I go in, I look at a lot of different shoes for style, color, and comfort. When I see something that I think I would like, I check for the appropriate size and try the shoes on. I walk around awhile in the shoes to see how they feel. I look in a mirror to see what they look like from a different angle. Often I take off that pair of shoes and try on another new pair. Sometimes I even put my old shoes on to remember what they feel like. The old ones almost always feel more comfortable unless the heel is so worn down that they are a little out of balance, and even then they seem comfortably familiar. After going through this process for a while, I often decide on a new pair of shoes to buy. Sometimes I even buy two different new pairs because I have invested so much time testing and comparing, and I can envision different occasions when one pair may match the situation better than the other pair. Sometimes I leave the store after a lot of trying on with only the shoes I wore into the store.

Trying on new ways of thinking, acting, or feeling is a lot like trying on a new pair of shoes. To try on an idea does not mean that I have to accept the idea I am being asked to examine. It does mean I am willing to consider or reconsider something from a viewpoint that I have not considered before, or perhaps have previously considered and rejected.

To try on a new behavior does not mean that I judge my former behavior as wrong. It means that I do not judge the *new* behavior as wrong. I am willing to see the benefits and disadvantages of different ways of behaving.

One can also try on a feeling that may seem new for the circumstance. To ask myself if I am actually feeling a particular, new emotion, distinct from one that I more readily admit to, offers me the opportunity to examine what that new emotion is telling me about what I may need in this circumstance. Different emotions carry different messages about what we need at a particular time, as will be explored in chapter 3. For example, some months after my father died, I found myself getting angry at my wife over petty things. My anger, which felt comfortable like an old shoe, kept my wife at a distance, especially because I was expressing anger *at her* when my anger was probably more about my father. I had plenty of reasons to be angry about how my father had not been present to me, about how he had not shown interest in who I had become and what I had accomplished. But that was only part of the story. My anger also kept me from facing into my grief and the fact that I would never see my father again. One evening after snapping at my wife for sometime she said, I realized I wasn't really angry at her. Something else was going on. She suggested that maybe I was really sad, not angry. When I tried on the possibility that I might still be deeply grieving my father's death, I realized I was not really angry at her for what she said. My anger was part of how I kept my sadness at bay and pushed my wife away so that I would not have to again face my sadness. When I admitted my sadness, my wife drew nearer to me and listened to me. I got what I really needed at that point. She accompanied me in my grief. When I had been angry, I was in effect telling her to keep her distance from me, and I did not get the comfort I really desired. The role of feelings and how we substitute one feeling for another will be further developed in the third chapter.

Trying on new ideas (content) and new ways of behaving (process) in multicultural settings is like trying on bicycle shoes that clip on to a special pedal, especially if you have never tried them. Wearing bicycle shoes for the first time causes a person to change some basic assumptions about shoes. Shoes are meant to protect your feet and make contact with the ground as you walk. They keep your feet from getting bruised, cut, or dirty and may be a fashion statement. Bicycle shoes also protect your feet, but they are not meant primarily for walking. The fact that they clip onto a special bicycle pedal means that your feet do not slide off the pedal. All the energy that your legs and feet bring to the pedals is transferred directly to the pedals. Because the shoes are clipped into the pedals, as your feet go through the revolutions of the crank, you can pull more efficiently on your upstrokes. With practice, these shoes make for much more efficient and faster riding. They can also be dangerous if you are not used to them. REI, a retailer of outdoor gear, states that the main disadvantage of this type of shoe-pedal system (which is ironically called "clipless" to distinguish it from a toe-clip system) is that "you'll fall. You will. Guaranteed. The foot naturally wants to slide backward when you're heading for tip-over. Clipless systems require you to move your foot out at a 45-degree angle."[4] REI recommends that you "find a soft grassy field and practice, practice, practice." After sixty times, for each shoe, they declare, you will get the hang of this system. These shoes are "multicultural" because, besides pedaling more efficiently, you can walk in them. And though your shoes click when you walk on a hard floor, they tell everyone you are an experienced biker.

Trying on new ideas and unfamiliar ways of acting in a multicultural setting also requires a willingness to examine basic assumptions and being willing to practice, practice, practice. The old idea or way of acting feels more familiar, more comfortable. In a multicultural setting, the new idea or manner of acting will not likely fit right away. Let me give an example from a multicultural congregation. Perhaps the new idea is that meetings or worship begin when people are ready or that it's okay for some people to arrive at 10 o'clock for a 10 o'clock service and for some people to arrive at 10:20 a.m. To fully appreciate what it means to try on this new concept, I need to realize that not all cultures understand time the same way. Most white people of European descent in the United States think in terms of being "on time" for events. They go by the clock. Many other cultures have a less rigid, more fluid sense of time. People from these cultures think of living in the moment, of being in the flow of one event until it segues into the next event independent of what the clock says. This is referred to as being "in time."[5] As a person raised to value my own time and the time of others almost apart from what is done in that time, being on time is a high priority for me. The notion of trusting that people can arrive in time because they are in multiple relationships that play out in their own time and that those relationships transcend the hours and minutes on a clock is a stretch for me.

To try on a different understanding of time may require a kind of conversion. Here the conversion required is seeing the issue of choosing the time of a service in a multicultural congregation as an *adaptive challenge* rather than as a *technical fix*. Ronald Heifetz and Marty Linsky, professors at the John F. Kennedy School of Government at Harvard University, characterize technical fix as the solution in which an authority applies current know-how to a problem. An adaptive challenge requires the people with the problem to learn new ways of working.[6] Using this framework, the working out of differences with regard to time in truly multicultural church is not a matter of a technical fix. The solution is not a matter of simply finding the right time (using current know-how) by saying, "Let's split the difference and begin at 10:10"—expecting that once congregation members decide on the new, agreed-upon time, they have solved the problem.[7]

In some multicultural settings, how one understands time and the expectations about when people will arrive is an adaptive challenge. People will need to discuss their cultural understandings of time and relationships. For some people, synchronizing with a clock—that is, being on time—will be important. For some of these people, time is money. Time is measured in terms of what work could be done in a given unit of time. Respect for oneself and for other people is related to not wasting time. Other people will have a very different understanding of time. For them time is more fluid: gatherings have an organic beginning and ending no matter what the clock says. Time is not measured in objective units; rather, time is related primarily to how I stay in connection with other people—people I am with now and will be leaving and people whom I am going to meet. People with this understanding of time speak about being in time. The point here is that trying on a multicultural approach to time, as an adaptive challenge, means that everyone has to learn new ways of relating and behaving. Seeking an authoritative solution would short-circuit trying on a truly multicultural approach.

Trying on a new perspective or method is often a cumulative process. Some ideas or ways of acting are acquired tastes. Similar to getting used to a new pair of shoes, one may need time to try out the benefits of a new idea or a new way of relating to others. Two things are important to remember about acquiring new options. First, if I don't try on anything new, I am stuck with the same old ideas and methods, and my learning will stagnate. Second, whenever I try on something new, I always have the option of going back to what I knew and believed beforehand or to the ways of interacting that have previously worked.

Learning to try on is essential if we want to investigate our differences, whether racial, cultural, ethnic, political, theological, liturgical, or philosophical. It offers us an inside look at differences that arise because of age, gender, sexual identity, status or power (student/teacher, clergy/laity, employer/employee), nationality, language, and so forth. The ability to try on other perspectives allows a congregation that operates in mostly monocultural ways to be transformed into a faith community that has the opportunity to embrace all its members' cultural values and ways of interacting.

When I think of this guideline theologically, I am aware that a primary way to image God is as creator. Insofar as we are made in the image and likeness of God, we are meant to be cocreators with God, the creator of all the diversity in the universe. What then does it mean, on an individual level, to be creating new life?

I live more in God's image and likeness when I am open to trying on new ideas and behaviors, especially when this means listening to the different experiences of other children of God. The try on guideline also helps me understand the work of the Holy Spirit, the Spirit that reveals new insights to the faith community, the Spirit that blows where she will.

The try on guideline can also be an invitation to an institution or community to think and act in new ways. In a seminary course I teach called "Creativity, Change, and Conflict," I invite students to imagine what a distinctively creative church would look like. What if the characteristic that most distinguished a congregation was neither its liturgical excellence, nor its wide-ranging social justice ministry, nor its music or education program, but rather its creativity? Suppose every aspect of its life and ministry was imaginative, inspired (filled with the Spirit), innovative. What if volunteers, staff, and visitors left worship, budget meetings, board meetings, and educational events feeling renewed, energized, revitalized, animated, eager for the next church encounter, fired up for their professional work, and enthusiastic about deepening their relationships with family and friends? What if folks in the town where the church is located said, "I'm not sure what doctrines or dogmas hold that church together, but they are the most creative group in this town? Any time people feel stuck in this town, they know all they have to do is gather a few folks from Creative Community Church and they will figure out a way through the logjam." Students, and most people I know, have trouble imagining that such a church could exist. Yet, inevitably the exercise of trying on that kind of community creativity frees up a lot of energy for thinking about what God might want to grow in somewhat barren places.

An attitude of superiority or internalized inferiority often underlies the violation of each of the guidelines. With regard to this first guideline, when I am in a position of dominance and I refuse to try on a new idea or way of behaving, at some level I am saying I know that my old way is *better than* this other way I am being invited to consider. When I am a position of less power, I may be saying I do not have the internal resources to try on this new way because I am not capable enough to do it. Thus, attitudes of superiority and inferiority hinder the exercise of trying on new ideas, feelings, and behaviors. When I see myself as superior or inferior to others, I am also contradicting the belief that all people are of equal worth in God's eyes, as Paul discusses in his analogy of the body (1 Cor. 12:12-26). More will be said about the notions of superiority and inferiority that undermine the ability to transform congregations in the chapter on power and difference.

It's Okay to Disagree; It's Not Okay to Shame, Blame, or Attack

Because the goal is to transform communities of faith through recognizing and valuing difference, it might seem obvious that a diverse group of people would disagree with one another and that this disagreement would be okay. My experience, however, has not always proved this assumption true. Sometimes groups with even a fair amount of diversity choose not to engage one another on topics about which they know they will disagree. A faith community may choose not to talk about politics at church or synagogue because they know they will disagree and they believe that disagreement will be divisive. Another group may have an implicit don't-ask-don't-tell policy about issues of sexual identity or eucharistic theology to avoid disagreements. The congregation may have a history of splintering when such topics are engaged.

When disagreement is not allowed, people don't show up as their full selves. If I am afraid that what I will say cannot be heard in a particular church, I may not join that church, or if I do, I will be always on guard when I am at church. I may even develop a type of split personality—bringing the acceptable part of me to church and sharing the part of myself that is not acceptable in other places. Such behavior will mean that I will not likely ever consider myself a truly committed member of that church.

Believing that disagreement is okay both honors individuals and their differences and is an act of faith that the community is mature enough to understand and embrace significant differences.[8]

The embrace of differences has a scriptural precedent in the differing stories of creation in Genesis and in the four different Gospel accounts of the life of Jesus, which cannot be reconciled into one smooth chronology or a completely homogenous theological picture. The two creation stories in Genesis come from different communities. Genesis 1:1-2:4a is generally believed to come from the Priestly tradition. Rather than a single author or a like-minded group of contemporaries, this tradition is seen as a school of thought that spanned several centuries. Its final form is thought to date from the exilic period when Israel's faith was under siege. As Israel sought to remain faithful to Yahweh while living in a strange land, surrounded by people who worshiped other gods, one issue became paramount: Israel must remain holy (set apart) as Yahweh is holy. Therefore, issues of ritual purity and legal cleanliness became important. And so the Priestly creation story avoids anthropomorphisms and has ritual and liturgical allusions.

Genesis 2:4b-24 is from the Yahwist tradition, commonly dated to the tenth century BC in the Southern Kingdom. Because of the glorious distinction God brought to the tribe of Judah during the time of David and Solomon, the Yahwist author presents God's communion with humans in an optimistic light. Despite the pervasiveness of sin, the Yahwist foresees victory in the moment of defeat—Eve's offspring will crush the offspring of the serpent (Gen. 3:15).[9] In the Yahwist tradition, human beings are not mere marionettes, as they are in the Priestly tradition. Individuals in the Yahwist tradition are allotted considerable freedom of action, bringing out both their strengths and weaknesses, as in the story of Adam and Eve eating from the tree in the middle of the garden.[10]

The two creation stories come from particular communities with their own special histories and concerns, which caused them to value their own way of telling the story of creation. Both the Jewish and Christian faith communities have received and treasured these different accounts. In a similar manner, each of the four Gospels comes from a particular community that valued a particular way of understanding Jesus. Mark's story can be seen to answer the twin questions, who is Jesus (culminating in the answer of Peter at Caesarea Philippi [Mark 8:29]) and what does it mean to be his disciple? Matthew presents Jesus as a second Moses to his mostly Jewish-heritage audience. Luke portrays Jesus more as a healer to his Gentile audience. John is generally regarded as more mystical and concerned with presenting the miracles of Jesus as symbols of God's action through Jesus the Word of God. For many people, the fact that the different evangelists present divergent pictures of Jesus is a bonus. In modern business jargon, the differences are value-added. Differences make the work of critical biblical scholarship and everyday belief more difficult, *and* they ensure that the story is richer and deeper.

Granting the reality of differences and the value of disagreement, one might ask, what are the limits of disagreement? The second part of the second guideline declares that shaming, blaming, or attacking others or oneself is not okay. In most faith communities, members do not physically attack one another. However, the number of stories about laypeople and clergy yelling at one another, name calling, stomping out of meetings, and refusing to speak to one another is surprising. In my experience, this kind of behavior is frequently a sign that some serious abuse of power has taken place during the congregation's relatively recent history. The norms of appropriate conduct have been so violated that the system can no longer behave with civility and grace. At other times, I suspect that people have so little opportunity to express their frustrations and fears in their families or their places of work that they act out inappropriately in a church setting where they feel that people have to accept them. Whatever the cause, when people attack, blame, or shame one another, "renorming" the community by teaching the guidelines on as many occasions as possible is an essential and immediate need. Once taught, the guidelines should be practiced religiously. In much the same way that an individual with a terminal disease can recenter herself through daily meditative prayer, so too a family or community can recenter itself relationally by practicing focused and consistent mindfulness in noticing, understanding, and appreciating difference—that is, by disagreeing without resorting to shame, blame, or attack.

Even when a congregation has not suffered the extremes of power abuse and people are emotionally competent and balanced, sometimes individuals violate the second half of this guideline:

"It's not okay to shame, blame, or attack oneself or others." For example, the chair of a committee may say to a new member, before even hearing out the speaker, "We tried that before, it never worked." Phrases such as, "How could you possibly think that?" and "No one who really loves God would . . ." are examples of shaming another person. Sometimes we shame or blame others through nonverbal body language, such as sighing deeply after someone says something we disagree with or find boring or rolling our eyes or dropping our head to avoid looking at the speaker.

We can also shame and blame ourselves, usually because on some level we believe that we are *less than* someone else in the group—perhaps the leader. Some simple phrases are clues to self-shame and -blame: "This may be a silly idea, but . . ." or "Probably no one would agree with me. . . ."

Theologically speaking, attacking, shaming, and blaming others with whom we disagree may stem from not valuing the vast diversity of goodness and beauty that God created. Some people feel a strong need to defend what they believe to be true, to control and manage the truth as if the world would whirl into chaos if this truth were challenged or amended. Or they may believe that they have been chosen by God to direct and manage others during a cataclysmic collapse of morals. Could this desire to control others represent a lack of faith that *God* is in control or at least a doubt that God is okay with the way creation is evolving? Jiddu Krishnamurti, the great Indian spiritual teacher, said, "Normally we thrive on blaming others, which is a form of self-pity."[11] Perhaps blaming others is a person's plea to be treated more compassionately. Pastorally speaking, those who blame and shame others or themselves need support in their fear, even as one works to ensure that others in the community can disagree without being abused. An experienced facilitator, whom the person trusts, might be able to ask him to slow down the interaction and look at his feelings. For example, look at the committee chair who says, "I don't know the other three people who volunteered to be on this committee. They never show up. They're just lazy." The facilitator might ask the chairperson to focus on his own feelings. If he is able to acknowledge that one of his feelings is fear—that he cannot do all the work by himself, that the project will not be completed, and that he will look bad—he may be able to shift from blaming the committee members to asking for help from them or from others once he has conveyed his concern. This focus on feelings leads directly to the next guideline.

Practice Self-focus

Practicing self-focus, the third guideline, has two parts. The first part has to do with using "I" statements—that is, making a commitment to speak in the first person singular about what one thinks, believes, or feels. Here the point is to avoid unsupported generalizations, such as, "People think . . ." or "Everyone believes. . . ." People use such generalizations as a way of saying what they think without taking responsibility for it. Furthermore, when I speak in generalities from a place of power or privilege, without acknowledging my status, I foster monoculturalism by speaking as if what I am saying is true for everyone, rather than simply my opinion or my privileged group's way of thinking. For example, when a white person says, "People feel scared in this neighborhood," he attributes his fear to others rather than saying, "I feel scared in this neighborhood." An even more honest or self-focused statement might be, "As a white person, I feel scared in this neighborhood." In a similar way, when a white person speaks about his own privileged neighborhood and says, "People feel comfortable here," he is generalizing and probably means, "I feel comfortable here" or "White people (my group) feel comfortable here." The generalization hides the unconscious monocultural assumption that if everyone were like me (a privileged white person) they would feel comfortable here.

In addition, broad, unsupported claims are often simply not heard. If someone tries to convince me of a general theory of life, the universe, and everything, even if it is mostly true, I lose attention quickly. I tend to tune out the person because such global statements are usually not true or they are so general that little of what is said is relevant or useful to the current issue. On significant issues, I don't expect everyone to be of one mind, so I am most interested in listening to the range of individual experience. When that person speaks from a place of self-focus, I am interested and stay tuned in. I can even lay aside some of my defenses and arguments to listen to someone who is speaking about her own personal experience, beliefs, thoughts, and feelings. From a tactical standpoint, self-focus—speaking your particular truth—makes sense if you want to be listened to.

As a trainer or consultant, I find that when I am genuinely curious about another person's reasoning, I need to avoid the trap of triggering that person's defensiveness. So I sometimes ask how a person came to think or believe the way she does. I find it much more effective to say, "Can you tell me more about . . . ?" than to ask, "Why do you believe . . . ?" Inviting a person to tell me more is open-ended and shows my interest in the person as well as the statement she just made. Asking a person why she said something strikes many people as questioning their motives or intelligence, and frequently triggers defensiveness. I am reminded of the times I angrily asked one of my daughters, in a demanding voice, "Why did you do that?" They were quick to learn that I was not asking for information but saying, "You should not have done that!"

Also true is that when I asked the same question out of genuine curiosity in a voice that conveyed a sense of inquiry rather than shame, I usually got an answer that told me about their decision making. The problem is that questions that start with *why* often trigger memories of shame and defensiveness. Therefore, I try to phrase a question that will elicit a story from a self-focused point of view. When I ask, "Can you tell me more about . . . ?" I generally learn a great deal about the person. If the person speaks in a self-focused manner, she is also more likely to learn why it is that she thinks what she does. Articulating the reason for her thoughts, beliefs, or actions may give her options for thinking or behaving differently.

The first dimension of practicing self-focus—using "I" language—largely benefits the speaker. Self-focus has a second dimension that is often overlooked. The perspective here is more that of the listener and the value of self-focus to me as a listener. In this dimension, self-focus means really listening to myself and the information from within that I often overlook. When I am truly self-focused, I am paying attention to the feelings that I am experiencing while someone else is speaking. As I am hearing their words and meanings, I am monitoring my own inner responses. I am aware that what is being said and what is not being said (what is left out of the conversation) are having an impact on me emotionally. Even if I do not know why I am having a particular feeling, I allow myself to become aware of my feeling state in the moment, and I take responsibility for it. Self-focus is being aware that these are *my* feelings. Something the other person said or did may have been a stimulus, and these feelings are *mine*. This sort of self-focus requires practiced discipline. When I am not exercising self-focus, I often "listen with my answer running." I confuse my response with universal right and good. I am also in danger of responding to the statement without paying attention to the speaker. Self-focus involves the discipline of noticing my feelings and asking myself what they may be telling me, before reacting to the content of what the other person has been saying (or not saying).

Sometimes people make the distinction between *reacting* and *responding*. Reacting generally means replying hastily to someone without fully taking in what they have said or replying to the statement and not the person. Responding usually connotes listening to the person as well as hearing the statement and in some way valuing the person. While I find this distinction useful, I am not at this point referring to the content of what I say in my response or even the manner in which I am saying it. I am pointing more specifically to the necessity of naming the feeling within me and understanding what that emotion is conveying to me about what I need. Therefore, this process of monitoring my internal feeling state can also be used when I am by myself thinking or reading. Even in such solitary moments, useful messages come to me not merely from the text I encounter or my intellectual processes. My feelings themselves have a history and can convey meaning to me. This notion of feelings as messengers is central to the role of feelings in transformation, which is the subject of chapter 3.

Theologically speaking, encouraging people to use "I" statements is a way of valuing the dignity of every human being. Each person's unique set of thoughts and beliefs has worth. Focusing on my own feelings acknowledges that God has created me as a thinking *and* feeling being. Employing this aspect of the guideline means using all the gifts and resources God has given me.

However, people from some cultures—for example, African, Asian, Native American—are reluctant to speak in the first-person singular. Their "we" statements are not generalizations as a way to avoid taking responsibility. For them, the use of *we* represents a deeply held belief in the primacy of community. For them, all actions of an individual, all thoughts, perhaps even feelings, exist because a person is grounded in a community. The notion here is, "Because we are, I am." When negotiating this guideline with people of diverse cultural backgrounds, one needs to make room for those who are not comfortable using "I" language for cultural reasons while at the same time inviting people of privilege to acknowledge their tendency to hide behind generalizations. The next guideline assists with this process.

Practice "Both/And" Thinking

People of European descent and therefore most white people in North America often have a cultural way of thinking that is "either/or"—right or wrong, good or bad, win or lose. Sometimes this is truer for men than for women. But the dominant cultural way of thinking in the United States is oppositional.[12] Underlying either/or thinking is an attitude, unusually unconscious and unarticulated, that I am superior to the person with a differing position, that the other person is inferior to me, or that if I win this argument my victory will mean I am superior. A person may not even notice how deeply either/or thinking is ingrained in his way of living because it is part of his worldview. Like fish swimming in water, people do not notice the water around them. Not all worldviews represent life in the same way. African and Asian worldviews tend to encourage thinking from a both/and perspective. We have already seen an example of the differences between European and African worldviews in the discussion of time under the try on guideline.[13]

Even though I enjoy or am accustomed to either/or thinking, I can *try on* both/and thinking. In my experience, both/and thinking feels artificial or awkward at first. I may even feel frightened, because I am giving up the strength and security of some deeply engrained beliefs. The both/and worldview assumes that a number of opinions and beliefs can coexist without canceling one another out. It applies to complex interactions and robust situations. The both/and worldview is also a practical way of valuing the difference inherent in another's point of view. Niels Bohr, the Danish physicist, expressed the importance of both/and thinking when he said there are "two sorts of truth: trivialities, where opposites are obviously absurd, and profound truths, recognized by the fact that the opposite is also a profound truth."[14]

The practice of both/and thinking often means substituting the word *and* for the words *but* or *however* in a sentence. This substitution is even more important when stating your opinion after someone has said something with which you disagree. Your *and* will let the other person know that they have been heard and respected and that what you are saying does not cancel out what they have said. Stating strong differences with both/and language can help prevent people with strongly differing views from slipping into defensive postures or predetermined solutions. It acknowledges the complexity of a situation and invites both parties to investigate why they see the situation differently. Using both/and language creates a path toward mutuality.

Both/and thinking is hard to exercise in an organization or a group where maintaining relationships of superiority and inferiority is of primary importance, where competition and being right are part of the culture, or where shaming and blaming are acceptable. For individuals to practice both/and thinking, it is important that others in the group or organization have been introduced to and are attempting to practice all the guidelines.

As a Christian, I ground both/and thinking in the Incarnation, my belief that Jesus is human *and* divine, and in my understanding that God sees us as we are in all our sinfulness *and* calls us to live in God's own image. Martin Luther spoke of human beings as saints *and* sinners.

Be Aware of Intent and Impact

The fifth guideline for recognizing and valuing differences is being aware of my intent and impact. *Intent* is my intention or motive in doing or saying something. *Impact* is the effect or consequence my speech or action has on another person or persons. Sometimes I make comments that I do not intend to be racist, sexist, elitist, or heterosexist, and nevertheless another person is deeply affected by my comment. The person who feels hurt or offended may then accuse me of inappropriate behavior and may even say that they think the remark was racist, sexist, and so forth. The conversation quickly escalates, and both of us become defensive.

Let me give an example. Perhaps I notice that another person has become very quiet or becomes quite defensive in response to a comment I have made. In such a case, rather than denying the impact that my comment has had on the other person by saying that I did not intend to treat her as inferior, I can take responsibility for the impact I have had on her. I can say that I am sorry. At the same time, I can examine myself to try to see if I am harboring or betraying any attitude of superiority toward that person. In such situations, it helps if I am curious about the response I have evoked from the other person and if I am curious about what role I may have played in evoking that response. In other words, I need to be careful not to assume that the response of the other person is her fault. I will talk further about blaming the victim, a modern form of oppression, in chapter 2.

When the tables are turned and I am feeling someone has misunderstood or sandbagged me, self-focus invites me to notice how I feel. I may feel angry that I have been abused or that some boundary has been crossed. I may feel sad that I have been misunderstood. I may fear that things are going to get out of control. Once I notice the emotional impact on me, I can combine this guideline with self-focus to determine what I need. The key here is to slow down the interaction. I can do this by telling the other person what the impact has been on me emotionally. The conversation then shifts from content (which is usually related to intention) to impact (which is usually related to feelings). For many people, this shift in the conversation feels awkward at first and takes some practice. It works best when people in the congregation or institution have been taught the guidelines and have had practice, often with a third-party facilitator or trainer, in slowing down the conversation. Implicit in this slowing down is the fact that one values how all the parties feel as well as what they are thinking.[15]

Often racist and sexist comments and behaviors, as well as other forms of personal level prejudice, are outside my conscious awareness. This is not to excuse these behaviors. For underlying them is an unconscious or unthinking attitude of power or privilege, an unconscious learned sense of superiority, which I do not intend to manifest. Not only do I need to become aware of the impact I am having on others, I also need to inquire of myself what attitudes of superiority or privilege may underlie my comments and behaviors that others experience as oppressive. In a similar way, people with less privilege or power need to reflect about the ways they have unwittingly learned to internalize or buy into their own oppression and thus also make an unconscious and unintended impact on others. This will be dealt with more in the second chapter.[16]

The intent and impact problematic is familiar to anyone who has read the letters of Paul. Paul writes, “For I do not do the good I want, but the evil I do not want is what I do” (Rom. 7:19). Ethically, I am accountable not only for what I intend but also for the impact I have on others that I may not have intended.

Take 100 Percent Responsibility for One’s Own Learning

When learning about and celebrating differences, each of us needs to take responsibility for our own learning. This means that I do not expect the people who are the most vulnerable or underrepresented in a group to teach me what I need to know if I am in a position of privilege. Often people who represent statistical minorities in a church or business become tired of trying to teach the dominant group. People of color are frequently called upon to teach white people what they do not know about the reality and the impact of their white privilege. Women are often relied on to do the relational work in an organization, and then their work is "disappeared," as will be discussed in chapter 5. Gay, lesbian, bisexual, and transgendered people often find themselves teaching straight people the history of discrimination against them as well as its impact on them. Rarely are these roles reversed, because people who are in the statistical minority in a culture or organization and those who are treated as inferior or less than have to learn the culture of those who are dominant as a matter of survival, while one of the privileges of the dominant position is not having to learn the culture of subordinates. Taking 100 percent responsibility for my own learning means not expecting others to do my work for me.

Some of the ways of taking responsibility include reading poetry, fiction, and history written by people who are not part of the majority culture; listening to music and attending theater performances of cultural groups different from our own; developing relationships with persons of another culture; living or working in an environment where we are in the minority; traveling to other countries to experience cultures as truly different from our own. I recently heard the story of a clergyperson who traveled to Mauritius, a small multicultural country in the Indian Ocean. She complained that she couldn't find a Starbucks coffee shop. Rather than taking responsibility for learning delicious new ways to drink coffee, she stayed in her place of privilege and decided that something was wrong with this country. It was *less than* where she was used to living.

The Gospels encourage each of us to learn the truth about God, ourselves, our neighbors, and all of creation: "And you will know the truth, and the truth will make you free" (John 8:32). Complete openness to the truth is impossible on our own; Jesus promises us to send the Spirit of truth. "When the Spirit of truth comes, he will guide you into all truth; for he will not speak on his own, but will speak whatever he hears, and he will declare to you the things that are to come" (John 16:13).

Maintain Confidentiality

Confidentiality, the seventh guideline, is important in one-to-one interactions, in learning groups, and in organizations. It has to do with boundaries and safety. On a personal level, I may choose to take certain risks or to try on new ideas and behaviors. I might even be willing to expose my assumptions or discuss my personal theology if I have a sense that what I am saying will not be made public outside of the context in which I am speaking. Most simply put, this guideline means that everyone agrees not to tell one another's personal stories.

In learning groups, I always emphasize my hope that people will share the content of the workshop or course as widely as possible. I encourage each person to share what she or he has experienced and felt. What they agree not to share is someone else's thoughts, feelings, or learnings.

In agreeing to each of the guidelines, people should be asked to make a commitment to each other and not just to the leader. This is most important with regard to confidentiality because people are agreeing not to tell each other's stories. To emphasize this, I always ask group members to look at each person in the group as they verbally assent to the guideline of confidentiality.

In congregations, schools, and agencies, a group may include people who, in another setting, report to someone else in the group. That is, a boss and his subordinate may participate in the same training workshop or may be members of the same governing board or small group in a congregation. This overlap in roles highlights another important dimension of confidentiality. In such situations, the leader of the group, as well as participants, should be aware that the person in the subordinate position may be afraid to speak freely because his boss is present. In a consulting or training situation when I do not know whether such situations exist, I ask if there are any people who have to report to someone else in the group. The reason for naming the reporting relationship is that the person in the subordinate position is in a more vulnerable position if he should disclose something during the meeting that could be held against him later in a performance evaluation. Thus the leader of the group should invite anyone who is in a supervisory position over another group member not to judge the supervisee's work performance based on interactions at the church. This separation of church life and work life—a dimension of confidentiality—is essential if the congregation is to become a safe place for people to learn new ways of thinking, feeling, and behaving around differences. The work environment may not hold the same assumptions and safeguards.

Reflecting theologically on confidentiality, I think of Jesus's concern for those who had less power in society. One of the primary reasons for confidentiality is to protect those who are most vulnerable—so that what they have shared in a group that has agreed to these guidelines may never be held against them or used to shame or blame them outside the group by people who haven't agreed to the guidelines. We note that while Jesus talks with the Samaritan woman at the well about her many previous marriages, he leaves it up to the woman to tell her own story. She is the one who goes back into the village and says that Jesus has told her everything she has ever done (John 4:4-42). The story of the woman caught in adultery inspires a similar caution. Here it is clear that those who have called for the woman to be stoned have not kept what they have found out confidential. Rather than publicly attacking the woman *or her accusers,* Jesus writes in the sand and says, "Let anyone among you who is without sin be the first to throw a stone at her" (John 8:7).

The guidelines I have laid out thus far are the ones I generally present to groups that want to better see, understand, and celebrate difference. When I ask for comments and additions, the two most frequent additions are "It's okay to be messy" and "Say ouch." I will say a word about both because they are important, even though I believe they may be contained in the above guidelines.

It's Okay to Be Messy

One of the primary assumptions of learning about and celebrating differences in order to transform people and congregations is that no one is perfect. We are all on a journey. Because we are human, we will make mistakes. In fact some successful business leaders suggest that the most successful organizations are the organizations that make mistakes the fastest. Fail faster, and learn from mistakes faster. Being messy is part of trying on. It's okay to have a negative impact and learn from it. It's forgivable. Others in the group will also learn. If I am constantly on guard about making mistakes or afraid of the impact I might have, it will be hard to try on new ideas and behaviors. Making mistakes and making them faster is not, however, an excuse for shaming or blaming others or for failing to account for one's impact on others.

Say Ouch

Interrupting shame, blame, or attack as quickly as possible is important, even if one does not know what to do next. When I am practicing self-focus and noticing a feeling of fear, anger, or loss, I might want to literally say ouch to alert the group to the impact that some words or actions are having on me. A skilled facilitator or another member of the group may then interrupt what is taking place to focus on what the impact has been on the person who said ouch. When the group agrees to this as a guideline, people are agreeing that it is okay to slow down the content to allow for processing feelings that have an impact on an individual, even if the intention was not to inflict hurt.

The Guidelines in Context

Having articulated the guidelines, next we turn to implicit and explicit assumptions people carry into group settings and about the process of establishing guidelines that in effect makes certain assumptions explicit and shared by the group. Because people can have very different assumptions about trust and safety, we will also look at these key concepts. Finally, we will consider the guidelines as a spiritual practice.

Implicit and Explicit Assumptions

Any time two or more people come together, they bring multiple sets of assumptions about proper conduct. These assumptions may be implicit or explicit. That is, they may govern the parties' conduct without ever being stated, or they may be articulated aloud. Most often both implicit and explicit assumptions are operating. For instance, the parties may all assume *implicitly* that they will not engage in physical combat, and they may *explicitly* state that each person has a right to his or her own opinion.

Their implicit assumptions may be in conflict with the implicit assumptions of other people in the group. For example, a man may assume that his opinion, as a man, is more important or better than any woman's opinion. In the same group, some or all of the women may assume that their opinions are just as important and beneficial as any man's opinion. The fact that the group may explicitly agree that each person has a right to his or her opinion does not mean that all believe those opinions will be equally valued. As people practice the guidelines, more and more of the implicit assumptions will come to the surface. The guidelines assist people in discovering their implicit assumptions and ascertaining whether others share those assumptions.

The Process for Establishing Guidelines

Some groups choose to take the time to build guidelines through a collaborative process. An assumption here, which may or may not be stated explicitly, is that guidelines arrived at through this process will fit the group better or have more buy-in from the participants. This may be true if the participants are interested in engaging in this activity at the beginning and if the leader is skilled at including everyone. Such a process can build community, trust, and a sense of accomplishment about working together. The disadvantage is an unskilled group may not choose adequate guidelines.

At other times, the leader of a group proposes some guidelines and asks if the other members would like to modify these guidelines or add any new ones. The assumption here is that a skilled, experienced leader may have a better idea of what guidelines are needed and that this particular group may also know something about its own needs and context that the leader does not know. The process of the leader beginning by proposing some guidelines may save some time if there is real assent to the proposed guidelines. The disadvantage is that an unskilled leader may try to force a set of rules on people in a way that leaves them feeling they have little power in the group.

While it is important for each group and its leadership to decide which process for establishing guidelines is most helpful to them, I have set out guidelines that I have found useful in a wide variety of settings. These particular guidelines can serve as a model for people who have little experience with explicit guidelines. Those with more experience can compare their guidelines with the ones I have articulated as a way of thinking about what they might need to include. The main point is that guidelines, especially when people are interested in working across differences, should be explicit and discussable. When they are not explicit and discussable, someone is likely benefiting and using power to his or her advantage. Others may be holding back from taking responsibility, either out of habit or out of fear. In the following chapter on power, we will examine how those who have been historically oppressed sometimes internalize their own oppression. Having historically had little or no input into the rules that govern groups, people who have been treated as inferior (racial minorities, women, people who speak English as a second language) may hold back out of habit even when they are encouraged to participate. Explicitly stated guidelines agreed to by all protect those in the group with the least amount of power. They ensure as much as possible that all will have the opportunity to participate as equals. The power shift that can occur with the articulation and implementation of guidelines is a major factor that enables transformation in a congregation, especially when the congregation represents many differences of race, culture, ethnicity, theologies, and lifestyles.

Guidelines, Trust, and Safety

When asked why a group needs guidelines, people frequently mention trust and safety. Guidelines help people trust their leaders, other individuals, and the group as a whole. It may even be that people who might tend to act unthinkingly in dominant ways are grateful for guidelines that remind them of the need for mutuality and greater awareness of others' needs and wants.

Often at the end of a semester or the end of a church leadership retreat, participants express appreciation for my leadership (or mine and a colleague's) in establishing an atmosphere where it was safe to take risks and thus possible to learn and grow. I always accept the compliment and then point out that the climate of trust was not simply the result of some magic I worked. The participants themselves created and agreed to the guidelines that made that trust possible. I do not say this to deflect the compliment. I point again to the guidelines to assure them that they too can create an atmosphere of trust by *explicitly* articulating guidelines for every group they lead or in which they participate.

Safety is a more complicated concept. People who have more power and privilege in society, in a culture, or within a particular group (for example, white people, wealthy people, people whose first language is English, and men) often like to talk about creating safety for everyone. While this goal is noble, these same people sometimes fail to acknowledge that they have more power or privileged status, more access to goods or resources, than others in the group. They sometimes fail to realize that when tension rises, people who have historically had less power, less privilege, less voice in a group are more likely to be adversely affected by any conflict that arises. They may be unaware that the feeling of safety they experience is not equally distributed.

On the other hand, people with historically less status and power in society or in a group (for example, people of color, people with low incomes, people who do not speak English or who struggle with English as a second or third language, and women) are deeply aware that the impact of decisions and the fallout from any conflict will redound upon them more than upon those who generally have more power. These people may not feel as safe as the people who have more power. Therefore, in a diverse group, people have different understandings and expectations for safety, depending upon their previous experience and their particular location in society or the group. Some people feel very little safety in a mixed group when they are in the minority, no matter how safe other people want them to feel. The range of feelings people have about their own safety in a group is worth paying attention to and naming in some situations.

The Guidelines as a Spiritual Practice

I try to live these guidelines as a spiritual practice in my family and friendships and with colleagues and students. I find that when I am in a conflict with someone, one or more of these guidelines have been violated. Sometimes at night I review the guidelines in a modern form of examination of conscience.[17] I recall my interactions with other people during the day both to give thanks and to acknowledge my shortcomings before God. When I recall an incident that was uncomfortable or that went awry, I look to see if I have violated one of the guidelines. When I am able to notice my shortcoming, I ask God's pardon and make a mental note (called a firm purpose of amendment in some traditions) to work on that guideline the next time a similar encounter occurs. When an interaction that had the potential to be problematic has gone well, I give thanks and note which guidelines may have made that success possible. Over time, I have begun to see the guidelines as a way of ordering the quality of my interactions with others and discerning the areas in my life where I need to ask God's grace for personal growth and transformation. The guidelines are that powerful for me.

I learned the guidelines I have presented when I was a participant in an antiracism, multicultural training workshop. I have used them in consulting with independent schools and nonprofit agencies, in church leadership retreats, and in a variety of workshops. I begin every class I teach at the seminary and all my online classes with a presentation and discussion of these guidelines. After I make my presentation, I always ask if people want to add any further guidelines. Sometimes participants add something that is important in their context or because of the particular history of their group that I would not have thought about. In all cases, even when the suggested addition seems redundant to me, I find that the addition itself or the possibility of adding a guideline means that the whole group feels less dominated by the leader. They feel a greater ownership of the guidelines, even if the guidelines have been largely presented by me as the leader. When I work with groups where some people have already been exposed to these particular guidelines and others have not, I invite those who know the guidelines to help present them, even as I suggest that all those who are present probably have some set of similar guidelines. I encourage all the participants to suggest guidelines that have worked for them.

This way of establishing guidelines underlines the fact that guidelines for a group's interactions affect both relationships and what the group can accomplish (products or goals). They create more mutual relationships by guaranteeing, as far as possible, that all group members are valued and celebrated through their participation and that the distribution of power is fairly equal. In diverse settings, guidelines in effect allow the complexity of a situation to be named and diverse and creative solutions to be put forward, even if they appear at first to be contradictory. In other words, guidelines allow for multiple ways of being and acting.

Both as a process and as an outcome, the notion that there exist multiple truths or perspectives that don't cancel each other out may be foreign to some people. Thus, the guidelines may require a change of mindset or a change of heart (*metanoia*).

Another way of saying this is that employing the guidelines requires, and perhaps facilitates, what Ronald Heifetz refers to as an adaptive change.[18] For Heifetz, a simple problem can be solved by a technical fix—an *authority* applies current know-how—as stated above. Diagnosing and treating a bacterial infection with antibiotics is an example of a technical fix. Singing a hymn in Spanish that the congregation knows and likes to sing as a step toward multicultural inclusion is a technical fix. Adaptive challenges require *the people with the problem* to adapt—learn new values and ways of behaving. This may require people to adjust their unrealistic expectations of and dependency on experts or authorities. It will require them to engage their own resourcefulness and to take more responsibility. Heifetz uses the example of working with a terminal cancer patient and her family to determine the specific end-of-life problems unique to them and the types of "treatment" they desire. This requires the adaptive work of all the parties, including patient, family, doctor, hospice providers, and so forth. Working with Spanish and English congregants to determine what type of worship, education, and fellowship best meets the needs of people on Sunday morning (or possibly other times) is adaptive work.

Learning the guidelines outlined in this chapter should be thought of as adaptive work, more than as a technical fix. For many people, the guidelines go beyond their current know-how, especially both/and thinking and the part of self-focus that attends to feelings. Practicing the guidelines is not simply the work of authorities, it is also the work of all who would be involved in transforming their congregations into more inclusive, welcoming, and lively communities of faith. The guidelines are not a technical fix applied by an expert to resolve conflict. The guidelines can assist people in conflict in acquiring new know-how—new values, attitudes, and habits of interacting—that will transform them. Practicing the guidelines will change how people understand themselves in relationship to others—challenging attitudes of superiority and inferiority alike. Often these very attitudes, as much as the ideas and behaviors about which people disagree, are what precipitate, maintain, and deepen the conflict.

2

Understanding Power and Difference

Race as a Primary Example

Speak out for those who cannot speak, for the rights of all the destitute.
Speak out, judge righteously, defend the rights of the poor and needy.

—*Proverbs 31:8-9*

For to be free is not merely to cast off one's chains but to live in a way that respects and enhances the freedom of others.

—*Nelson Mandela*[1]

This may be the most liberating chapter of the book for some readers. For others, it may be quite unnerving. We cannot explore significant differences and transforming communities without exploring power and privilege. In my experience, our ability to examine and our comfort in examining issues of power and privilege depend in large measure on how much power we have, or think we have, in various aspects of our life—and how much privilege we think we may lose if our privilege comes under scrutiny. Even if we are willing to look at issues of power and privilege—especially as they affect us personally—this examination may be difficult if we are used to thinking about power and privilege as something earned or acquired by individual effort. Those of us who are born white or male or in a wealthy family have certain economic and political advantages compared to those who are born persons of color, female, or poor. These advantages or disadvantages have more to do with the groups we are born into than they have to do with our effort or personality. Power and privilege are not randomly or equitably distributed, and so some of us may feel guilty about our comparative good fortune or angry about our relative ill fortune. Those of us who benefit from the inequality may be uncomfortable discussing it. Those of us who experience economic injustice or who struggle to attain greater access to power are often more than willing to speak about who has power and how the dynamics of power and privilege affect them.

By *power* I mean the ability to do or to be. The ability to do is often the capacity to bring about a change in oneself, in one's circumstances, in relationships, even in the wider world. The ability to be refers the ability to be oneself, to be free, to express one's true thoughts and emotions. However, both the ability to do and the ability to be are largely conditioned by our social location or position in the world. Finally, power does not have to mean aggression—power *over* another person—or the limitation or diminishment of others.[2]

By *privilege*, I mean the benefits conferred to members of a dominant group simply by virtue of their membership in that group. Such privilege is unearned, not the result of achievement or work, but conferred by the virtue of an unjust system of power distribution.[3]

For those of us who move through life with little, or much less, power relative to those around us (for example, people of color, women, uneducated people, people who are poor), talking about power and privilege ensures that conversations about differences will have substance rather than avoid the elephant in the middle of the room. For example, most people of color and women have a practiced facility in discussing power and privilege, for they see how white people and men respectively have privileges and exercise power that affects them on a regular basis. For these people, discussions of differences that include reflections on privilege and power are liberating, though often painful. The very naming of privilege accorded to dominant groups of people and noticing how power functions between and within groups are steps toward equalizing the power differential. We can't change it if we don't see it.

Some people, by virtue of membership in dominant groups (for example, white people, men, well-educated people, people who are rich), have a significant amount of power, privilege, and access to resources relative to others.[4] Reflecting upon this imbalance of power, privilege, and access can be frightening if we have not done it before or if our prior reflection has been in an adversarial context. We may fear loss of power, privilege, status, or the ability to have things our own way simply from the act of noticing our privilege. We may prefer to think that we have earned the power and status we have: we have worked hard to get what we have, and we sure as heck don't want to give it up. Our fear is amplified if we believe we live in a zero-sum world—that when one person gains power or resources, someone else has to lose. In such a case, we may fear that we will have to give up life as we know it if we understand that we are given unearned power and privilege simply because of our race or gender or accent.

I am speaking here about looking at ourselves *as members of particular groups* (for example, white people, men, well-educated people, people who are rich, clergy) and the kinds of privilege and access to resources that come simply from being members of one particular group within a category (for example, race, gender, educational level, socioeconomic class, ordained or lay status, and so on). Conversely, belonging to other groups (for example, people of color, women, people who are poor, laity) within that category may mean that we are *targeted* to receive fewer goods, privileges, and access to resources.

The truth is, we all belong, or have belonged, to both types of groups. By that I mean if we pick one particular category or variable (for example, race, gender, socioeconomic class, educational level, religion, age, ordained or lay status, sexual orientation or identity, physical or mental ability, citizen or immigrant status, or language), we may find we have experienced more power, more privilege, and more access to resources than other groups in that same category. Initially, comparing within one category is important in order to understand the model. For instance, considering the category of class, we find that those of us who are middle or upper class will have more power, privilege, and access to public and private resources than people who are poor. If we look at another category, we might find that we have (or had) less power, privilege, and access to resources than others. Choosing the variable of age reveals that all of us as children have experienced having less power, privilege, and access to resources than those who were adults.

What makes the task of examining power, privilege, and access to resources difficult and often confusing is that we may belong to several groups at the same time—some that are dominant or privileged groups and others that are subordinated, less-privileged, or oppressed groups. *Dominant groups* are those whose members—simply by virtue of their belonging to that group—have more power, privileges, and access to goods and resources than other groups in the same category (race, gender, class). *Subordinated groups* are those groups whose members—simply by virtue of their belonging to that group—have been or are targeted by those who are dominant in society to have less power and privilege or to receive fewer goods and services relative to other groups in the same category. To give a simple example, if we look at educational level, a *well-educated* woman has more power and access to resources than uneducated women have. And, if we look at gender, *as a woman*, this person generally has less access to power and resources (earning power or access to leadership in most organizations) than a man with the same education. I am talking here about status *as a group member* and what power, privilege, benefits, and access to resources generally are granted or denied to a member of a particular group *within a specific category.* A particular woman may indeed experience more power and have more access to resources than a particular man. Similarly, a particular African American or Latino/a may have greater wealth, better education, more prestige, a better job than a particular white person. But these will be exceptions.

Why is it important to talk about the groups to which we belong? Isn't it enough to recognize individual differences? The primary reason to talk about the groups to which we belong is that by virtue of belonging to particular groups, we may engage in destructive and ineffective interpersonal behaviors or patterns, often unconsciously. These behaviors are based in attitudes of superiority and inferiority and can be destructive to others as well as to ourselves. If we become more aware of the behaviors or patterns, and the attitudes that underlie them, we can choose more positive alternative behaviors.

A Theological Basis for Valuing Differences

Before discussing specific behaviors or patterns related to belonging to particular groups, I want to return to the thesis of this book: that God intended the amazing diversity of human beings and of the entire creation, and that differences are good! In the book of Genesis, we read that on the fifth day, God "created the great sea monsters and every living creature that moves, of every kind, with which the waters swarm, and every winged bird of every kind. And God saw that it was good" (Gen. 1:21). And on the sixth day, "God made the wild animals of the earth of every kind . . . and everything that creeps upon the ground of every kind. And God saw that it was good" (Gen. 1:25). Even humankind, created in God's image, is diverse: "male and female" God created them (Gen. 1:27). And when God saw everything that was made in all its diversity, "it was very good" (Gen. 1:31). In a similar way, Paul talks about the diversity of the church and the gifts of ministry within it, comparing it to a human body in which all the parts are valuable (1 Cor. 12:12-31). In light of this appreciation of difference, we can assert that communities of faith are at their most vital when they recognize and value differences.

Furthermore, faith communities can *become* vital through recognizing, understanding, and celebrating differences. Differences, of course, are not always valued. The early church struggled with the differences between followers of Jesus who were of Jewish ancestry and those who were not. They argued about assimilation: was circumcision for men a requirement for baptism and belonging to the community? In the end, they opted to recognize and value differences of culture and religious background. Today many of our communities are diverse culturally, racially, ethnically, educationally, theologically, and with regard to class status. Even the more homogeneous congregations are diverse with regard to age and gender. The thesis of this book is that recognizing, understanding more deeply, and celebrating these differences rather than ignoring them or taking them for granted will vitalize our faith communities.

The Multicultural Process of Change

To understand what this transformation looks like I present on page 39 a diagram (figure 2.1) developed by VISIONS psychologists and educators Valerie Batts, John Capitman, and Joycelyn Landrum-Brown.[5] They call this kind of transformation the "Multicultural Process of Change." Because it involves recognizing and valuing differences of all kinds, the process itself is multicultural. They designed the particular model or tool primarily to help individuals, groups, and organizations to work against racism. While racism is not the only form of oppression, a specific focus on racism is important in itself and also as an especially clear example of domination and subordination because of the particular history of the United States in which European immigrants slaughtered indigenous people and brought African peoples here as slaves. These events are part of the founding story of this country and have often been downplayed or misrepresented.[6]

The multicultural process of change begins by recognizing the way power affects how our communities are structured and how people treat one another. The VISIONS model shows the effect of power on four levels: On a *personal level*, how we think about ourselves and others is frequently superimposed with judgments of better than and less than. Power affects our interactions with others on an *interpersonal level.* It also affects the policies and practices that create and sustain our communities on an *institutional* level. And on a *cultural level*, those who dominate in society define what is "good," "true," and "beautiful"—or the opposite.

Monoculturalism and Pluralism

To understand how power is related to our view of differences, let's begin by looking at the two contrasting worldviews rep-

Figure 2.1. Multicultural Process of Change

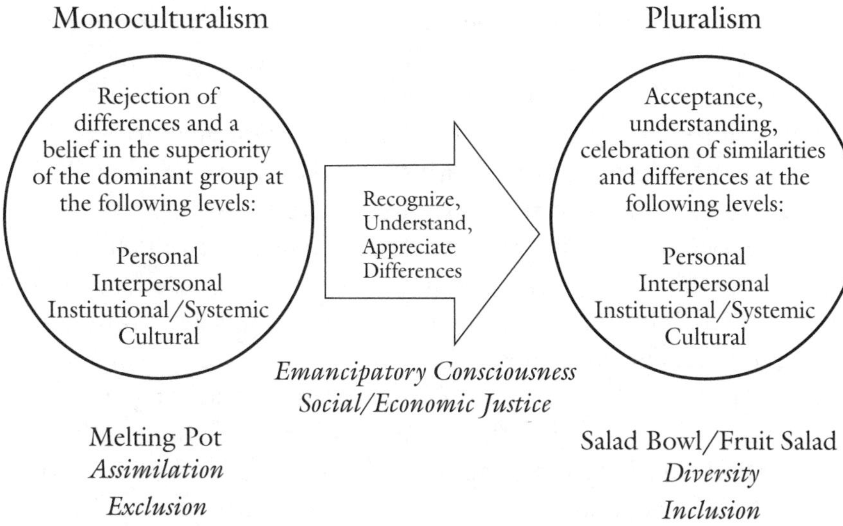

resented in the diagram—neither of which exists in pure form. One worldview sees differences as better than and less than, or higher and lower, and uses power to reinforce the superiority of those who are dominant. In effect, this worldview, which is called monoculturalism, excludes differences. It corresponds to what Paul speaks of as creation subjected to futility, sin, and death. This is the *old creation*. In this worldview, people with the most power treat those who are different from them as less than themselves. In essence, they believe that for anyone to join their community, other people have to become as much like them as possible. They must assimilate or be excluded. This attitude of superiority today is exemplified by English-only movements or by the decision of a congregation to have zero tolerance for a theology that deviates from the theology of the leaders.

The other worldview, pluralism, accepts, understands, celebrates, and utilizes differences. It refuses to see differences as better than and less than, higher or lower. Paul speaks of "the freedom of the glory of the children of God," which is the *new creation* (Rom. 8:21). This attitude of justice and equality is exemplified today in congregations that sing and pray in the diverse languages spoken by their people and in "open and affirming" congregations that welcome and incorporate gay, lesbian, bisexual, and transgendered people as equal members. The movement from a dominant, power-over, judgmental worldview to a more just, more equitable set of relationships takes work and time. The process is ongoing and occurs on many levels.

Monoculturalism is deeply engrained in unconscious attitudes of many white people in the United States. I remember being taught as a child to be proud that my country was a melting pot. I did not realize until much later what many white European immigrants had to give up to become "Americans." When I was growing up, my grandmother, who was born in Hungary, lived with us. She and my father almost always spoke Hungarian with one another. My father refused to teach my brother and me anything more than a few words and phrases and one nursery rhyme in Hungarian.[7] As a child, I thought my father was trying to preserve a secret language that he could speak with his mother and that I would not understand, and that it wasn't worth his time and energy to teach us Hungarian because there would be so few people we could speak to. He told me later that he didn't teach me Hungarian because we could really be "American" if we only spoke English.[8] As a result of my father's decision to assimilate in this way, I was kept from learning a second language in my own home, although that would have been relatively easy. Not learning a second language at home was a price I paid to belong to the melting pot—the culturally dominant, white, English-as-primary-language, "American" society.

Oppression and Internalized Oppression

Monoculturalism is another way to talk about *oppression*. VISIONS training materials use this definition: "Oppression—the systematic mistreatment of the powerless by the powerful, resulting in the targeting of certain groups within society for less of its benefits [for example, quality health care and education],—involves a subtle devaluing or nonacceptance of the powerless group."[9] For this reason, VISIONS theorists refer to groups that have been systematically oppressed as "target" groups, and those groups who have been in dominant or privileged positions as "nontarget" groups. Oppression may be economic, political, social, psychological, and theological. Oppression, VISIONS trainers add, "has occurred historically and over time. Oppression includes the belief in the superiority or 'righteousness' of the group in power."[10]

The failure to positively value differences and the belief in the superiority of a dominant group are also woven into the attitudes of many people of color, women, poor people, and other groups who perceive themselves as less than or inferior. When people take for granted their socially constructed positions as less than or fail to notice that they are being treated as inferior, we speak of this situation as *internalized oppression*. Internalized oppression is particularly insidious when the laws of a country or the rules of an organization have eliminated overt forms of oppression. In such situations, equality or near equality may theoretically exist for individuals, and yet they continue to act as if others are superior and they are inferior.

In some parts of U.S. culture, people are still legally and formally treated as second-class or inferior people. Some denominations restrict ordination to men only. Women who wish to be ordained in those denominations are clearly treated as less than or inferior. Similarly, in most states in the United States and most countries in the world, gay and lesbian couples are treated as less than or inferior with regard to their right to marry a partner of the same gender.

The Myth of the Melting Pot

Only recently did I learn that the popularity of the melting pot image came from a play by the same name, written by the British-born novelist and playwright Israel Zangwill, one of the earliest interpreters of Jewish immigrant life in the United States. The play opened in 1908. President Theodore Roosevelt, who became one of the play's most extravagant boosters, was in the audience. *The Melting Pot* is a love story involving David Quixano, a gifted Jewish composer living in New York, and his beloved, Vera Revendal, a non-Jewish Russian exile. Quincy Davenport, the only major native-born "American" character in the play, is an unemployed millionaire who owns a symphony orchestra and has hired the talented German conductor, Pappelmeister, to orchestrate David's symphony. According to Joe Kraus, assistant professor of English at the University of Scranton, the millionaire Davenport ironically prefers low-brow, comic opera and lacks the "genuine American sensibility that Pappelmeister appreciates and that David embodies."[11] According to Kraus, Zangwill intends Davenport's crudeness to characterize him as less "American" than the immigrants (such as Kathleen, the Irish maid) who populate the play. We thus encounter a cultural hierarchy that inverts the economic hierarchy.[12] The central scene of the play comes when David describes the conviction that underlies the symphony he has written:

> America is God's Crucible, the great Melting-Pot where all the races of Europe are melting and re-forming! Here you stand, good folk, think I, when I see them at Ellis Island, here you stand in your fifty groups, with your fifty languages and histories, and your fifty blood hatreds and rivalries. But you won't be long like that, brothers, for these are the fires of God you've come to—these are the fires of God. A fig for your feuds and vendettas! Germans and Frenchmen, Irishmen and Englishmen, Jews and Russians—into the Crucible with you all! God is making the American.[13]

The play was itself a melange of melodrama, farce, burlesque, and rhetoric. It sought to entertain people of different cultural and economic backgrounds, and it succeeded everywhere but in New York, where according to Kraus, critics were beginning to dictate the correct way to stage a play appealing to an elite and homogeneous audience and with well-defined expectations about dress and decorum. According to Kraus, this New York taste for formal theater, without the mixture of styles appealing to heterogeneous audiences, became a force in American socialization. Kraus writes:

> Once critics began asserting that only one type of theater was acceptable, once they began denying varieties of aesthetics in the theater audience, they created a situation in which the audience really was in a position to conceive of itself as being a group of "fused Americans." It was the theater, the homogeneous, formally insistent theater that New York heralded, that would help transform melting-pot immigrants into Americans. Whatever may have succeeded or failed on the stage of *The Melting Pot,* the real show was happening in the audience.[14]

The process of establishing a dominant white culture in the United States, which began with the elimination or decimation of many indigenous nations and the importation of African peoples as slaves, was continuing in a new way. Whether we focus on the play itself or the New York theater, a movement was clearly afoot to strip many white Europeans of their "old world" cultures and their ethnic differences. Socially elite whites were establishing a hierarchy within white cultures. Speaking only English and assimilating into the Anglo-American culture became a priority. Even white newcomers to the United States were expected to shed their languages and many of their customs. In spite of the fact that my white teachers from kindergarten through high school suffered to varying degrees a loss of their European cultures, the melting-pot understanding of America was always presented by them as a positive notion. Some of the resistance of white people to pluralism is embedded in the internalized oppression they experienced when they lost their cultural differences in order to become American. Thus, assimilated immigrants sometimes take the attitude toward newer immigrants, "If I had to change, you have to as well." Like my father, some European Americans resist pluralism because they still believe "English only" is better than, and being multilingual is less than.[15]

That being said, we must bear in mind that while a cost was exacted (for example, a loss of family history, culture, and language ability) for non-English speaking white Europeans who came to the United States, it was not the same as the cost borne by others who often were not even allowed to assimilate. Africans who came to this country were not part of the melting pot. There was no expectation that they would assimilate. They were brought as slaves. People of Asian decent were denied citizenship as late as 1952. Eduardo Bonilla-Silva, professor of sociology at Duke University and a major scholar and author on race and ethnicity and their connection to stratification and political economy, speaks to this point in a video entitled *The House We Live In*. Speaking of the melting-pot understanding of the United States, Bonilla-Silva says the "melting pot never included people of color. Blacks, Chinese, Puerto-Ricans, et cetera, could not melt into the pot. They could be used as wood to produce the fire for the pot, but they could not be used as material to be melted into the pot."[16]

Target and Nontarget Groups

The grid on page 45 (figure 2.2) illustrates forms of oppression that spring from monoculturalism and the rejection or subordination of differences by those who have the most power.[17]

This chart represents multiple ways power imbalances can and do occur in U.S. society and in the rest of the world, although parts of it will not apply in or need some adaptation to other settings. I have added clericalism to the VISIONS list, because it is a particular type of oppression that must be addressed if we are to transform congregations. Other forms of oppression could be further specified, depending on circumstances. To better understand the difference between being a member of a dominant or nontarget group and being a member of an oppressed or target group, I suggest that you stop reading and engage the following exercise.

Figure 2.2. Target and Nontarget Groups

Types of Oppression	Variable	Nontarget Groups	Target Groups
Racism	Race/Color	White	People of color (African, Asian, Native, Latino/a Americans)
Sexism	Gender	Men	Women, Transgendered
Classism	Socioeconomic class	Middle, upper class	Poor, working class
Elitism	Education level Place in hierarchy	Formally educated Managers, exempt, faculty	Informally educated Clerical, nonexempt, students
Religious Oppression Anti-Semitism	Religion	Christians Protestants Christians	Muslims, Hindus, others Catholics Jews
Militarism	Military status	World War I and II, Korean War, Gulf War Veterans	Vietnam Veterans
Ageism Adultism	Age	Young adults Adults	Elders (40+ by law) Children
Heterosexism	Sexual orientation	Heterosexuals	Gay, Lesbian, Bisexual
Ableism	Physical or mental ability	Currently able-bodied	Physically or mentally challenged
Xenophobia	Immigrant status	U.S. born	Immigrant
Linguistic Oppression	Language	English	English as a second language Languages other than English
Clericalism	Ordination status	Clergy	Laity

Questions for Reflection

1. Looking at the chart "Target and Nontarget Groups" on page 45, identify the nontarget groups to which you belong and the target groups to which you belong.
2. Choose one nontarget group to which you belong.
   a. What are some strengths that come from your experiences as a member of this group? Write down the words that come to mind to describe these strengths.
   b. Think about a time you were treated as better than because of your membership in this group. Write down the words that come to mind to describe being treated as better than.
   c. Think of a time when you found yourself treating a person in a target group as less than. This may have been intentional or unintentional, conscious or unconscious at the time. Write down your thoughts and feelings about this incident.
3. Choose one target group to which you belong.
   a. What are some strengths that come from your experiences as a member of this target group? Write down the words that come to mind to describe these strengths.
   b. Think about a time you were treated as less than because of your membership in one of your target groups. Write down the words that come to mind to describe being treated as less than.
4. If you do this exercise as part of a group, pair up and share with your partner the responses you are comfortable sharing. It might help to form pairs that share some similar target and nontarget characteristics. For instance, if the group includes only two people of color, they might choose to share their responses with one another.
5. After the pairs have shared, the group can discuss what they have learned by doing the exercise.

Levels of Oppression

When people begin to discuss the various types of oppression, confusion often arises because an individual from a particular target group, for example a woman, may not feel she has suffered any oppression by virtue of being in that group—in her case being a woman. I can recall several instances when I was consulting in independent schools and older, white, female teachers told me that they had never experienced any personal prejudice because of their gender. They told me that they had applied for and got good jobs at the same pay as men, and they had advanced in their careers. They did not experience themselves as inferior or less than *on a personal level.* At the same time, "women working full-time year-round still earn only about 77 cents for every dollar earned by men—and women of color fare significantly worse," according to Jocelyn Samuels, vice president for Education and Employment, National Women's Law Center, in her testimony before the U.S. Senate Committee on Health, Education, Labor and Pensions on April 12, 2007.[18]

One way to deal with these two realities—not feeling personally oppressed and being statistically at a disadvantage regarding earning power—is to realize that all the types of oppression, all the "isms," can occur on four levels.

Personal Level

Oppression on this level has to do with attitudes, beliefs, and feelings that one group (whites, men, clergy) is superior and that others (blacks or Latino/as, women, laity) are inferior or that their differences are not acceptable. These attitudes or beliefs can be conscious or unconscious. They can be learned directly from teachers, parents, ministers, or others in positions of authority. They can be "caught" through indirect messages, by observation, or by example. *Prejudice* occurs on this personal level. It is a negative attitude toward a person or group arising from a prejudgment or evaluation based on one's own standards or the standards of one's group. We maintain the prejudice by finding "facts" to explain it. An example would be, "Blacks should be separate; they are different." This type of prejudice is an example of cognitive misinformation—that is, the conclusion (blacks should be separate) is based on an untested or erroneous belief or value (blacks are different in such a way they must be segregated). At other times, a feeling, for instance a fear, is presented as fact. In this case, I gather other facts to support what I have decided to be true on the basis of my feelings. An example would be, "It's so hard (read, I'm uncomfortable) working with Mexicans; they're lazy and just don't care about quality."[19] Other examples of personal level oppression or prejudice include thinking that men are better managers than women or that white doctors are superior to doctors of color.

Interpersonal Level

The interpersonal level has to do with behaviors that may be subtle and outside the actor's awareness. Thus the oppression may be intentional or unintentional. We become aware of the oppressive nature of these behaviors and their impact on others when we feel discomfort or tension in a cross-cultural interaction or when someone points them out to us. The behaviors arise from a conscious or unconscious assumption that we are better than another. An example of an oppressive behavior on this level would be for a white person at a meeting to speak after a person of color has spoken very clearly and say, "What I think Renae was trying to say was . . ." For a member of a dominant group to always speak first in a diverse group or to need to have the last word is also a form of interpersonal oppression. Other examples of oppressive behaviors and internalized oppression follow.

Institutional Level

The institutional level has to do with formal laws, written and unwritten rules, as well as practices and procedures that govern an organization and that function to the advantage of the nontarget or dominant group and to the disadvantage of the target or subordinated group. These rules and practices help to maintain the superiority, power, and privilege of the nontarget group. Oppressive institutional level practices include holding meetings when members of nondominant groups cannot attend, advertising for new job openings in venues that ensure the organization will maintain the same racial and ethnic imbalance, hiring a "token" representative of a minority group and failing to support that person with adequate training for the environment, and failing to train current homogeneous groups of employees regarding multicultural issues in order to make a smoother transition to a more diverse workforce.

Cultural Level

At the cultural level, the group in power also maintains superiority by determining what is "right," "acceptable," "good," "true," "moral," or "beautiful." Members of this group may also determine that the actions, thoughts, and expressions of others are negative, unacceptable, or inferior. Batts observes, "Conformity to the dominant culture is then viewed as 'normal' when in fact the myth of the inherent superiority of the group setting the standards is operating."[20] Thus individuals will have to conform their behavior to that of the dominant group in order to be accepted as suitable or competent. Examples of cultural level oppression include displaying artwork of only one culture, requiring employees to speak only English when on breaks, providing only "traditional" (read "white European") music in a multicultural congregation.

Old-Fashioned Racism and Modern Racism

For more than forty years, since the civil rights movement made overt racial oppression illegal, sociologists, psychologists, and antiracism trainers have been making a distinction between old-fashioned racism and modern racism. As we will see, this distinction applies to many other forms of oppression as well. *Old-fashioned racism* refers to the explicit belief that blacks and other people of color are inferior to whites. White superiority or white supremacy is the ideology of this overt prejudice. Overt racism in education was sustained by the law of the land in the United States until 1954. Appendix B, "Institutional and Cultural Oppression in the United States," gives an outline of the checkered history of laws and Supreme Court rulings regarding race in this country. Old-fashioned racism operated on all four levels. Whites overtly proclaimed attitudes of their superiority and blacks' inferiority (personal level). Whites called blacks by their first names and expected submissiveness from blacks, such as being called by an honorific or "sir" (interpersonal level). Blacks were required to attend separate and inferior schools, use separate drinking fountains and bathrooms, enter buildings by separate entrances, sit in the balconies of movie theaters and churches, and ride in the backs of buses (institutional level). Blacks were "targeted" to receive fewer goods, benefits, and resources. Whites restricted black voting. Movies and advertising portrayed white people as average Americans. Blacks and Latino/as were absent or portrayed as inferior (cultural level).

Modern racism is the name given to racism after the passage of the Civil Rights Act in 1964, when many explicitly racist practices became illegal. Prejudice and oppressive attitudes continued in a more hidden, indirect form. Modern racism, according to Batts, is "the attribution of non-race related reasons for behaviors that continue to deny equal access to opportunity to black and other targets of systemic oppression."[21] These subtler, implicit, new forms of racism continue to oppress targeted groups. The subtlety also functions to hide oppressive attitudes and feelings from the very people who have them. This obfuscation of their racism leads to whites acquiring what Peggy McIntosh, founder and codirector of the National SEED Project on Inclusive Curriculum (Seeking Educational Equity and Diversity), refers to as "the invisible knapsack of privilege" that whites experience and take for granted today.[22] While modern racism is now more prevalent, old-fashioned racism still operates in places where people feel cultural support for overt expressions of oppression. For example, predominantly white churches will say that they do not need to consider black candidates for senior pastor openings "because we need someone who fits in (read, who is on our level)." Both forms of racism rely on the myth of the superiority of the dominant group.

Modern Racism

VISIONS analysts Mary Sonn and Valerie Batts identify five types of modern racism behavior: (1) dysfunctional rescuing; (2) blaming the victim; (3) avoidance of contact; (4) denial of cultural differences; and (5) denying (or not understanding) the political, social, economic, historical, and psychological significance of differences.[23] These modern racist behaviors can be seen in a congregational setting and in behavior related to clericalism, another form of oppression.

Dysfunctional Rescuing

Dysfunctional rescuing is most easily described as help that doesn't help. This form of oppression is based on an assumption that the person in the target group is inferior and cannot help herself. The behavior is patronizing and condescending, and it is often motivated by guilt. It may be conscious or unconscious and is cloaked in a shroud of politeness that makes it hard to recognize and challenge.

For instance, the governing board appoints one of the few persons of color in the congregation, a relative newcomer, to chair a new committee. The board believes that appointing this woman will be a good way for her to get to know others, help her feel that she truly belongs, and raise her standing in the congregation. The board fails to recognize that this tokenism may be a setup for failure, given that others who believe they have more experience may resent her appointment and be unwilling to work with her. Truly diversifying a committee or a congregation means that people will have different values and different leadership styles.

White people may need to realize that *they themselves* will have to make some changes and adapt if people of color are to have an equal place.

Or the pastor spends an hour explaining the previous year's budget to the new treasurer, who is the president of a large accounting firm. The treasurer's attempts to inform him that she understands the budget are met with "I'm just trying to show you how things are different here at the church." The pastor is unaware that he is treating the professional financial person as inferior, perhaps because she is a layperson, perhaps because she is a woman. Her knowledge of budgets probably exceeds his own.

Blaming the Victim

Blaming the victim, another form of modern oppression, ignores the impact of historical and current systemic oppression on the oppressed or target group. The nontarget person accepts little or no responsibility for current inequalities. Nontargets set up target group members for failure and then blame them for negative outcomes after providing inadequate support for them. Sometimes this blame is public and aimed directly at the target person. Other times members of the nontarget group speak among themselves about how "those people" should have done things differently, without ever having shared their expectations directly with the people they are critiquing.

For instance, the sole Latina member of the worship committee becomes depressed and begins to withdraw from participation when her ideas for hymns, prayers, and special celebrations are continually rejected or ignored, even though the percentage of Spanish-speaking people in the congregation is growing. It turns out that the committee had no intention of significantly changing the style of the worship; therefore they did not value her suggestions. They merely wanted the appearance of a diverse planning group so that they could claim that Spanish-speaking people were represented. In addition, the white members of the committee view the Cuban, Puerto Rican, and Honduran people as one group of non-English speakers. When the Latina committee member's suggestion for a hymn was tried and some of the Spanish-speaking congregants said they didn't know it and preferred another hymn from their culture, the Latina committee member was blamed. The committee chair suggests that she be replaced by a different Spanish-speaking representative "who understands the worship style of the congregation better"—probably meaning one "who likes traditional white liturgies."

Or the newly ordained, single, assistant pastor complains to the senior pastor that the lay couple who has successfully led the youth group for four years doesn't have a theological understanding of ministry. Though they were busy starting their careers and raising a family, they agreed to lead the youth group because they had met each other in a youth group and stayed connected to the church through college because of their positive experience in religious youth activities. The assistant pastor believes that he is superior to them with regard to theological education. He does not value their lived faith experience and ability to relate to the young people because they do not have his sophisticated theological language and understanding. Their differences in style on a weekend retreat and the assistant's condescending attitude toward the lay couple result in some of the young people choosing not to attend for several weeks. The assistant blames this on the lay couple's theological incompetence.

Avoidance of Contact

As a form of modern oppressive behavior, avoidance of contact is operating when members of the nontarget group make little or no effort to get to know, understand, or value members of the target group personally or professionally. Sometimes nontarget group supervisors avoid stepping in to correct a target group employee or to settle a dispute between two target group employees for fear of being called a racist, when they would have intervened had the employees been white. This lack of experience in dealing with target groups means that members of target groups nearly always understand the people in the nontarget group better than members of the nontarget group understand people in the target group, because it is necessary for the survival and success of target group members to know how to function within the nontarget environment.

For example, members of the Bible study group that meets in different parishioners' homes continue to suggest that they meet in one of the three "centrally located" homes of white parishioners, rather than accept the hospitality of the "more distant" black or Latina members who have offered their homes as a meeting place. All the members of the diverse group live within five miles of the church.

Or a clergyperson refuses to mediate in a heated dispute between two lay people for fear of being too domineering, when she would mediate in a similar dispute between two members of the clergy.

Denial of Cultural Differences

The most common manifestation of denying cultural differences is "color blindness," minimizing physical and behavioral differences or cultural preferences of target group members as a way to mask discomfort with those differences or to completely deny their importance and to enshrine nontarget cultural preferences. It often takes a form similar to this: "What difference does it make if he is black? We're all human, after all!" meaning, "What difference does it make if he's black, as long as he never challenges me, and he acts like a white person?"

For instance, white people in one congregation never use the words *black* or *African American* to describe the only black family in their congregation or the words *white* or *European American* to describe themselves. Members of a congregation say they want to make people of color feel at home in their congregation but insist on maintaining their traditional European American or white, Anglo-Saxon service format and music without ever talking about its style.

Or clergy make lay participation difficult or impossible by holding important diocesan meetings during afternoon hours or national meetings over several weekdays—times when most lay people have to take vacation time or comp time to be away from work.

Denying (or Not Understanding) the Significance of Differences

Another form of modern racism is denial of or not understanding the political, economic, historical, and psychological significance of differences. Here nontarget group members minimize the influence of these factors on members of the target group. Cultural differences may be seen as simply interesting minor points to be acknowledged if time, energy, or money allow. This form of oppression is the anchor of white supremacy, patriarchy, and Western-worldview domination. It denies that the dominant group is acting in oppressive and domineering ways by keeping the dial tuned to its own culture. As a way of denying the historical, structural, and systemic disadvantages that function to maintain a radical imbalance in access to power and resources, it holds up examples of a single member of a target group who has been able to succeed. In ecumenical and interfaith settings, we may find denial of or failure to understand the theological significance of differences.

For instance, passages from the Gospels in which "the Jews" are presented in negative manner are read without comment. Sermons avoid addressing overt anti-Semitism in the text. In a congregation with a large percentage of recent African immigrants, discussions about the starting time of meetings and services fail to consider different notions of time in African and U.S. cultures.

Or the senior pastor, who is paid in accordance with denomination guidelines for clergy compensation, suggests that the congregation hire a parishioner at substandard salary rather than hire the parishioner or someone else in accordance with the American Guild of Organists' compensation guidelines. On a systemic level, churches rarely compensate lay and clergy equally, even when their educations are identical.

Internalized Oppression Behaviors

We have looked at one side of the dance of oppression—a set of behaviors employed by nontarget persons, by people acting out of their power and privilege. The other side of the dance that sustains oppression has to do with those who have little or no power or less access to resources—those who are target persons.

Oppression is insidious. Those who have been treated as inferior by a whole society or institution often respond by internalizing an attitude of inferiority and engaging in submissive behaviors that may have once been necessary as a means to success, if not for their very survival. Batts calls this attitude of internalized oppression "the incorporation of negative or limiting messages regarding our way of being and responding in the world by targets of systemic oppression."[24] Here, Batts says, members of a target group "define their uniqueness as inferior or different in an unhealthy or un-useful manner."[25] Internally oppressive behaviors begin as *survival* responses in situations where members of the target group detect a threat. As oppression decreases, more options become available and target group members can behave differently. If they continue to engage from a reactive posture, as though they are indeed inferior to others, they are said to have internalized the oppression or to be acting out of internalized oppression. The circumstances of oppression have changed, but they have not.

For members of a nontarget group to attribute internalized oppression to target group members is not really possible, because only target group members can sense if they are threatened or in a survival situation. Target group members need to be responsible for assessing if a threat still exists for them, or if they are acting according to a learned pattern or old habit that served them well when conditions were oppressive and dangerous.

Sonn and Batts describe five types of internalized oppression behaviors that can again be illustrated with congregational examples regarding race or culture and clergy or lay status: (1) system beating; (2) blaming the system; (3) reactive avoidance of contact; (4) denial of cultural heritage; (5) lack of understanding or minimization of the political, social, economic, historical, and psychological significance of racial oppression (or another specific oppression).

System Beating

System beating can be seen in target group member attempts to get around the system by "manipulating others or the system through guilt, psychological games, or illicit activities," Batts writes.[26] By internalizing an attitude of inferiority, the target group member believes that she does not have the power to succeed by being herself or being direct. Often the target group member will try to take care of the feelings of the nontargets for fear of being viewed unfavorably. For example, when a black person is angry, he may suppress his anger because he believes that even though his anger is legitimate, it will frighten white people or make them feel guilty.

At other times, the target group member will play dumb or attempt to be invisible. For instance, in a mostly white congregation, a wealthy member of color makes a very small pledge while serving on the capital campaign committee, knowing that he can accuse someone of being a racist if he is challenged on this. Or a layperson never says no when the pastor asks her to do more volunteer work, thus taking care of the pastor's need to easily find assistance with pressing tasks, even though her family relationships are suffering as a result. The pastor never asks her if taking on a new task would result in her neglecting herself or family obligations.

Blaming the System

Blaming others or the system for one's failures is another internalized oppression behavior. Blaming the system is a way of giving up one's power to bring about change. The blame and anger sometimes mask a deep underlying sense of hopelessness regarding the possibility of change for the better.

For example, a Chinese parishioner runs for the church board without submitting the required paperwork and then blames the system when he is not seriously considered. A committee member of color misses half the committee meetings and is late to most of the rest and then complains that the white people are making decisions without his input.

Or a lay outreach minister, who is a paid staff member at a large congregation, takes on a second, very demanding job. She says the pastor is too demanding when she is criticized for not meeting deadlines and the benchmarks she herself set when she first took her church job.

Reactive Avoidance of Contact

Reactive avoidance of contact[27] has two expressions. In its first expression, reactive avoidance of contact takes the form of avoiding members of one's own target group because they are "not black enough," "not Korean enough," or "not feminist enough." The second expression is an avoidance of nontarget group members whenever possible because one has an exaggerated suspicion of them or a fear of rejection. Reactive avoidance of contact may also take the form of avoiding work or relationships all together by escaping "through fantasy, dreams, drugs, alcohol, sex, food, or withdrawal," Batts writes.[28] The sense of inferiority is so great it leads to a hopelessness that results in avoidance of members of one's own group as well as others.

A black parishioner will work on committees having no other people of color as members because, in his opinion, "they always slow the process down." A layperson refuses to seek spiritual counsel from a member of the clergy because he believes that clergy cannot understand his life circumstances.

Denial of Cultural Heritage

With this internalized oppressive behavior, denial of cultural heritage, members of a target group conspire to accept the label of inferiority ascribed to their group. They defer to the nontarget group. They devalue or reject their own heritage. They overvalue the customs, culture, beliefs, and practices of the nontarget group as superior or as the norm.

For instance, a Latina member of the church board criticizes others of her culture who only attend the Spanish-language worship service at her congregation. "They should come to the main ten o'clock service if they really want to be members," she says. A parishioner refuses to use the committee structure established by the church to advance her project. "I can't be bothered with that. I go to the boss [the pastor] when I want to get something done." She believes that other lay members are inferior to the clergyperson, who is the one who really counts.

Lack of Understanding or Minimization of the Significance of Racial Oppression (or another specific oppression)

I have maintained the specific focus on racism with regard to internalized oppression because of the current political tendency to deny the pervasive nature of racism and the unwillingness of many people to understand that the historical legacy of racism remains with us. Just as important, when white people are able to see internalized racial oppression in people of color as a response to white dominance, white people can begin to overcome the cultural pressure not to examine racism. Once it is understood, this dynamic serves as an example for understanding other forms of internalized oppression.

The effects of racism continue to deeply affect the lives of blacks in this country as well as other peoples of color. One of the consequences of this legacy is that people of color continue to collude in their own oppression. Batts writes that the manifestations of this form of internalized oppression include:

> Being passive and unassertive; feeling powerless (learned helplessness); misdirecting anger to persons with less power; having difficulty expressing anger; avoiding conflicts at all costs; turning anger inward, resulting in high blood pressure, strokes, ulcers; buying copiously (symbolic status striving, resulting in conspicuous consumption of goods such as clothes and cars); in-group fighting; displaying sexist or other "ism" behaviors, e.g. heterosexism, classism; taking advantage of the lack of information or feelings of powerlessness of other people of color.[29]

Examples of a lack of understanding and minimizing or trivializing the political, social, economic, historical, psychological, or theological significance of oppression include a black Sunday school teacher who is more demanding of black students in her class, even when she knows that white students are not paying attention and doing their assignments. She is afraid to confront the parents of white students. Or a lay church employee always takes the side of the clergy when a member of the congregation has a complaint, even when he thinks the complaint is justified.

The Dance of Modern Oppression and Internalized Oppression

Like many other dysfunctional relationships, modern oppression and internalized oppression can be viewed as a dance. Oppression on both the target and nontarget sides of the equation is most likely to continue when there are two partners who are willing to engage in dysfunctional behaviors. White people who are prone to dysfunctionally rescue people of color are likely to find people of color who will accept the rescue as a way to get around the system. If the white person then recognizes that the person of color is cutting corners to beat the system, the white person may blame the victim, who in turn blames the system. A complex, vicious cycle begins with more than enough blame to keep it going. The next step of the dance may be avoidance of contact when the white person decides it doesn't pay to deal with folks of color, thereby cutting off any further contact with them ("We tried that and it didn't work"). The person of color in turn decides not to trust any white people, engaging in reactive avoidance of contact.

The diagram on page 61, "Behavioral Manifestations of Modern Oppression and Internalized Oppression," illustrates the relationship between oppressive behaviors of members of nontarget groups and the internalized oppression behaviors of members of target groups.[30] (See figure 2.3.) We all engage in behaviors on both sides of the chart, depending on whether we happen to be considering ourselves as members of a nontarget or a target group in a specific transaction. The diagram also names the alternative behaviors that can break the vicious cycle of oppression. While the cycle can be broken by someone on either side taking responsibility for their behavior and acting differently, it is crucial to remember that on the target side, the behaviors are usually learned as survival behaviors in times of overt oppression.

Figure 2.3. Behavioral Manifestations of Modern Oppression and Internalized Oppression (Alternative Behaviors in Italics)

Modern "Isms" **(Nontarget Group Behaviors)**	**Internalized Oppression** **(Target Group Behaviors)**
Dysfunctional rescuing *Functional helping*	System beating *Confrontation or standing up*
Blaming the victim *Problem solving*	Blaming the system *Owning responsibility*
Avoidance of contact *Mutual contact*	Reactive avoidance of contact *Sharing information from our different cultures*
Denial of differences *Recognizing differences*	Denial of my cultural differences *Recognizing differences*
Denial of the significance of differences *Recognizing the political significance of cultural differences*	Lack of understanding of the significance of differences *Sharing information on the impacts of cultural differences*
Problem solving at the personal, interpersonal, institutional, and cultural levels can be used to generate ongoing multicultural structures and processes as alternatives to all oppressive behaviors and internalized oppression behaviors.	

For target group members to employ alternative behaviors, the balance of power needs to have shifted in such a way that they are convinced their survival is not in question and that acting as equals will not result in retaliation for "being uppity."

Before looking at how we break cycles of oppression, I invite you to reflect on which behaviors in the dance of oppression and internalized oppression you are most likely to engage in.

Questions for Reflection

The following two questions might be shared in pairs or as part of a larger group discussion:

1. Looking at the behaviors listed in figure 2.3, in which oppressive behavior are you, as a member of a nontarget group, most likely to engage in a cross-cultural situation (for example, dysfunctional rescuing, blaming the victim, avoidance of contact)?
2. Looking at the behaviors on the same chart, in which internalized oppression behavior are you, as a member of a target group, most likely to engage in a cross-cultural situation (for example, system beating, blaming the system, reactive avoidance of contact)?

Breaking the Cycle of Oppression on the Personal and Interpersonal Level

How does one break this cycle of oppression? The first step is to admit that oppression still exists—that the "isms" are alive and functioning. On the institutional level, many laws have changed to make certain forms of oppression illegal. On the personal level, most of us at times still engage in behaviors that that are oppressive to others or to ourselves. I find that I also need to do more than simply acknowledge that the "isms" exist. For me it is helpful to look at my behaviors toward others to see if I am acting in ways that are oppressive. I do this in two ways. Privately, either in a journal or by making an examination of conscience at the end of the day, I ask myself which of the nontarget behaviors I might have engaged in during the day. Frequently, my cue for surfacing such behaviors is recalling an interaction across difference that felt uncomfortable to me or one in which another person expressed a discomfort with what I had said or done. For instance, I am planning a workshop with a colleague of color. She and I are both engaged and contributing ideas about the format and content. At some point, I realized that she had withdrawn from the conversation. As I look back on the exchange, I am aware I had said that when I attempted to present the content she was suggesting, "it" didn't work. I took no responsibility for the possibility that what didn't work may have been my style of presentation or that she might be more familiar with the material and a more appropriate person to present it, given who she is.

I also examine the places where I am acting out of a habit of internalized oppression—times when I fail to speak up because I am judging myself to be inferior or helpless. For example, because my parents were working class and did not go to college, I am sometimes intimidated by upper-class people and withdraw from discussions, even though I have several graduate degrees.

My second approach to changing my behavior is meeting for peer supervision with others who know the tools I have described in this chapter. For a number of years, I have been a member of a daylong, once-a-month, peer supervision group of white people where we talk about our interactions across difference. Because the group includes men and women and people of different ages and sexual identities, we look at both our nontarget and our target identities and how we act toward each other in the group, as well as report on our professional and personal interactions across differences. In addition, because my professional colleagues at the school where I teach use the VISIONS tools, we are able to call one another on our behavior toward each other and toward students, staff, administration, and trustees. For instance, when I am bending over backwards and about to compromise standards in grading a paper written by a student of color, I can confer with a Asian or African American faculty member who may suggest that I am engaging in dysfunctional rescuing by giving a grade the student doesn't deserve or avoiding contact because I do not really want to talk with this student of color about her performance. The fact that we have a common language and theory means that we can see our failures not simply as personal flaws, but as part of the inherited system of oppression that has affected us all.

Confronting History and Institutional Level Oppression

Some years ago, I co-led a travel seminar to South Africa. It was a life-changing experience. The first night our group stayed at Resurrection Haven, an HIV/AIDS shelter for women and children. That night a baby we had met earlier in the day died. She was buried, as were many others, on the grounds with her favorite toy as a grave marker. Many other experiences on that trip made me look at what it meant that I am white and at the unearned privilege that comes with being white. Nearly everyone we encountered on the trip assumed that I was the leader, even when my black, female, faculty colleague had made prior arrangements with a particular host or was introduced as one of the coleaders. I also encountered what it was like to be viewed as a "race traitor."[31] I was the object of the most hateful stares I have experienced in my life by white people when my female black faculty colleague and I dined in restaurants together—ten years after the end of the apartheid government.

However, the most chilling experience of the fourteen-day trip for me took place in the Apartheid Museum in Johannesburg, South Africa.[32] About one-third of the way through the museum, I turned a corner and came face to face with an entire wall of black plaques. There must have been more than one hundred plaques on the wall. I drew closer and began to read the plaques. There was one plaque for each racial law passed beginning in 1948, the year I was born. I was deeply distraught by the cold calculation with which year after year, elected officials carefully crafted new laws to take away civil and human rights from people, laws to legally separate mother and father from each other and from their children, laws to protect perpetrators of outrageous violence, laws to strip people of their language, culture, dignity, freedom, and life. I had prepared for this trip and was aware of the horrors of apartheid. What I was not prepared for was the coldly deliberate, "rational" determination with which white supremacy had been legalized and maintained.

Recently, I enrolled in a course on race law taught by Charles Walker Jr., chief counsel for the Division of Professional Licensure for the Commonwealth of Massachusetts and former chairman of the Massachusetts Commission Against Discrimination. Even before the course, I had some awareness of the negative racial laws that are part of the history of the United States. I assumed that most of them originated in the South. I was not prepared for the extent to which "rational," well-educated, political leaders from the North, South, East, and West continued to push for and sign legislation to strip people in my own country of their language, culture, dignity, freedom, and life. Taking the race law course made me aware of the how pervasive racism has been and continues to be on the institutional and cultural levels.

In similar ways, all oppressions have been and can continue to be enacted into laws and written into policies that govern schools, businesses, governments, and churches—locally and nationally. Reversing institutional level oppression means taking a close look at the ways our forebears and our current leaders have organized our corporate life to the advantage of some groups and the disadvantage of others. In appendix B, I have compiled a list of laws and judicial decisions, along with a few significant historical events—primarily regarding race—that I hope will serve as a reference for some, not all, of the important turning points regarding institutional level racial oppression. For those of us who may need it, this list may be a wake-up call regarding the tendency to legitimize systemic injustice based on race and color. Perhaps someday one of our museums will have a wall of remembrance and atonement, similar to the one in the Apartheid Museum in Johannesburg to remind us to never again commit such injustices.

Multicultural Audit

How can local congregations recognize and transform institutional oppression, especially regarding race and culture? The first step is to do a multicultural audit. This audit could have many dimensions. First, you might compare the racial and cultural demographics of the neighborhood served by the church with the racial, ethnic, and cultural demographics of the church itself. Has either of these demographics changed over time? Look at leadership statistics as well as membership data. Have individuals from racial, ethnic, and cultural minority groups participated in committee and worship leadership? Has the congregation ever interviewed minority (target group) candidates for clergy leadership positions? Is the ability to speak more than one language seen as a significant *asset* in hiring staff members? Does newcomer recruitment and incorporation take into account that people who are different from the racial, ethnic, and cultural majority might have needs, interests, and gifts to share that are different from people of the dominant group?

Looking at the constitution, bylaws, and vision and mission statements of the church, is there any reference to race, ethnicity, or culture? If not, the underlying assumption might be that race and culture are not significant or that members are assumed to be white. My experience has been that black, Latino/a, and various Asian majority congregations include something about their cultural heritage in their historical documents and vision and mission statements. Generally speaking only white congregations are "color-blind" to their assumptions about racial and cultural heritage, though they may allude to a particular ethnic heritage, for instance Polish, German, or Irish.

Are there prayers, hymns, and special celebrations that acknowledge and celebrate racial, ethnic, and cultural diversity? Do these represent the diversity of the congregation and even a wider diversity than is present in the current congregation? Is this diversity represented throughout the year or only during Black History month or some similar designated time? Are preachers of different races, cultures, and—here I would add, different denominations or faith traditions—ever invited to lead worship or preach?

Is the curriculum for the education of children and adults multicultural? Are there workshops and forums specifically on topics of racial difference or multiculturalism? Do people of color have a significant voice in deciding curriculum or forum topics? Are people of different cultures and traditions invited to talk about how their race or culture affects their faith development?

How are power and money viewed with regard to missionary and outreach activities? Is a better-than/less-than attitude (possible dysfunctional rescuing) inherent in mission or outreach work? For instance, is the emphasis in Habitat for Humanity or Honduras construction projects on helping these people who are so much poorer than we? Or is the emphasis on building relationships over time and learning from other members of God's family who may have very important things to teach us about faith, hope, or family life?

These are but a few of the questions that could be part of a multicultural audit. If engaged as a truly educational and transformative process, it will lead to many more questions. The audit is not meant as a checklist. The point is to engage as many people as possible in seeing and acting differently by seeing and celebrating as much difference as possible.

While I have focused on race and culture, a truly inclusive multicultural audit would include examination of differences regarding class, gender, age, theological perspective, sexual orientation, and laity and clergy.

Activities to Promote Multicultural Awareness

In my experience, teenagers are extremely open to issues of justice and equality. I recall my own daughters often seeing injustice and being outraged by situations where I had become inured to the inequity. Whether the injustice they perceived was my own father's comment about "lazy Mexicans" (on a personal level) or the construction of barriers to immigration (on an institutional level), my daughters named what they saw as injustice and advocated change. Sometimes their questions about why it was so were aggravating. I labeled them "young and idealistic." Does that mean I was old and had lost my ideals?

Congregations can capitalize on the energy many teenagers have for social justice. The youth group or a high school church class could do research and develop a timeline to present at a workshop or adult forum on institutional racial oppression using the timeline in appendix B. The timeline could be posted on newsprint around the walls of the church, auditorium, or a large classroom, or it could be mounted on large poster board in the nave of the church. The students could act out certain segments of the history, such as the principal arguments on both sides of the Dred Scott case or *Brown v. Board of Education*. They could find out if any of the significant historical players were members of their denomination—heroes to be celebrated at a Sunday worship service for advancing racial equality. Or conversely, they could investigate representatives of their denomination who held back the progress of justice. They could research whether the denomination had (or has) a position on issues such as slavery, desegregation, integration, immigration, or affirmative action, and whether the positions changed and who was responsible for those changes.

A variation of this exercise would be for the youth group to search the history of the congregation to find instances of ancestors, laity and clergy, who took stands on issues of racial, ethnic, or cultural oppression. In a parish I served in Massachusetts, I was aware that four people had participated in the Selma to Montgomery march in March 1965. One was still a member of the congregation. I am embarrassed to say I never learned the names of the others or found a way to celebrate their courage and faith. The story I remember, whether mythical or real, was that the pastor decided to join them after they had committed themselves to going "because he was afraid they'd get into some kind of trouble"! This same congregation set up their own transportation program, with overnight housing in parishioners' homes should a snowstorm require it, for black students from the inner city to attend their local suburban school. The church took on this program because the volunteer, state-sponsored program had not yet reached their suburb twenty miles from the inner city. The same church also used some of its endowment to finance low-percentage mortgages so that black families could buy houses in their town.

Another program I would recommend was inspired when I attended the Workmen's Circle Bat Mitzvah of the daughter of close friends at Brandeis University.[33] Of the eight or so students who were celebrated for coming of age in their Jewish identity, the majority were adopted—from China, the Philippines, and Central and South America. Each student spent several months putting together a storyboard about their racial, cultural, and ethnic heritage. The stories included their own personal background, their cultural heritage, and the history of Jewish people in their birth country. The members of the class also wrote and personally delivered a letter to a major children's retail store in which they opposed the company's use of child labor outside the United States to manufacture the company's products. Students preparing for confirmation could develop similar personal and cultural histories of their faith ancestors and share these stories through the parish's newsletter or through displays in the church hall following the confirmation ceremony. They could also highlight stories of ancestors who spoke out or took action to promote racial justice.

Using the race law timeline of appendix B as a resource, the adult education committee or the social justice committee could develop a five-week adult education series, perhaps for Lent. The program would look at five periods of U.S. history, focusing on religion, race, and culture: (1) European arrival through writing the U.S. Constitution; (2) post-Constitution through Civil War; (3) Reconstruction through World War II; (4) post–World War II through the Civil Rights Era (1960s); (5) 1970 to the present. In each period, the program would focus on issues of racial justice, ethnic and cultural assimilation, celebration of racial and ethnic differences, and the role religion played in oppressing or liberating people of various racial and cultural backgrounds. Attention could be focused on whether leaders (attorneys on either side of court cases, judges, presidents, movement leaders, plaintiffs, or others) were members of the local church's denomination or whether the denomination took positions on any of the issues. Stories of congregations that took stances for racial justice and equality could be highlighted—for example, Ebenezer Baptist Church in Birmingham, Alabama, where black leaders and others gathered during the early 1960s or the churches in Altadena, California, which stored property for Japanese families who were interred during World War II.[34]

The purpose of the program is to make racial oppression and liberation and their relationship to religion discussable in order to motivate people for the hard work of overcoming institutional-level racial oppression. Obviously, it is also important to challenge other forms of oppression such as sexism, heterosexism, clericalism, anti-Semitism, and so on, at the institutional level. Similar programs about these differences could be designed for youth groups, confirmation classes, and adult forums using these examples as models.

Much of the focus of this chapter has been on differences of power, privilege, and access to resources that lead to racial injustice and cultural oppression. On a behavioral level, examples of clericalism were also given. The specific focus on race has been intentional because of the long, clear history of racial oppression in the United States and the fact that racial oppression continues today in modern forms. Political power is not generic; political power is held and exercised by specific individuals and groups over other particular individuals and groups to maintain specific unearned privileges and rights—the right to speak first at meetings, the right to avoid surveillance in a department store, the right to marry, the right to be seen as oneself and not as the representative of a group, and so on. Real-life behavior has led theorists like Batts to develop a paradigm of behaviors that can be recognized in other forms of oppression such as sexism, classism, ageism, heterosexism, and so forth. When I notice that in a particular category (race, gender, class, and so forth) I am more privileged and I am in the group that tends to see itself as *better than*, I can examine my behaviors in relationship to the nontarget side of the figure 2.3 on page 61 and think about what alternatives I have. In a similar way, when I see myself as having less power, privilege, and access to resources or find myself or others valuing me as *less than*, I can examine my behaviors in relationship to the target side of the chart and look for behaviors that are alternatives to internalized sexism or internalized classism, for example. In this way, all white, affluent congregations can learn the model presented here and reflect on differences within their own congregation regarding age, gender, theological belief, or sexual orientation. They can also examine the attitudes of superiority or inferiority that accompany or drive various forms of oppression and internalized oppression.

Questions for Reflection

1. On a personal level, what spiritual practices (prayer, examination of conscience, spiritual reading) might lead you to better recognize, more deeply understand, and more passionately celebrate multicultural differences? Include the many differences outlined in figure 2.2 on page 45. What spiritual practices might help you notice and change attitudes of superiority (thinking of yourself as better than and others as less than)? What religious practices might help you deal with fears you might have of people who are different from you? What spiritual practices might help you overcome inferiority attitudes (I am less than) in regard to people who are different from you racially, culturally, sexually, educationally, and so forth?
2. On an interpersonal level, who might be spiritual companions to you in the work of changing oppressive behaviors or internalized oppression behaviors? Who can you count on to help you employ the alternative behaviors mentioned in figure 2.3?
3. What programs would you be willing to organize or attend at your church, library, local college, or university

3

The Role of Feelings in Individual and Community Transformation

But when they saw him walking on the lake, they thought it was a ghost and cried out; for they all saw him and were terrified. But immediately he spoke to them and said, "Take heart, it is I; do not be afraid." Then he got into the boat with them and the wind ceased. And they were utterly astounded, for they did not understand about the loaves, but their hearts were hardened.

—*Mark 6:49-52*

A little kingdom I possess,
where thoughts and feelings dwell;
And very hard the task I find
of governing it well.

—*Louisa May Alcott*[1]

The Honeymoon Is Definitely Over: Part 1

The first position I took as a solo pastor was in a suburban, pastoral-sized congregation with two Sunday services and a combined attendance of 140 people. The congregation was progressive liturgically and theologically. Inclusive language was the norm in hymns, Scripture readings, and preaching. Forty children participated in two youth choirs and by serving at the altar. The church was the most socially active congregation in the town of fifteen thousand people. The town food pantry was housed at the church and open five days a week. Members of the parish had participated in civil rights marches in Alabama in the 1960s. In 1967, when a voluntary state program to expand educational opportunities for inner-city children did not reach this suburban town, parishioners organized transportation for inner-city black students to attend the town's public school and provided homes for those students during snowstorms. The parish had always had male senior pastors until the female interim, who was the minister for the eighteen months immediately before my arrival. Three women had served as associate clergy during the tenure of the two previous pastors.

When I was hired, the parish search profile said that the congregation wanted and needed more than one professional minister. The budget had funds designated for a part-time youth minister with the expectation that we would hire someone in that role shortly after my arrival. After sixth months, other funds, in addition to money already designated for a part-time youth minister, became available to sustain a twenty-five-hour-per-week professional position. The needs of the congregation were discussed at several board meetings. The board made the decision to hire an assistant pastor, half of whose time would be devoted to supporting Sunday school teachers and the youth program. The other twelve hours would be devoted to visiting parishioners at home and in the hospital and preaching once a month. We wrote a job description and advertised the position. I informed the leadership that all other things being equal, I would prefer hiring a woman. I seemed to have the support of the church board because a woman as preacher and worship leader would complement my ministry in those roles. The two senior elected lay leaders of the congregation agreed to serve with me as the search and selection committee.

I was excited about the prospect of having a colleague. The amount of work was growing, and the liturgical, pastoral, and outreach demands were considerable. The lay leaders and I had begun to review resumes and schedule interviews. And then it happened.

A senior woman who had served in various capacities at the church for more than forty years, including currently chairing the committee that operated a secondhand clothing store as part of the church's mission and outreach, wrote a letter to the board.

She placed the letter in all the board members' mailboxes at the church, intentionally omitting my mailbox. On the morning of the next board meeting, the author's daughter, who was on the board, asked me if I had seen the letter and then gave me a copy of it. I was shocked—partly because I had been bypassed and partly because of the content of the letter.

The letter was five pages long, handwritten, and signed. It made a strong case for a youth minister and then demanded that this person not be a clergyperson and not serve as assistant minister. It said that I had not been pastor long enough to deserve an assistant and that as we knew from politics, senior people hired assistants to do their work for them. I was smart enough to know that this letter was not about me, and I was still enraged. What happened at the board meeting only made me more angry.

Though we had a lot of other business on the agenda, the board spent more than two hours discussing this woman's letter. Many board members showed a great deal of deference to her. They related the many ways she had served the church, and they said that she probably spoke for other people as well. Other people had a different opinion of the woman. They agreed that she was a pillar of the church, but they said she had tried this kind of thing before. They were clear that the congregation was in favor of hiring an assistant, and they believed that this woman spoke for very few people. They suggested that the letter was inappropriate—especially because she had not given me a copy. They suggested that the two senior officers of the board speak with her to explain the board's decision to hire an assistant who would meet and surpass all her articulated expectations regarding youth ministry. The board decided to continue with the hiring process with one change to the job description.

During the discussion of the letter, a few people began to discuss the fact that the previous pastor's work had overlapped with the work of one of the assistants. They noted that both the pastor and the assistant occasionally visited a hospitalized parishioner together. They suggested that this was an unnecessary duplication of ministry. I agreed and said that it would never occur to me to have two clergy make a visit at the same time to a hospitalized parishioner, though we might alternate visits. A few people then began to talk about not having the new assistant present at the 8:00 a.m. service unless he or she was preaching. This would free more time (about an hour per week on average) for other duties. I suggested that the time saving was small compared to the advantage of clergy knowing the people at both services and not treating the smaller early service as second class. As more people joined the "no attendance unless preaching" camp, I acceded to this change in the job description, even as I said applicants might think this was a strange thing to put in the job description. With the job description settled, the board decided that the interviewing (which was already scheduled) and hiring could proceed, and the officers made plans to visit the author of the letter.

I had spoken very little during the meeting. This was the first bump in the road since I had begun serving this congregation. In fact, it was a sizable New England pothole. I knew that the proverbial honeymoon was over. I was quiet in part because I was still stunned that someone would think that giving a letter to the entire board and not to me would prevent me from knowing who sent it and what it contained. I was hurt that I was being compared to lazy politicians—not that I assume all, or even most, politicians are lazy. I was also quiet because I wanted to listen and to observe how the members of the board would deal with this issue. I suspected that I would learn more at this meeting about the health of the congregation and the competence of the lay leadership than I had learned in the entire six months I had been at the church.

At the end of the meeting, I said that I never thought of the new hire as *my* personal assistant, but rather as another member of the clergy staff accountable to the board and the congregation as well as to me. I told the board that I was glad that we were proceeding with the hiring. I said that I had learned a great deal during the meeting and that there were some significant things that puzzled me. Primarily, I was puzzled as to how they had allowed one person to hijack more than two hours of their time—even though they had a full agenda and several people believed the sender's not including me in the distribution of the letter was inappropriate and that the content of her letter was hurtful and off base. I said that if the board continued to second-guess their carefully thought-out decisions in this way, we were in store for a lot of long, unproductive meetings. I asked them if they would be willing to meet the next week at the home of one of the officers for two hours with only one agenda item—to talk about how they had come to second-guess their decision and to allow their regular agenda to be taken over. I said I had some ideas about what had taken place, and that I wanted to learn with them about how to prevent this from happening again. With less reluctance than I had anticipated, they agreed to meet.

Much of what was going on in this situation was unstated and perhaps even outside the awareness of the participants. Like an iceberg, 90 percent of the substance was below the surface. I believe the core of what people do not see often has to do with feelings—with the emotions of the participants in a story. So to grasp the full story, we need to uncover the role that feelings play in individual and community transformations. Feelings carry with them information we need about how to act in a situation. I believe that many lay and clergy leaders in congregations and agencies are overtrained on an intellectual level and underskilled emotionally. Because our reasoning skills are finely honed, we often rely on them to the exclusion or impairment of our affective abilities. Few of us, especially men, have been encouraged to become affectively competent.[2] Throughout this chapter I use *emotional* and *affective* interchangeably to refer to the feeling dimension of knowing and learning. I also talk about emotional *literacy* and affective *competence* as almost identical, though literacy refers more to how we come to know what we know and our ability to *read* our own and other people's feelings, and *competence* speaks more to the ability or power to integrate the affective dimension into our behavior, especially in the service of bringing about a transformation or change. Competence is related to the application of what our feelings are telling us.

Becoming affectively competent means that we develop a repertoire of skills to employ in addition to our reasoning skills and our imaginations. Affective competence helps us and those with whom we are engaged get what we need from an interaction, especially when repeated attempts to reason through a situation come up empty. Put simply, when you find yourself having the same intellectual exchange with another person for the third time, trying to convince them of the importance of your idea, it is likely the problem is not intellectual but emotional. The source of the discrepancy is not in the cognitive realm but in the affective dimension of the interchange. Change happens only when we are emotionally ready. Even the most correct thinking will not bring about conversion from racist, sexist, or other oppressive attitudes and behaviors if a person is overwhelmed by their own fear, sadness, or anger.

The Role of Feelings in Learning and Transformation

Before returning to the expired honeymoon story that begins this chapter, we will look at the role of feelings in learning and transformation. Human interactions and learning happen in at least three different dimensions: cognitive, affective, and behavioral. Learning itself is a process of transformation—the acquisition of new ideas, the implementation of new behaviors, the exploration of new feelings. It follows, then, that for individuals and organizations, change happens in these three dimensions as well. Figure 3.1 shows a way to imagine those dimensions.

Individuals take in information from all three dimensions. For some people, cognition is the primary way of learning. They are conceptual learners. They read the directions about how to assemble something before they even open the packages that contain the parts. Other people learn by doing. This manner of gaining knowledge is called behavioral learning. These folks don't bother with the "Read Me" computer files or the bright-colored package inserts that say, "Read all the instructions carefully before beginning assembly." They immediately install new software and begin to play with it to see how it works. Others learn primarily through their emotions. Such people sometimes talk about "having a feel for something" or knowing it intuitively. No one way is right. And while each of us likely has a default manner of learning, some of us are skilled at more than one method of learning, depending on the circumstances.

Figure 3.1. Three Dimensions of Learning and Change
The wavy line illustrates how the affective dimension of change is like an iceberg and often lies below the surface.

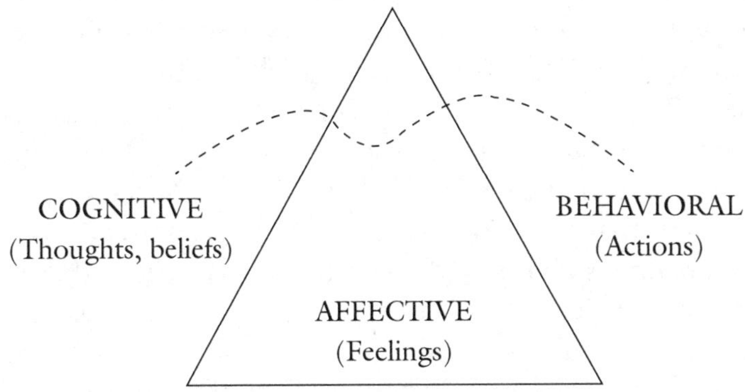

Emotional Illiteracy

On a cultural level, North American society, heavily shaped by dominant white heterosexual masculine values, favors the cognitive and behavioral dimensions. Value is placed on "right thinking" (*orthodoxy*, a term coined in 1630) and "right action" (*orthopraxy*, 1852). In U.S. culture, less value is placed on the affective dimension. *Orthopathy*, the Greek term for "right feeling," has not yet found its way into the *Oxford English Dictionary.*[3] I remember being taught "feelings are neither right nor wrong; they just are. It's what we do with them that counts." I suspect that the intent of this aphorism was to say that it was okay to be angry, but that it was not okay to hurt someone because of my anger, and so on, for other feelings. While I still agree that feelings are not good or bad, I believe this construction—"Feelings are neither right nor wrong; they just are"—devalues the use of feelings in knowing and transformation. We do not say that thinking or behaving is neither right nor wrong, that they just are. Feelings contain knowledge about what we need in a given situation. Feelings bear messages about how to act ethically toward ourselves and in relation to others. When a feeling is congruent with the stimulus that evoked it, we get a clear message about what is needed. In this way we perceive something is *right* about feelings. I suggest the term *orthopathy* for this congruence, which is further explained when I talk about the substitution of feelings later in this chapter.[4]

The difficulty in becoming emotionally literate is that most of us have been taught to be suspicious of our feelings, not to trust them. This is so pervasive that when we speak of people from cultures that give more respect to feelings, we tend to question that people's ability to think rationally. I believe that built into Western society is a tendency to view thinking as clearer and more important than feeling when it comes to learning and engaging in transformation. The hierarchy of cognitive and behavioral learning as *greater than* affective learning can be a form of oppression we exercise against ourselves. Because many of us are emotionally illiterate, we do not know or value the range of our emotional capabilities. And because of this we are affectively incompetent—that is, we do not know how to use our emotions and the emotional abilities of others to bring about transformation. This very lack of knowledge inhibits change. In addition, blocked or substituted emotions actually prevent transformation. Further complicating the tendency to distrust emotions is the gender and racial stereotyping that accompanies the thinking/feeling dichotomy. According to this stereotype, white men arrive at decisions by thinking and women and people of color make decisions intuitively or by accessing their feelings.[5] A powerful example of this stereotyping occurred at the 2004 Democratic National Convention in Boston. Commentators said that Teresa Heinz Kerry—the wealthy businesswoman and wife of presidential candidate John Kerry—should have told more personal (read, affective) stories about her husband. She was not supposed to be so "opinionated." She responded that she wished people would speak about women as also being "smart and well-informed."

The phrase "feelings are not facts" sometimes associated with 12-step recovery programs, also tends to devalue the importance of feelings. As a mantra the phrase may stop people from drinking, but it carries a danger with it that people will distrust their feelings rather than their bad reasoning. Here is an example that sets the context as I see it. I feel depressed; the world seems to have turned against me. My habit at such times is to tell myself, "I'm depressed; a drink or two will make me feel better or at least take my mind off my troubles." The problem is not the feeling of depression. The problem is the rationalization that alcohol or drugs are the solution. Yet people do not say, "Thoughts are not facts." I believe the goal is to avoid the inaccurate, non*fact*ual conclusion that drinking or drugs or overeating is the solution to feeling bad (that is, angry, sad, scared). My point is simply that in the service of a good cause, interrupting addictive behavior, we are told to be suspicious of our feelings or taught to degrade feelings.

Feelings as Messengers (FAM)

The theory or tool I present here as a way of honoring and employing the affective dimension of our being is called "Feelings as Messengers," or FAM. It is one of a variety of tools developed by VISIONS, Inc., for use in multicultural training and consulting.[6] FAM invites us all—men and women—to be more emotionally literate. It invites us all to be affectively competent. The theory proposes that feelings carry messages about what we need to do to take care of ourselves and to be fully present to ourselves and others in any situation—a liturgy, a pastoral visit, a business meeting, an attempt at community transformation, inviting and welcoming new members, and reflection upon any of these events. The theology that underlies affective competence asserts that feelings are a significant dimension of our beings as God created us. Such a theology points to the expression of feelings throughout the Scriptures, including the attribution of feelings to God, as a way of legitimizing and valuing feelings.[7]

FAM talks about six primary feeling families: powerful, joyful, peaceful, mad, sad, and scared. Each feeling family has a spectrum of feelings within it, as illustrated in *The Feeling Wheel* developed by Gloria Willcox, which can be found in appendix C.[8] Each feeling is a response to a stimulus. Something happens and a feeling arises that we may or may not attend to. Unlike some theories that stress that feelings "just are," FAM emphasizes that feelings carry important messages that give us useful information about what we need in a particular situation. When we are in touch with our feelings, when we attend to them, we receive information about a suggested response or behavior. Figure 3.2 details the six primary feelings or feeling families, along with the most common stimulus, message, and need or response.

Figure 3.2. Feelings as Messengers Grid

FEELING	STIMULUS	MESSAGE	NEED or RESPONSE
POWERFUL	Accomplishment or anticipated success	I am competent.	Keep on keeping on!
JOYFUL	Inner gratitude, awe, wonder	I am excited, happy.	Keep on keeping on!
PEACEFUL	Deep awareness of connectedness	I am centered.	Keep on keeping on!
MAD	Real or perceived violation	My boundaries have been crossed.	Reestablish boundaries. Get safe.
SAD	Real or anticipated loss	I am experiencing or anticipating bereavement.	Find space and support to grieve and let go.
SCARED	Real or perceived danger	I am threatened or in peril.	Arrange for support and protection.

This grid, developed and copyrighted by VISIONS, Inc., has been slightly modified. Used by permission.

The *powerful* family of feelings includes: confident, worthwhile, successful, respected, and faithful. These feelings are stimulated by an accomplishment, such as finishing a major project at work or cooking a wonderful meal for guests. The feeling of being powerful can also be stimulated by an anticipated success or simply the sense that "I am capable." I feel powerful when I have done everything to prepare for a meeting and anticipate that it will go well for everyone. Powerful is about the ability to be what I want to be or to do want I want to do. Feeling powerful here does not mean I exercise power over or dominance of others. When I feel powerful, the message is "I am competent," and the need is to "keep on keeping on!" That is, the feeling is telling me to continue being who I am at this moment or doing what I am doing.

The *joyful* family includes: excited, energetic, playful, creative, sensuous, optimistic, and hopeful. *Joyful* connotes an outgoing expression. When I am joyful I want to share the feeling with others. The stimulus for joyful is a sense of awe or wonder. I am joyful when I am at a party with friends whom I really like. When I saw my daughter take her first steps, I felt joyful. She felt powerful, if a little hesitant. When I feel joyful, the message is "I am excited and happy" and the need is again to "keep on keeping on!"—to continue being who I am and doing what I am doing to prolong the feeling.

The *peaceful* family includes: content, intimate, trusting, relaxed, serene, thankful, and loving. Peaceful is a more inward feeling than joyful; the energy is calmer. The stimulus for feeling peaceful is a deep awareness of being connected. I feel peaceful when I have written a difficult letter and know that I have spoken honestly about what needed to be said to reconnect with someone. I feel peaceful when I am in right relationship with those who are important to me. When I feel peaceful, the message is "I am centered." My need is for things to stay as they are. I want to continue in the state I am in.

The *mad* family includes: angry, hateful, hurt, critical, jealous, irritated, frustrated, distant. The stimulus for feeling mad is a real or perceived violation, the sense that a boundary has been crossed inappropriately. I feel mad when what I say is completely ignored in a meeting or when someone breaks into my house. The message is "I am being, or I have been, violated." What I need is to reestablish appropriate boundaries. The feeling of anger (mad) is dealt with at the end of this chapter. In figure 3.2, the response to anger is reestablishing boundaries and getting safe. Being clear about my boundaries is especially important when the stimulus (violation) is from someone with whom I have little or no relationship or from one who has, or is perceived to have, significantly more power than I have. Insofar as I am able to renegotiate boundaries *within* a relationship, anger can be seen as highly relational with the possibility of ultimately bringing me closer to the person with whom I am angry.

The *sad* family includes: ashamed, depressed, lonely, isolated, bored, tired, grief-stricken, apathetic, stupid, inferior, and remorseful. The stimulus for sadness is a real loss, such as the death of a parent, and anticipated loss, such as a child who is about to go off to college. The message of sadness is that I am experiencing a loss or I am about to experience a loss. Thus apathetic, bored, and tired are indications of a loss of motivation, a loss of interest, a loss of sleep—something is missing. When I am sad, I need time and support to grieve my loss, to let go of what once was. This need is easy to understand when someone is grieving a death. But what about when a person is tired? I recall what a friend said after her first child was born. She talked about the energy it took to function as a milk factory and the endless nights of sleep deprivation. "I am tired all the time. After a while I came to realize that I can be tired all the time and still function in a fairly normal way." She had found the time and support to grieve her loss of sleep and energy.

The *scared* family includes: bewildered, discouraged, embarrassed, overwhelmed, frightened, confused, anxious, insecure, and submissive. The stimulus for feeling scared is a real danger, such as a powerful person verbally or physically attacking me, or a perceived danger, such as being unable to pay my mortgage if I don't find a job. The message associated with feeling scared is

"I am in danger." The need I have is to arrange for protection or support.

Each feeling is a response to a stimulus. Something happens and a feeling arises. For infants, the stimulus ⟶ feeling pattern is clear. When an infant is frightened, he startles and may gasp or cry. He needs to be calmed, supported, protected. If an infant is hit, he cries. His comfort and security have been violated. He wants the boundary reestablished. If an infant is being entertained, she is joyful, she wants to continue to receive the stimulus—the singing of the parent (keep on keeping on!). If she is peaceful, she may also want this feeling to continue, and so keeping on may mean not adding further stimuli. The point is that when we are very young, the pattern of stimulus ⟶ feeling ⟶ message ⟶ need is fairly straightforward, especially if the basic needs continue to be satisfied. A problem arises when the needs are not met in a predictable way or when we are told it is not right to have or express certain feelings. When this begins to happen, we are on our way to losing the innate, natural connection between stimulus ⟶ feeling ⟶ message ⟶ need. As adults, recovering this connection is the task of developing emotional literacy. *Emotional literacy* means that I am aware of what feeling(s) I am experiencing in response to a stimulus at any given moment. It means that I am paying attention to the message that the feeling is sending me so that I can choose whether and how to respond. The challenge is to strive for the congruence between feeling and stimulus that is natural for us as infants. I believe this gives new meaning to the words of Jesus: "Truly I tell you, unless you change and become like children, you will never enter the kingdom [realm] of heaven" (Matt. 18:3).

Substitution of Feelings

One difficulty many of us face regarding emotional literacy is that we were raised to acknowledge or value only certain feelings. We were taught that only some feelings are legitimate to express. Sometimes this message was "caught" or sensed rather than explicitly taught. In any case, we may substitute one feeling for another, usually without being aware that we are doing so. Such substitution is generally a habitual behavior that was self-protective when it was learned.[9] In the context in which I first began to substitute "more acceptable" feelings, expressing the natural feeling—that is, the feeling that was congruent with the stimulus—probably was not safe or sanctioned. The substitution becomes a problem if I unconsciously replace an original feeling with a substitute feeling when I am no longer in a context that "requires" me to substitute my feelings. When I substitute a feeling, perhaps out of habit, I get the response associated with the substituted feeling—instead of the response I really want or need that is associated with the feeling I have failed to recognize or express.

In my family of origin, it was okay to be sad or scared. It was not okay for me to be angry. My father was the only one who was allowed to get angry. When I experienced a violation of boundaries, I could be sad, even cry, and seek comfort or I could be afraid and seek support and protection. I could not express anger that someone had come into my space or crossed an emotional boundary. This restriction meant that in my family, if I was angry, I had to substitute an acceptable feeling of sadness or fear. Thus, at the precise time I needed space or distance (to reestablish boundaries), I had to give the message (through an expression of sadness or being scared) that I wanted someone to come closer to comfort or protect me.

Little boys being taught not to cry when they experience a loss is another example of substitution. Generally the substitution for feeling sad about a loss is feeling powerful. This gives the message, "I am okay." People around him may then come to the conclusion that he doesn't need anything, when what he may really need is to grieve and receive support for his grieving. His expression of control pushes others away precisely when he may want them to draw nearer. The substitution of a more acceptable or more familiar feeling for the natural one deprives him of what he needs and gives off a signal to others that is confusing or misleading because it is not congruent with what is taking place.

Anger is generally seen as legitimate only for *white men* in the North American context. Here anger is about power over others, not about relationship. That's why a white *boy* isn't allowed to express anger and is even discouraged from feeling it or naming it as anger. When he becomes a man, being angry will become his "right"—and, of course, his trap, because then anger may be the only emotion he is allowed to express.

As a corollary, North American culture says that men of color and all women and children are not permitted to express anger because they are not supposed to have power. I discuss a more relational aspect of anger later in the chapter. The point here is to notice how cultural norms around power play a role in the feelings various groups of people are allowed to express.

Emotional Literacy as a Personal Discipline

Emotional literacy is knowing what feelings are congruent with the stimulus I am experiencing. It can also apply to the capacity to notice when another person's feelings may seem incongruent with a particular stimulus. If I suspect such an incongruity, I can inquire about it, though it is up to the other person to discern the harmony or disharmony between the stimulus and the feeling. Emotional literacy is a discipline that requires much practice. It is a form of self-focus that may seem artificial until one has grown accustomed to it over time. Practicing self-focus may require slowing down an interaction and taking the time to ask myself what I am actually feeling and what I need before reacting to what someone else says. Getting in touch with my most genuine feeling, and its attendant message, may give me more options for speaking or acting in a situation and lead to a different quality of interaction.

For many people who have a lot of privilege or power, and for white men in particular, focusing on their feelings seems unnatural, in part as a result of social and cultural conditioning. Until relatively recently, noticing, talking about, and acting upon most feelings, with the exception of anger, has been countercultural for white men. Even now, thinking is split off from and valued over feeling in most public or work settings. While men are increasingly encouraged to express their feelings in intimate relationships or home settings, the same is not as true for men in the business environment. Though women seem to have more permission to express feelings in a business environment, many work settings continue to exhibit a general inhibition regarding emotions. Rules about feelings in ministry settings seem to straddle the line between familial and business codes of behavior. This means that churches may be a place where white men, in particular, can learn to become more emotionally literate. It also accounts for the fact that when a person sees someone else substitute feelings in church (for example, displaying anger in place of sadness or fear), that substitution may seem radically out of place. Because a church is familial, the expression of feelings is usually more acceptable and congruent, and therefore men should be able to express sadness or fear and women should be able to express anger.

We can also think of FAM as a tool for deepening relationships and bringing about communal transformation. FAM has the capacity to deepen relationships because it helps individuals know themselves better. It helps them be more aware of what they need in a given situation. This allows people to be more genuinely present to one another. In a similar way, FAM enables a group of people to notice substitution patterns where the flow of stimulus → feeling → response is not congruent. As a tool, FAM can also help people identify which feelings are generally acceptable, or regularly prohibited, within a group or community. It can also help them change their substitution patterns and express the more congruent feeling. Increasing the affective competency of a community means that the community can recognize the messages carried in people's feelings and begin to deal with their needs more consciously. One of the primary barriers to change, on both a personal level and an institutional level, is the failure to take time to process people's feelings. When people have not processed their feelings, it is very hard for them to listen to reasons for why they should participate in a change process. Chapter 7 deals at length with the role of feelings as part of transformation. Here I simply want to acknowledge that giving people more information about a change will not facilitate transformation if people have feelings of anger, fear, or sadness connected to the change that they have not expressed. The expression of the feelings allows for responses to be made and for needs to be met, which frees people's energy to focus on cognitive aspects of the change. In addition, processing feelings is more difficult if people have substituted feelings. For instance, if a group of long-time parishioners expresses anger about moving the altar forward or changing the hymnal and the leadership focuses only on their anger, the parishioners may never find the time and support to express their sadness associated with the loss of the church design or furnishings to which they were so accustomed or the loss of the music which brought them such joy and comfort.

Guidelines and the Use of FAM

Before applying FAM to transformation, relating this tool to the guidelines articulated in chapter 1, "Guidelines for Recognizing and Valuing Differences," is essential. While the guidelines are important for all interactions, intellectual and emotional, particularly vital is articulating them in settings where the expression of feelings and the messages they convey has been inhibited or undervalued. Furthermore, the guidelines are necessary to better safeguard those who have less power in the setting. The use of FAM by an unscrupulous or unskilled leader might be dangerous. Such a leader probably would not articulate or follow the guidelines I have presented or similar ones—perhaps in order to maintain power. Thus, teaching the guidelines first, then teaching FAM to members of a congregation or an organization, as well as to staff, is important so that all constituents are empowered to use the FAM theory and are better able to protect themselves against possible misuse or abuse of the theory.[10] Because of the power inherent in their positions, leaders, supervisors, mentors, and trainers should avail themselves of ongoing supervision in order to examine their own thinking and feelings in interactions with those they lead, supervise, train, or work with as colleagues.

The Guidelines for Recognizing and Valuing Differences should always be explicitly stated and agreed to by all parties as an ongoing practice. Should meetings get particularly tense or the relationship become static or frayed, an explicit return to the guidelines can be most useful. They should definitely be restated if a third-party intervention is required. Finally, the guidelines may prevent confusion between learning and therapy. The role of feelings suggested here is to foster mutual learning and to bring about individual and communal transformation. People often think that a focus on feelings implies a move toward therapy or therapeutic work. Feelings are also an important component of education and leadership and being recognized as such is essential.[11]

Personal Applications of FAM Theory

On the personal level, applying FAM theory means asking oneself a series of questions. Think of a situation in which you felt engaged and from which you believe you still have a lot to learn. Place yourself mentally in the situation as if it were happening right now. Ask yourself these questions:

- What am I feeling in this situation?
- Is this my natural feeling (congruent with the stimulus) or a learned, substitute feeling?
- What is the message for me in this feeling?
- What is this feeling telling me I need?
- How might I choose to respond?

These questions can also be asked of a parishioner by a pastor or by a lay member of a pastoral care team. A fair amount of skill is required in asking these questions of another person, especially because most of us have learned various substitution patterns that seem so familiar that we do not notice that they are substitutes. The pastor or lay caregiver runs the risk of substituting feelings while she is working with the parishioner and of projecting her own congruent or substitute feeling on the other person. The person receiving pastoral care might also believe a feeling is congruent because he has habitually substituted that feeling for the more congruent one. In other words, it may be hard for both the caregiver and the receiver to trust their answers to the questions. Practicing this process of slowing down improves effectiveness.

Another way to help process feelings is to look at the need or response column of the FAM chart (figure 3.2). If one can name the need or response, one can then look across the chart to the left to see which feeling is congruent. For example, if I am aware that someone keeps cutting me off when I am speaking and I establish my right to complete what I am saying (establishing boundaries), then I am probably angry. If my response to this situation has been to be sad, to withdraw, or to cry, it may be that those were the only safe options I had at one time and developed a habit of substituting sadness or fear for anger. Working backwards (right to left) on the chart is another way of becoming aware of my substitution pattern or helping someone else do the same. It promotes emotional literacy.

Applying FAM theory is different from simply asking a person what he is feeling and "staying with the person on an emotional level," as distinguished from "staying in one's head." FAM theory states that a person's congruent feeling *gives a message* about what he needs, even if he cannot always acquire what is needed in the immediate situation. Helping him understand the message and the need means more than simply being with him as he expresses a feeling. It means helping him determine if the feeling is congruent with the stimulus, as distinct from a substitute feeling. It also means clarifying what message is associated with the feeling and what need or response is associated with that message. FAM is action oriented. It points to possible responses. It is more than passively being with someone else in his feelings.[12] Men often present anger in place of fear or sadness. Women often present sadness or fear in place of anger.

Even knowing this theory, the first priority for a leader is to focus on being emotionally literate about her own feelings, in order not to project her feelings onto others, and to know what she needs in a particular situation. For instance, if a leader is scared and knows that she can get support or protection, she is less likely to project her fear upon a parishioner or group member. If a leader is sad, she can identify the loss and begin or continue to grieve. In either case, the leader's ministry will likely be more effective, and the leader will be practicing good self-care. This in itself can be a model for other members of the faith community.

Theological Reflection, Scripture, and Feelings

Theological reflection can be an important tool for personal or community transformation. In the church this discipline has a long history, which I will not rehearse here.[13] For theological reflection to be most effective, we need to understand the role of feelings in it. When we use theological reflection as part of the process of transformation, the goal is not to engage in proof texting—citing a particular passage of Scripture as if the author or God had our situation in mind when the text was written, and therefore using the text as a way of engineering an outcome we had in mind before even considering the text. Rather, members of the community try to recall passages of Scripture, generally stories, that may resonate with the situation to open it up in rich and profound ways. The Scripture may support or challenge our plans or merely offer alternatives not previously thought of. The ability to refer to an analogous story from Scripture allows us as members of a modern community of faith to be in conversation with a treasured historical community of faith. The underlying theological belief is that the same God who spoke to our ancestors may have something to say to us, when we listen to a particular Scripture story that has meaning for us in the present. What is the same is the process of listening for God's intention, not the particular circumstances or situations.

Rather than select a scriptural passage to fit a particular transformational challenge, I want to explore a number of passages that resonate with the six primary feeling families we have discussed. The purpose is to notice the feelings in these passages from the Bible and to gain a sense of how they might relate to our own feelings.

For example, we might explore the story of Jesus and the moneychangers in the temple and reflect on the violation that Jesus experienced, his anger, and his attempt to reestablish boundaries (Mark 11:15-19; John 2:12-25). Similarly, one might delve into the story of Mary and Martha and ask about the violation Martha experienced that led her to complain, "Lord, do you not care that my sister has left me to do all the work by myself?"(Luke 10:40b). Notice that such an inquiry does not assume the perceived violation is either intended or grievous. In fact, one can even inquire whether Martha is substituting anger for sadness. Perhaps she is really sad that she has not "chosen the better part" (Luke 10:42). The passage from the sixth chapter of Acts about the neglected Greek widows also suggests a violation (Acts 6:1-6). Or one might look at Jesus's sadness at the death of Lazarus (John 11:32-35) or his look at Peter after he denies knowing Jesus (Luke 22:61). Clergy and members of lay pastoral care teams might reflect on the story of Ruth and Naomi and inquire into what loss a parishioner has incurred and what possible responses to the sadness might be available (Ruth 1:1-22). The stories of Jesus in the garden—"Let this cup pass from me" and "So, could you not stay awake with me one hour?"—and of Mary's visit to Elizabeth may speak to fear and the need for support (Matt. 26:39, 40; Luke 1:39-56). The story of Job offers a wide range of encounters with deep emotions.

One of my favorite stories is the one about Bartimaeus (Mark 10:46-52). Here the apostles project their fear onto Bartimaeus, saying, "Take heart"—in effect, asking him to not be afraid (v. 49b). Is there a less scared person in the Scriptures than Bartimaeus? After all, he is shouting, "Jesus, Son of David, have mercy on me!" (v. 47). He doesn't care who hears him. He may be brash, even obnoxious, or perhaps just desperate. But he certainly is not afraid. He does not need someone telling him to take heart. For me, this story illustrates the feeling of being powerful in spite of being blind and a beggar, of being proactive—after all he stops Jesus in his tracks. The woman who engages Jesus at the well (John 4:7-42) also exemplifies the feeling of being powerful. The father of the prodigal son is joyful (Luke 15:11-32). Stories of Jesus, his mother, and Paul contain examples of people who feel peaceful even in stressful situations.

The point is not to have a list of passages to apply to various situations. Instead, leaders and members of a congregation allow themselves to freely associate and then examine the biblical passages that occur to them, using what they know about feelings as messengers as one way of breaking open the situation. In the end, the discussion returns to the situation, and one can ask, "What might God be saying to me in this situation if I attend to my feelings and the messages they contain?"[14]

Feelings and Relationship

Examining the role of feelings from a relational perspective, not simply from the point of view of one person's experience of his or her own feelings, is also important. Feelings, including anger, are modes of connection. Beverly Wildung Harrison, retired professor of Christian social ethics at Union Theological Seminary in New York and the first woman president of the North American Society of Christian Ethics, powerfully conveys the relational perspective of feelings in her article, "The Power of Anger in the Work of Love: Christian Ethics for Women and Other Strangers." Harrison writes:

> Anger is not the opposite of love. It is better understood as a feeling-signal that all is not well in our relation to other persons or groups or to the world around us. Anger is a mode of connectedness to others and it is always a vivid form of caring. To put the point another way: anger is—and it always is—a sign of some resistance in ourselves to the moral quality of the social

> relations in which we are immersed. Extreme and intense anger signals a deep reaction to the action upon us or toward others to whom we are related. . . . Such anger is a signal that change is called for, that transformation in relation is required.[15]

Harrison goes on to discuss what happens when anger is denied. She explains the substitution of boredom or moralistic self-righteousness for anger, which destroys relationship:

> We need to recognize that where the evasion of feeling is widespread, anger does not go away or disappear. Rather, in interpersonal life it masks itself as boredom, ennui, low energy, or it expresses itself in passive-aggressive activity or in moralistic self-righteousness and blaming. Anger denied subverts community. Anger expressed directly is a mode of taking the other seriously, of caring. The important point is that where feeling is evaded, where anger is hidden or goes unattended, masking itself, there the power of love, the power to act, to deepen relation, atrophies and dies.[16]

The Honeymoon Is Definitely Over: Part 2

When the board met at the home of one of the congregation's officers, a palpable tension was in the air. I suspected board members were embarrassed that they had spent so much time discussing the letter from the disgruntled senior. Perhaps some were also angry that I had called them to account. I myself was very nervous—scared would not be too strong a word. I thought that this might be a watershed meeting, and I feared the water might be a tsunami that would wash away my credibility with the board. I was also excited. I thought that if things went well, we would establish a deep working relationship. I thought that I would learn a great deal in this meeting, and that too was exciting.

When the meeting began, I asked the board members if they could tell me how it was that they let go of their agenda for the previous meeting and spent more than two hours talking about the letter. At first someone said that the author was a long-time parishioner who had served in many important capacities and that she deserved to be taken seriously. Someone else said that perhaps they had misjudged the sentiment of the community and that maybe there wasn't much support for an assistant because people thought we might not be able to support the salary.

After a few more similar comments, I agreed that listening to all members of the community is important and granted that we might not have understood the extent of the resistance to hiring an assistant. I then asked them if they would be willing to entertain another explanation. They said they wanted to hear my idea.

I said that when I was interviewed for the position of pastor, I did some research. I found out that the pastor that preceded me got divorced just about a year before he resigned from the church and took another job. Two years later, just before I was hired, he got married to one of his former assistants. They, of course, knew the story. In fact, the parish rented a bus, and more than forty people traveled eight hours to attend the wedding! The pastor before him had broken his marriage and ordination vows by becoming involved in a relationship with a parishioner, thus abusing the trust placed in him as her pastor. He was forced to leave the parish by the judicatory.[17] The board knew that story as well. Sitting in the room, as a member of the board, was the former husband of the woman with whom the second pastor had an abusive relationship. After I recalled the history of my two predecessors (both apparently beloved by many people), I said I thought the resistance to my hiring an assistant was because most people knew I would hire a woman, all other things being equal. I said I believed that people were afraid that I would divorce my wife, leave my two small children, and marry the newly hired female assistant.

The first response to my statement was laughter—a nervous "You've got to be kidding" sort of laughter from many in the group. I said that I really believed fear was behind the letter and other resistance in the congregation. As evidence of my opinion, I cited the reference to my being like a politician, the statement that I had not been there long enough to deserve *my own* assistant, the comments about both the former pastor and assistant (now happily married) making joint hospital visits, and the job description restricting the new assistant to attendance at the early service only when preaching. At that point, one woman said, "You know, when you first mentioned the story of our former pastors as part of the resistance, I thought 'Yeah, maybe that's it!' Then, I dismissed it. You don't seem at all like them." Then a man said, "It didn't occur to me at all until you mentioned it. But now I think you may be on to something. At least we ought to talk about it." And so we did for nearly two hours.

This story is a good illustration of the power of feelings and the tendency of most groups to ignore feelings and focus on intellectual or cognitive explanations for nearly everything.[18] Had I known the FAM theory at the time *and* had it been part of our common vocabulary and practice, I might have asked the board at that first meeting not what they *thought* but how they *felt*. It might be that the anger directed at me by the long-time parishioner was not simply misdirected anger that was meant for the former pastor. She may have been substituting anger for sadness or fear. It may be that this woman was also sad that she had lost a beloved pastor (she went to his wedding). She may have felt scared that it would happen again. It may also be that the board was busy substituting peacefulness for their own fear. They were certainly working very hard to find a way to placate the author of the letter without dealing with any of their own fears, anger, or sadness.

Some of my musings may be those of a Monday morning quarterback, since this story took place more than a dozen years before I learned the FAM theory. At the same time, I am certain that had I and the board known the theory, our discussions in those two meetings and about other events for the next six years I was pastor would have been richer and probably more productive. Yet even without a specific knowledge of the theory, we did spend time processing what each individual felt. The board was transformed into a tighter community of individuals, and they worked more proficiently. Board meetings that had lasted three-and-a-half hours under previous pastors rarely went beyond two hours. A woman assistant was hired within the month. The focus of her ministry was youth work. She and I both made hospital visits, but not together. She and I are still happily married, but not to each other!

Summary of FAM Theory

North American culture often teaches us that thoughts and feelings are dichotomous. The theory of Feelings as Messengers allows one to think about feelings, to attend to the energy present when one's feelings are engaged and acknowledged. It also invites inquiry into the message implicit in the experienced feelings—data about what is needed and what possible responses might be helpful. As applied to others, FAM goes beyond responding empathetically and moves toward understanding patterns of behavior and new options once those patterns are seen. The theory posits a close connection among the cognitive, affective, and behavioral dimensions of learning and living. It offers a way to become more emotionally competent in exercising self-care, pastoral ministry, and leadership for transformation. Finally, it is more than a technology for ministry, leadership, and theological reflection. Embedded in the messages of feelings is the possibility of sustaining and deepening relationships. The messages tell us what we need to know to respond ethically to others and ourselves.

A Group Exercise on the Role of Feelings

Developed by VISIONS consultants, the kinesthetic exercise that follows is most powerful when done with a group of people who actually move about in a room as described below. Individuals can also respond to the exercise questions by themselves while reading this book.

After explaining the Feelings as Messengers Grid (figure 3.2) and the concept of substitution of feelings, illustrating with examples, the facilitator places six larges sheets of paper around the room—either on the floor or taped to the walls. On each paper is the name of one of the feeling families: powerful, mad, peaceful, scared, joyful, sad. I usually place the sheets around the room in that order so that neither side of the room is seen as "positive" or "negative."

The group is asked to gather in the center of the room. As each question below is asked, participants move in silence to the feeling that best answers the question. Everyone is asked to look around and notice where people are and who is next to them. Individuals are given the opportunity to process by briefly commenting on why they chose to go to a particular feeling. Not every person needs to comment. After a few comments, participants are asked the next question, and the process continues until all the questions are finished.

1. In your family of origin, what feeling did you have most permission to express? Go to that feeling. Process. (The leader invites individuals to say why they have a particular feeling.)
2. In your family of origin, what feeling were you not given (or rarely given) permission to express? Go to that feeling. Process.
3. What feeling did you most often substitute for the denied feeling? Go to that feeling. Process.

Now think about your current congregation (or with some groups, your place of employment or significant social setting, such as a club, reading group, parents' group, and so forth).

4. What feeling do you have most permission to express? Go to that feeling. Process.
5. What feeling are you not encouraged to express? Go to that feeling. Process.
6. What feeling do you most often substitute for the denied feeling? Go to that feeling. Process.

The following story illustrates the kind of learning that can develop from the above exercise.

The Happy School

Recently I presented FAM to a group of primary school teachers as part of a long-term multicultural training and consulting contract at a kindergarten-through-grade-twelve, independent school in a wealthy, white suburb. Before the presentation and processing (using the six questions above) took place, the teachers were asked to "check in" with one word describing how they were feeling as we began the training session. A second question asked them to share a recent multicultural success or challenge.

One teacher said she felt distressed and went on to describe her challenge. She had an African American boy in her mostly white, second-grade class. She said he had not done his homework. Because he was quite bright, she guessed that it was not because he didn't understand the assignment or couldn't do it. She knew that he was bussed to the school from a poor inner-city neighborhood. She knew he was being raised by a single mother and that there had recently been violence in his neighborhood, including a shooting on his street. She asked him if he was okay. He smiled and said he was fine. She said he always smiled and appeared happy, even though the teacher knew that there was turmoil in his house and neighborhood. She said the challenge was figuring out how to help him talk about his situation. She wanted to make contact with the boy.[19] When the check-in was finished, the FAM theory was explained along with substitution of feelings. Then the group began to do the exercise by moving to the feelings in response to questions one to six above. For questions four, five, and six, the participants were asked to think about the school as their setting. The overwhelming majority moved to joyful as the feeling they had most permission to express at the school (question 4). Most people said they were discouraged (question 5) from expressing fear. Some said they were discouraged from expressing anger or sadness. When asked what they substituted for the discouraged feeling, most of the group went back to joyful, some went to powerful.

"So," I asked, "how would you describe the feeling culture of your school?" "We're the Happy School," a teacher replied. "We're constantly told to put forward our best face," another replied. "Yes, and we tend to be pretty upbeat and optimistic anyway," a third teacher added.

A light dawned for me as I recalled the story the second grade teacher told about the African American boy during the check-in forty-five minutes earlier. "So how do you think your school culture might affect the African American second grader we talked about during check-in?" I asked. "Oh my gawd," several people gasped at once. Then someone said, "We're setting up our kids. We're telling them that the most acceptable feeling is happy. Our culture doesn't like scared, and we are teaching that to all our students, not just the black ones." Energy filled the room. The exercise wasn't just personal anymore. It had professional consequences. Another teacher said, "I felt sorry for some of our poorer kids. I felt powerless to change their home situations, their neighborhood environment. Now I realize that what needs to change is *our* environment. If we as adults find it hard to express our feelings of fear, anger, and sadness here at school, how can we expect our students to do it? We have work to do." Indeed, we all have work to do.

4

The Role of Imagination in Transformation

But, as it is written,
"What no eye has seen, nor ear heard,
nor the human heart conceived,
what God has prepared for those who love him"—
these things God has revealed to us through the Spirit;
for the Spirit searches everything, even the depths of God.
—*1 Corinthians 2:9-10*

At that time the disciples came to Jesus and asked,
"Who is the greatest in the kingdom of heaven?"
He called a child, whom he put among them, and said,
"Truly I tell you, unless you change and become like children,
you will never enter the kingdom of heaven."
—*Matthew 18:1-3*

It is above all by the imagination that we achieve
perception and compassion and hope.
—*Ursula K. Le Guin*[1]

Transforming congregations into more multicultural, just, compassionate, and reconciling communities requires that we have a different way of conceiving how we can live, work, and celebrate together. This reconception requires imagination, the capacity to see what does not yet exist or form a picture or mental image of something in the future. As religious people, we might say that this image is inspired by God's Spirit breathing within us. Sometimes this inspiration takes the form of dreams or visions (Joel

2:28, Acts 2:17-18). In Romans 8, Paul writes, "We know that the whole creation has been groaning in labor pains until now; and not only the creation, but we ourselves, who have the first fruits of the Spirit, groan inwardly while we wait for adoption, the redemption of our bodies" (vv. 22-23). Being open to the Divine Spirit requires that we open ourselves to the unexpected. The discipline of daily prayer or meditation, stepping back from our busy routines, may allow us the time and space to try on the mind of God. At other times, reading, painting, dancing, playing or listening to music, walking in the forest or along the beach may inspire us to see differently, to open ourselves to a wider view, to align ourselves with God's desire for us and for all creation. When we actually try to live this new (future) vision of reality in the present, theologians and scholars of Scripture talk about the reign of God being proleptically present, from the Greek word πρόληψισ, for "anticipation."

The word *proleptic* means the representation or assumption of a future act or development as if presently existing or accomplished. Thus when female voices carry as much weight as male voices in a meeting or when persons of color have as much power on a board as white people, we can say we are proleptically living the out the reign of God. The notion here is that the future (God's justice, compassion, and reconcilitation) is coming toward us. We are anticipating God's full reign even if we are living it only momentarily. Our imaginations, inspired by God's spirit, allow us a foretaste of what it will be like when we will truly be living as God's children respecting the dignity of all creation. So Paul writes of how God anoints us, sets a seal of ownership on us, and puts God's "Spirit in our hearts as a first installment," guaranteeing what is to come (2 Cor. 1:21-22, also 2 Cor. 5:5). In Ephesians, the author tells us that God chose us before the creation of the world to be God's adopted children, redeemed and forgiven in Christ. And God

> has made known to us the mystery of his will, according to his good pleasure that he set forth in Christ, as a plan for the full-

> ness of time, to gather up all things in him, things in heaven and things on earth. In Christ we have also obtained an inheritance, having been destined according to the purpose of him who accomplishes all things according to his counsel and will, so that we, who were the first to set our hope on Christ, might live for the praise of his glory. In him you also, when you had heard the word of truth, the gospel of your salvation, and had believed in him, were marked with the seal of the promised Holy Spirit; this is the pledge of our inheritance toward redemption as God's own people, to the praise of his glory (Eph. 1:9-14).

The word αρραβωυ, translated here as "pledge" of our inheritance, refers to earnest money or the deposit that guarantees that the transaction will be completed. It is an actual foretaste of what is to come—in this case the blessedness that is God's reign.

How do we enact this theology? How does the Spirit help us set goals and take action that leads to a more just, less oppressive world? Most of us believe that it is God's plan for us to live as equals. What prevents us from living out that belief? How do we close the gap between our current reality and the fullness of God's reign? For me, the process involves more than an intellectual exercise. It begins with a *desire* rather than with sense of *obligation* or *duty*. Let me give a simple example on a personal level.

Over many decades, I have tried to make both New Year's resolutions and Lenten resolutions, mostly to little avail. I tell myself that it would be a good idea for me to get more exercise or to lose weight or to be more faithful to daily meditation or the reading of Scripture. Generally, my resolution is framed in terms of an obligation or duty to myself, something I *should* do. And unfailingly I manage to stay with this sense of obligation for only a few days or weeks. It's not that my thinking or planning is bad. I just don't seem to have the energy or commitment to follow through. And then when I fail at my good intention, I inevitably feel bad about myself and make it even harder for me to try a similar resolution in the future. One significant exception to this pattern stands out in my life, and for many years I didn't really understand why I was successful in making the change I envisioned. Now I think I know why, and it's really rather simple. Let me tell you the story.

About eight years ago, I was again considering a New Year's resolution. I decided that I really wanted to invent some new meals my family could enjoy. One of my daughters was studying abroad, so I had more room to experiment, because I had only three palates to please. So I decided that I would prepare one new meal each week. The meal could be from a cookbook, from my mother's old recipe box that I had inherited, something I made up, or an adaptation of a meal I had eaten in a restaurant. The only stipulation was that it couldn't be something we were used to eating at home, which left a lot of room for experimentation.

I managed to keep my resolution for about four months—a Guinness record for resolutions in our house. At the end of the time, I had more than fifteen new meals to add to our cooking repertoire. I shared the cooking responsibilities with my wife, which meant that, when it was my turn to cook, if I cooked only my new meals, I wouldn't repeat a meal for a full month. Only some time later did I realize that my approach to this resolution was different from all my previous New Year's and Lenten attempts. I did not tell myself what I *ought* to do. I did not "should" on myself. Rather, I was approaching the entire enterprise as an adventure, almost a game. I didn't exactly imagine myself as a gourmet chef, but I did believe that it was possible for us to have a genuinely enhanced dining experience over time, because I could already almost "taste" the difference. Something playful guided this endeavor. I now understand this playfulness that took place for me through the lens of transactional analysis.

Beginning Transformation with the "Natural Child"

Transactional analysis, TA for short, is the popular name given to a psychological theory developed by the psychiatrist Eric Berne in the late 1950s in California.[2] TA is a post-Freudian theory of both personality and communication. According to Berne, every individual has three distinguishable ego states: Parent, Adult, and Child. The ego states are psychological realities, not roles; and the terms are capitalized to distinguish them from actual parents, adults, and children. Each ego state is a "system of feelings accompanied by a related set of behavior patterns."[3] According to Berne, people are operating from a Parent ego state when their behavior resembles that of parental figures. People are acting from an Adult ego state when making an autonomous, objective appraisal of a situation, stating problems perceived, thought processes used, and conclusions made in a nonprejudicial manner. People are acting from a Child ego state when their feelings and manner of acting are those they would have had as a child.

The Parent ego state has two expressions: direct and indirect. The direct expression refers to a person acting in the same way as a parental figure. The indirect expression refers to a person who is acting in accordance with messages given by a parental figure, even if this is not how the parental figure would have acted ("Do as I say, not as I do"). The Child ego state also has two expressions: *adapted child* and *natural child*. The Adapted Child acts in response or reaction to parental influence. He or she behaves as the mother or father (or other parental figure, such as teacher or pastor) wanted the child to behave—by complying. Or the Adapted Child adjusts by withdrawing, complaining, whining. The Parent *causes* an effect in the Adapted Child. The Natural Child acts spontaneously, creatively; her behavior is not a reaction to the Parent. Great energy for transformation is inherent in the Natural Child.

Berne and his followers use this basic scheme to analyze human interactions and complex organizations by looking at the feeling and behavioral tapes (or scripts) we acquire in childhood and examining how these are active in the various ego states. TA theorists assist people in breaking unhelpful or destructive habits and help them untangle miscommunication, which they refer to as crossed or covert (duplex) transactions—talking across ego states without realizing it. The goal is generally to engage in complimentary transactions. For example, complimentary transactions occur when two people speak to one another from their respective Adult ego states (A: "I'm going to quit the board"; B: "What led you to that decision?") or when person Y, speaking from the Parent ego state, responds to person X, who is speaking from the Child ego state (X: "I feel sick, I think I have a fever"; Y: "I'm so sorry. I'll get you some aspirin"). My interest here is not in analyzing individual transactions, but rather in understanding how the various ego states assist or inhibit transformation.

Bringing about a desired transformation means moving from one state of being or set of circumstances to another that is more beneficial or advantageous. Such a transformation can be initiated from any of the three ego states. The Parent ego state would tell us what we *should* do. The Adult ego state would analyze all the possibilities, weighing their merits, and calculating the best objective outcome. The (Natural) Child ego state moves from a place of spontaneity, remembering previous successes and the sheer delight that comes with accomplishing something new or desired. Each of these beginning points has merit.

The Parent ego state can judge or nurture. Many civil rights advances came about because laws telling people what was right or wrong, and what they were required to do, were changed. By talking about moral imperatives or about how we need to act to care for those who are "the least of these who are members of [our] family" (Matt. 25:31-46), preachers encourage people to change their oppressive behaviors. The prophets in the Hebrew Scriptures frequently functioned from the Parent ego state when they were berating the sinfulness of the people who had turned from God's ways.

Leaders act from the Adult ego state when they solve problems. For instance, in a congregation experiencing declining membership, the leaders may do a demographic study to determine whether the church can grow and, if so, what types of people are most likely to be attracted to their church and under what conditions. They might pilot some advertising and neighborhood canvassing or employ a consultant who has demonstrated success in increasing the size of similar congregations.

The Child ego state may be the least often employed of the three when it comes to initiating change. Here and in what follows

I am speaking of the *Natural* Child because this ego state offers the greatest opportunity for radical transformation. For this reason I describe it in greater detail: Think of a small child about a year old who is just on the verge of walking. The child has most likely learned to crawl with considerable expertise and speed—getting where she wants with relative efficiency. She has seen other people walking and has formed some image of what walking would be like for her—she has pictured herself as a walker. Most likely, the parents have held her hands as her feet flail in crawling and walking motions. And then, at some moment, it all comes together. She takes those first steps—with an assisting hand or holding on to the coffee table or couch. Very soon she is darting across the room, falling occasionally at first, but with a tremendous grin or even shrieks of complete glee.

My suspicion is that most of us did not learn to walk because we were doing what our parents (or Parent ego state) were telling us to do. In other words, an "ought" or a "should" did not direct our behavior and feelings. Nor were we acting from the Adult ego state. We were not consciously problem solving or calculating the motions that would result in successful perambulation. Rather, an image coalesced uniting "me" and "walker." We imagined ourselves as walkers. If you watch a child on the verge of walking, you can almost see the cartoon bubble over her head that shouts in glee, "I'm walking!" even before it happens. I don't mean to say that the child has intellectually worked out the idea of walking. It is more an image, a dream, a vision. Woven into that image is a feeling of competence (power) and joy. It's as if she is saying, "I can do it! I love it! Look at me!" without even knowing what *it* is or the component parts that contribute to the success and joy. In a sense, walking proleptically comes from the future to meet the child in the present. It is in her before it is fully exercised. She *imagines* walking and the walking begins—not all at once, but the impetus is irrepressibly there. She sees herself as a new creation *and* she is that novel, inventive creature.

As an educator and in my capacity as director of theological field education, I know that students and supervisors are more likely to learn if they create goals and objectives for their learning, if they are intentional and self-motivated. When I have asked students and supervisors-in-training to articulate their goals for the course or workshop in which they are participating, they very often formulate these goals from the Parent or Adult ego state. The participants are telling me and themselves what they *need to* or *should* learn based on a message they internalized from some parental figure who acted as the students believed they should act or who told them what proper behavior should be. Other times they have intentionally reflected on problems they have encountered, and they have calculated that certain intellectual tools or new ways of behaving might be more effective in meeting the challenges they face. Setting goals from these ego states will likely be of more assistance than engaging in the course with no thought about what they hope to accomplish. Therefore I believe that goal setting should be encouraged. But I now have an alternative method that invites students and supervisors to *imagine* new ways of thinking, behaving, and feeling.

Within the past few years, I have invited supervisors, initially, and then students to formulate goals from the Child ego state. I generally first invite them into the process and then explain it after they have done the exercise; so, that is what I will do here. I first encountered the method I am describing when I worked as a campus minister in the late 1970s. I learned another variation of the same method in setting personal goals for multicultural change through training created by VISIONS, Inc.

Exercise for Imagining Personal Transformation

Imagine yourself in a training course or workshop that extends over several days, weeks, or months. (Or alternatively, imagine reading this book as your course or workshop.)

Take a moment to relax. Use whatever method of relaxation works best for you. After reading the directions, you might find it helpful to close your eyes. Focus on your breathing. Breathe slowly and deeply. As you take in breath, take in God's spirit; the spirit of life; the spirit of creativity, wisdom, health, and well-being. Breathe in all that is good. As you exhale, let go of as much tension as you can. Release all that troubles you and holds you back or holds you down. Let go of what oppresses you—as much as it is possible for you to do. Continue to breathe slowly and deeply for a few minutes. As you do so, relax your body. Let go of tension in your limbs, your torso, your shoulders and neck, your face and scalp. Notice any place where you feel tense, and go to that place and make peace with whatever pain or tension you find there. Relax as much as you are able, and be at peace with what you cannot change.

Now take a moment to imagine that your time of learning is finished. The course is complete. You have turned the last page. The training workshop is over. You have engaged with the material to the best of your ability. You have connected with those around you. You have learned, and you have taught others in the process. It has been a mutually enriching experience. You have accomplished everything you hoped to accomplish, given the time and energy at your disposal. You have even exceeded some of your hopes for learning and growing. Imagine that this has been the experience that you really desired, and you are different because of this experience. It has changed your life in positive ways. You are a new creation. You are at this point—at the end of this learning chapter of your life—all that God has created you to be at this time.

Now take a moment to think about how you are different, how you have changed, how you have been transformed by the Spirit of God. Be as specific as you can. Imagine yourself at the end of a training period. Perhaps it is May, and you have been learning and growing over an academic year. Or perhaps it is Friday and the end of a weeklong workshop. Imagine yourself at the end of the time of learning and say *in the present tense* what you are *thinking differently* about yourself, the church, or your work; what you are *doing differently*, and *how you feel*. Use these sample sentences to formulate how you are changed. Remember to state your changes in the present tense.

1. It is *May* (or Friday or some other specific endpoint to a learning session). I have finished this time of learning. I have been successful in accomplishing what I desired. It is *May*, and I am thinking (differently) . . . (State here some of your new ideas, beliefs, learnings.)
2. It is *May* (or Friday or some other specific endpoint to a learning session). I have finished this time of learning. I have been successful in accomplishing what I desired. It is *May*, and I am doing (differently) . . . (State here some of your new behaviors.)
3. It is *May* (or Friday or some other specific endpoint to a learning session). I have finished this time of learning. I have been successful in accomplishing what I desired. It is *May*, and I feel . . . (State here how you feel about yourself, what you have learned, how you are acting differently.)

My experience with this process of goal setting for learning and personal transformation has been remarkably positive, though it is not easy. For some people, doing the guided imagery and imagining themselves in the future is hard. Also difficult is speaking in the present tense about how they only *hope* to think and behave in new ways. Nevertheless, claiming these anticipated learnings *in the present tense* is important, because it is a way to practice the difference between *is* and *ought*. It is an exercise in embracing God's transformative power in us proleptically. When people do use the present tense to talk about a significant projected learning or an important new way of thinking or acting, you can hear a remarkable conviction in their voices. And more important, they hear it themselves. When a person expresses his or her *voice* in this way, I have often had the person tell me a month later that he has made an incredible breakthrough in how he is acting, or how she is thinking about herself and others or about community. In a group setting, giving voice to a possible new way of being or acting allows that way of being or acting to be *heard* into reality. The relational speaking and hearing brings about the possibility of a new reality.[4]

When the voice comes from the Natural Child ego state, generally tremendous energy, creativity, and a sense of almost unlimited possibility accompanies it. The difference between this voice and the voice that emerges from the Parent ego state with its "shoulds," "oughts," and "musts" is almost palpable. The statement, "I am preaching with clarity and conviction," spoken with enthusiasm (Child) is much more likely to bring about the desired result than "Preachers ought to be clear and convincing" (Parent) or "My goal is to preach clearly and with conviction" (Adult).

Imagining Community Transformation

Faith communities, ministerial agencies, and other institutions also can bring about transformation by engaging the Child ego state of participants in imagining the future. The advantages of this are similar to the engagement of the Child for personal transformation. Many of us resist messages that come from the Parent about what we *should* do. Often goals initiated from the Adult seem well-reasoned but do not gather the energy of the community or group that is needed to implement those goals. Engaging the Child ego state of participants generally ensures energy abundant enough to imagine significant organizational transformation and overcome the resistance to change. Even more energy is usually needed to sustain the process through implementation. This additional energy is also more likely to come when the Child continues to be engaged.

My introduction to planning for transformation by engaging the Child came many years ago when I was working in a middle-class, suburban congregation. A consultant came to the church to assist us with welcoming and incorporating new members. He asked us, "If Emmanuel Church were an ideally effective church, fully living out God's unique call, what would it look like? What would you see happening?" I am sure the consultant neither made an allusion to transactional analysis nor at the time did I hear the question in light of that theory. Nevertheless, there was something different about the question and the energy it unleashed in the group. We were not being asked what we thought we *should* do. We were not asked to focus on membership as a problem and discover ways to solve that problem. We were invited to imagine our future as alive and vibrant and to describe in the present tense and in specific detail what we saw happening. After that, we looked for common responses, set priorities, and made some action plans. Unlike other daylong planning events I had attended, people went away from that day with more energy than when they arrived. No one seemed to regret having spent a beautiful Saturday indoors at church when they could have been working in their yards or playing at the beach.

Today I would understand the work we did those many years ago as similar to appreciative inquiry, though I don't believe we did all the steps of that process, which had not yet been developed. Today the process of appreciative inquiry is widely accepted in both corporate and ecclesial worlds. Because it is highly effective and allows for the recognition and celebration of differences, I offer an overview of the assumptions, theory, and practice and encourage readers who wish to delve deeper into this approach to community transformation to consult Sue Annis Hammond's *The Thin Book of Appreciative Inquiry*[5] and Mark Lau Branson's *Memories, Hopes and Conversations: Appreciative Inquiry and Congregational Change*.[6]

Appreciative Inquiry

Appreciative inquiry (AI) is an organizational development process that builds upon what is positive in an institution or community in order to bring about renewal and change. It is as much an art or adventure of transformation as it is a science. AI was developed by David Cooperrider and Suresh Srivastva at the Weatherhead School of Management at Case Western Reserve University in the 1980s.[7] AI attempts to discover what animates a system—that is, what in the system is most alive and responsive to its members and to its environment. It involves asking questions (inquiry) about what is working well (appreciation) in order to strengthen the capacity "to apprehend, anticipate, and heighten positive potential."[8]

Appreciative inquiry is built on a number of assumptions that are compatible with the tenets of most faith communities. To summarize, the similar, key assumptions offered by Hammond and Branson are:

- In every organization or faith community, some things work well.
- It is best to focus on what works well, because what we focus on becomes our reality.
- One way we focus is by asking questions, and the very process of asking questions brings about a change in the organization.
- Asking questions designed to tap into the best practices of a community leads the community in a positive direction.
- As people make this journey into the future, they carry parts of the past with them.
- In making this journey, we should carry the best parts of the past into the future.
- Differences are valuable; they should be recognized, understood, and celebrated.
- The language we use creates our reality.[9]

To these assumptions, which Branson shares with Hammond, he adds three more:

- "Organizations are heliotropic"—that is, they turn toward the sun or the light.
- "Outcomes should be useful."
- "All steps are collaborative."[10]

A theological basis for AI can be found in the letter to the Philippians: "Finally, beloved, whatever is true, whatever is honorable, whatever is just, whatever is pure, whatever is pleasing, whatever is commendable, if there is any excellence and if there is anything worthy of praise, think about these things" (Phil. 4:8).

The importance of these assumptions can best be seen by comparing AI to traditional problem solving. Problem solving is essentially a deficit model that begins with the identification of a problem or a set of inadequacies. Its focus is on what is wrong. Because what we focus on determines our reality, it is easy to devolve into negativity. The second step in problem solving is to analyze the cause(s) of the problem. Unfortunately, sometimes the causes are unknown or unchangeable. Not knowing the cause of the problem or being unable to do anything about it can lead to further negativity. In the easiest cases, analysis of causes can lead to possible solutions, which are also analyzed in order to develop an action plan. Recalling the earlier discussion of transactional analysis, we can note that this method of traditional problem solving relies heavily on the Adult ego state and thus has the limitation that it does not attract much energy from participants.

Appreciative inquiry is a process designed to build cohesiveness in the community or organization even as it imagines what the organization can become. Leaders working with AI begin by introducing participants to the assumptions of AI and deciding on a focus of inquiry by asking a series of questions designed to uncover where people have found vitality in their faith community or organization. Leaders then ask questions to discover what the community did best in the area under consideration. They encourage participants to tell stories about best practices and to imagine "what might be" by developing provocative proposals or propositions for the future as people build consensus around their dreams.[11] This process initially engages the Child ego state and only toward the end involves the Adult and Parent ego states as consensus is built toward "what should be." This process is iterative; at each stage the leader asks more questions about what has gone well and participants tell more stories about previous successes so that the energy builds. As many people as possible are involved in the process so that there is communal energy and maximum endorsement when the implementation stage is reached.

One of the key dimensions of appreciative inquiry is the formation of provocative proposals. In my experience, leading a group in developing these proposals is difficult because the process involves building the necessary energy and consensus to carry out the implementation while at the same time refining the goals or dreams so that they are clear and possible and still a stretch for the community. How does a leader do this? As was the case with the personal level resolutions or goals, the leader invites the group to state these proposals in the affirmative and the present tense, as if they are already happening. The leader takes care to see that the proposals are grounded in the experience of the community, based on the best data available, so that they are achievable. The leader helps stretch the organization by uncovering and challenging current assumptions and practices. If the community does not examine its beliefs about itself, its environment, its strengths, and its limitations, it will not move.

Even when a community is poised for change and willing to examine its assumptions and beliefs by developing provocative proposals, significant transformation requires new learning and new relationships. The thought processes and knowledge that sustained the old way of being are not sufficient for imagining a new reality and for implementing and sustaining a new vision. The community most likely needs to acquire a new level of emotional literacy and affective competence as well as new information and systems for sharing that information. New interdependent relationships, in which power and expertise are shared, are required. More will be said about these relationships in chapter 5, which explores relational theory.

Finally, the implementation needs to be monitored carefully and key players need to be supported. It is helpful to think about this process of implementation on all four levels of intervention and change that were discussed in chapter 2. On the personal level, individual attitudes, beliefs, and thought processes need to be examined. Preaching and teaching are primary ways to articulate alternatives and options. Information needs to be shared. The vision needs to be grounded in the faith that has been handed to us by our ancestors—in its best practices and most authentic, lived tradition. People also need opportunities to understand and express their feelings.

On the interpersonal level, leaders' responsibilities include noticing when oppressive behaviors and those that result from internalized oppression arise. Two common behaviors that can quickly undermine the appreciative inquiry process are avoidance of contact and denial of difference or denial of one's cultural heritage. The most common form of avoidance of contact is the failure to invite certain groups into the planning process (youth; non-English speakers; those who are employed at night or weekends, when the planning usually takes place; members of racial and ethnic minority groups). Denial of difference and denial of one's cultural heritage occur when leaders or participants rush to vision—that is, when people do not take the time to examine the nuances of the differing stories about what has been vital in the past. Arriving too quickly at consensus about past successes or about wishes for the future means that there will not be support at the stage of implementation. The people who were assimilated into the process without their genuine consent will opt out or rebel.

On the institution level, the faith community needs to examine rituals, customs, bylaws, and rules that might prevent the dreams from becoming a reality. The organizational structures need to change with the vision in order to support it. In the later stages, one person can sabotage the whole transformation process by appealing to an old regulation or bylaw that was not updated. More important, the formal structures of an organization or community are like the skeleton that holds the body upright and enables movement and flexibility. It needs to be kept in good health.

Last, cultural level change is at the heart of the AI process. The outcome is a new set of definitions of what is good, true, and beautiful. When the dream is realized, people sense that they are living in a new cultural setting. In many cases, this means the inclusion of a greater diversity of people who are visible and whose voices are heard and celebrated. On the most profound level, the cultural shift is experienced as God's reign breaking into the present in new and unexpected ways.

Exercise for Imagining Communal Transformation

This exercise is designed for use with a church board on a weekend retreat where the goals include community building and setting board goals for the coming year. It can also be used with a larger group as part of a daylong leadership or parishwide retreat. The questions are based on sample questions in the appendix of Branson's *Memories, Hopes, and Conversations.*[12]

Opening Questions

Think back over your entire experience at Your Church (name your church). Remember a time when you felt alive with God's spirit and deeply engaged in the life, ministry, and mission of the church. What were you doing at that time? Who else was involved? What was happening? How did you feel?

Relationships

Recall the relationships at this church and your other spiritual homes during your life. Who are the people through whom and with whom you have grown most spiritually? Who are the people with whom you have most experienced your own vitality, your power and effectiveness, a yearning to learn and grow, a sense of self-worth, and a desire for deeper relationship?[13] Let those people come into your presence and offer you a word or phrase of blessing.

Now think about relationships here at Your Church in which you feel most alive. What do you most value in these relationships? What groups do you participate in that you value the most? What groups help you understand and live out your faith more authentically and courageously? As you think about the wider church community, what is most important about how we connect to one another? Tell a story about a relationship that has been inspiring to you.

Spiritual Life

Reflect on all of your experiences at Your Church. What events, programs, and relationships have contributed most to your spiritual life—to a deeper awareness of God's presence and activity in your life? Describe one such event, program, or relationship.

As you think of the wider faith community, what events, programs, and relationships have been most significant in developing the congregation's relationships with God? When this congregation is growing spiritually, what do you seeing happening? Describe an event when the congregation is growing spiritually, when people are growing deeper in their relationship to God and one another. Who is involved? What are they doing?

Understanding and Valuing Differences

Think about the composition of Your Church. What are the racial, ethnic, and class differences you notice? What about differences in theology, lifestyle, family composition? Tell a story of demographic change in your church or community.

When Your Church has been at its best, how have participants and members gone about noticing your differences and understanding and valuing them at a deeper level? When you have been at your best, how have you celebrated your differences? Who was involved? What did you see happening? Tell a story about when you were involved in getting to know someone quite different from you. Tell a story about how the congregation has deepened its understanding of differences or celebrated differences.

God's Mission in the World

Think about your personal ministry and mission beyond Your Church. When have you been engaged in ministry, outreach, or mission that has been enriching and rewarding? What contributed to the satisfaction? Tell the story of your involvement.

Think about how Your Church has been engaged in your community and in the wider world. Tell a story of ministry and mission that goes beyond the membership of the congregation. Who was involved? What took place? What do you think was most significant in that event?

When Your Church is at its best, what is it known for in the community? How does Your Church express God's justice, compassion, and reconciliation in the local and global community?

Your Contributions

Take a moment to remember that God has brought you into life and into this community to be a unique expression of God's love, wisdom, and creativity in this corner of God's creation. No one else is like you. No one else makes the contributions that you make to the world.

If your life were to end soon and someone were to write your obituary or give a testimony about your greatest contributions at Your Church and in your community, what would that person say? Don't be too humble. What are the most vital ways you contribute to this faith community? Think about who you are and what you do—your personality, your beliefs, your skills, and your activities. Give examples of how you contribute to the vitality of your church and community.

Summary Questions

Imagine that you are a reporter writing about the vitality of all the faith communities in your town. What do you tell people is the most important, life-giving characteristic of Your Church? When it is at its best, what is the single most important value that characterizes Your Church? Summarize that value in a word or phrase.

Wishes

Imagine that God is abundantly blessing Your Church now and into the future with vitality, courage, and productivity. The mustard seed has become a tree (Luke 13:19), and the leaven has raised three measures of flour (Luke 13:21). Make three wishes for the future of Your Church. As these wishes come true, describe what it looks like. What do you see happening?

I have used these questions (often omitting one or two questions in "Relationships" through "God's Mission in the World") as part of a church board retreat to help people experience the benefits of the appreciative inquiry process. I give people about fifteen minutes to write their answers or make notes individually in silence, with soft music in the background, or by going outside if the weather is nice. Participants are then asked to interview each other in pairs, using the questions. They are asked to choose someone they do not know as well as others in the group or someone who is different from them. They are given about thirty minutes for the interview. They then return to the larger group. I first ask people what the exercise felt like, hoping to maintain the energy of the Child ego state. People usually find the exercise very energizing. What takes place next depends on the type of group gathered, the amount of time available, and the goal of the group. My goals have generally been to give the group a taste of the appreciative inquiry process, as distinct from other goal-setting processes based on problem solving. I also want them to experience the kind of community building that takes place by doing this exercise together. Ideally, this experience becomes one of the vital activities in their corporate spiritual life.

Based on its experience with this exercise on a retreat, the board of one small church decided to assign to each board member one other adult in the congregation for a mutual interview. The board members felt that this would help them share the energy and excitement they felt on the retreat as well as begin to teach the AI process to others in the congregation. They then planned to ask the enlarged group (the board and newly interviewed people) to make one more set of mutual interviews with parishioners not yet interviewed—thereby involving nearly all the active adult parishioners in the process. They focused more on the summary questions and the wishes and intended to use those to determine a focus area for dreaming and planning about their future during an upcoming all-parish planning event.

The full AI process requires several months of hard work and the involvement of a large group of participants. It requires diligent note taking, communication back to the participants and the wider congregation, continual refinement of focus, development of action steps, and careful monitoring to see that differences are valued and not lost. For that work, I strongly recommend having the leadership read and discuss either Branson or Hammond. The congregation should also employ a consultant to guide the process so that the lay and clergy leaders can participate fully without having to be concerned about the mechanics of the process.

My purpose in this chapter has been to call attention to the role of imagination in bringing about transformation and the importance of focusing on what is working well. In essence, this means trying to see ourselves and our future as God sees us. When we try to adopt God's vision, all things are possible. At the same time, bringing about the new reality God has in mind for us is essentially collaborative work. It is the work done *in relationship with* God and others. It requires attending to and building relationships that recognize, understand, value, and celebrate differences. The following chapter articulates a theory of relational development that both honors differences and forms a foundation for transforming communities. Equipped with a new relational theory of human development and interaction, our provocative proposal might be: We are doing justice, loving kindness, and walking humbly with our God (Mic. 6:8).

5

Relational Theory as a Way of Valuing Differences

I discovered I was most truly myself
when I was open to relationships with others,
when I knew that I belonged to a community.

—*Margaret Bullitt-Jonas*[1]

The unrelated human being lacks wholeness,
for he can achieve wholeness only through the soul,
and the soul cannot exist without its other side,
which is always found in a "you."

—*Carl G. Jung*[2]

One of the most significant and consistent areas of growth for me in the thirty-plus years since I have been ordained has been in regard to my relationships and how I think about self and relationship. People who know my history would be chuckling now. I can picture both of my daughters saying, "Well, yeah! You started out as a celibate Roman Catholic priest, and now you're married and have two daughters!" They would be right, of course, to point to that obvious change. The intimacy of a long-term, committed relationship with a woman is very different from living in community with a varying number of men who come and go as their work assignments take them to different parts of the world—where their ministry takes precedence over intimate relationships. But the change I am speaking about is more fundamental than the shift in priority from work to relationships.

I was raised to think about *self* as the primary category when thinking about human development. I don't mean this in a self-centered way, that *my* self is most important. I mean self as the fundamental reality, the primary building block of society. I bought into the idea that my goal in life was to develop into an independent, autonomous, mature human individual. I believed that if I did that in a relatively successful way, *and only if I did that*, I might then be able to have mature relationships with other people who were also able to develop as independent selves.

This bias about the self as the primary category of analysis and development was subtly reinforced in my parochial school experience and in church. For the most part, as I remember it, ethics and morality had to do with how an individual lived in the pattern of Jesus. The second great commandment, "Love your neighbor as yourself" (Mark 12:31), was interpreted to imply that one's *self* was a primary category. *Relationship* was something two selves could engage in, but it was not itself a primary category. Even though most of the Ten Commandments have to do with how a person lives in community or in relationship to others, they were presented in my early schooling as a checklist for appropriate individual behavior or, more accurately, as a list of prohibitions about what the good man or woman should not do. This code of individual ethical behavior was reinforced by the practice of individual private confession in the secrecy of a darkened, somewhat soundproof confessional. Clearly, most behaviors had relational or communal implications, but those implications did not get much emphasis in my early education. Even performing restitution for stealing or slander had as much to do with a requirement for getting one's *self* back in God's grace as it had to do with healing the broken relationships.

When I first studied psychology, the great psychologists I was assigned to read (Sigmund Freud, Carl Jung, Alfred Adler, Abraham Maslow, Erik Erikson, Lawrence Kohlberg) just happened to be men and just happened to have used their research to create norms about men and then generalized that research to all people. Even Freud, who studied women fairly extensively at the beginning of his career, went on to reject what women said about being sexually abused because it did not match what he had come to assume was true about men's experience and because his male colleagues would not accept what he initially reported the women had said.

As I began to do antiracism and multicultural training and as I studied relational psychology, I started to see three problems with the notion that self is the basic category of human understanding and development. First, the emphasis on the self reflects the individualistic bias of Western European and modern North American cultures. In Asian, African, and Native American cultures, the community is the fundamental category. The South African (Zulu and Xhosa) concept of *ubuntu* asserts that persons and groups form their identity in relationship to one another: "I am because we are."[3] Second, focusing on self inevitably creates a deep split between self and other—a split that invites comparisons with inevitable better than/less than judgments, along with subsequent power disparities. Third, self, like race, is a social construct. As the relational theorists Jean Baker Miller and Irene Stiver point out, "The term [the self] has become so reified it's worth remembering that there is no such *thing* as a self. It is a *concept* made up by psychologists and sociologists."[4]

Influenced by the relational theorists, whose work I present in this chapter, I have come to understand *relationship* as the primary category in human development. Human development does not take place except in relationship, in interactions with others. Therefore, rather than focusing on individual development, one focuses on mutual development. One looks not at the *self* but at "the connection between" two or more people.[5] This connection does not belong to any one of the people; it belongs to both or all. Yet each person experiences this connection as her own—a part of her.

Trinity: God as Relationship

The theological corollary to seeing self as the primary category of human development is seeing three *persons* (read, *selves*) in one

God. As a child in church and in religious education, I remember a lot of stress was placed on the distinction and autonomy of the persons and on the oneness or identity of the Godhead or the Divine Being. Certainly, emphasis on identity was in line with the *mono*theism of Judaism, which distinguished the Hebrews or Jews from many of their neighbors. The Shema, "Hear, O Israel: the LORD our God is one LORD" (Deut. 6:4 KJV), is the prayer that all Jews are taught as children so that they may say it as their final words before dying. Jesus, as a Jew, lived this belief. Certainly, Christianity is a monotheistic religion. However, when Christianity tries to work three persons into this emphasis on the identity and oneness of God, things get messy. No wonder that most discussions of the doctrine of the Trinity begin and end by saying it is a mystery! While I grant that human categories are inadequate for describing the Divine, notice how easy the concept is to grasp if we start with relationship, rather than self or identity, as the fundamental category.

I have come to think about God as relationship or community. Far greater minds than mine have struggled with the enigma of the Trinity (how to have both *three* persons and *one* God), so I do not pretend to have solved this great theological puzzle.[6] I simply want to say that imaging God as relationship helps me make sense of the doctrine of the Trinity in a way a three-persons-in-one God does not. Try this on: In the beginning when the Divine Community created the heavens and the earth . . . (Gen. 1:1). Or: In the beginning was the Word, and the Word was of the Divine Relationship (John 1:1). Seeing God as relationship does not take away the difficulty of explaining the ineffable in limited human concepts and language, but it does change the nature of the theological problems.[7] When we conceive of God starting with three persons, we struggle with how they are equal and how there is only *one* God. When we start with relationship, we struggle to understand what these "entities" (there is no good word) are when they are not in relationship. They are not selves. They are not separate beings. They are not aspects or dimensions. And they are *never* out of relationship, even theoretically. If relationship/community/connection is primary, they can be seen as "persons" only *in so far as they are* not *in relationship*. In other words, "person" is what they would be if there were no relationship. *Connection* or *connectedness* is more important than and prior to *what* is connected. This relational view of God also offers a new way to understand Genesis 1:27. If we think of God as an entity, a self, being created in God's image has something to do with having the Divine within us or being a reflection (mirror image) of the Divine. If we are created in the *relational* image of God, male and female, then relationship comes before identity, and masculinity and femininity are more about *how we are in relationship* than about *who* we are.

Looking at human relationships, when we use self as the fundamental category, the self/other dichotomy is inevitable; whereas, with relationship as the fundamental category, self is what you have when you don't have relationship! Self becomes an empty concept. The great Jewish philosopher and theologian Martin Buber expressed a similar view. In speaking about human relationships, he wrote that "meaning is to be found neither in one of the two partners, nor in both together, but only in their dialogue itself, in this 'between' which they live together."[8]

The Relational Revolution in Psychology

Beginning in the 1970s, a revolution began to take place in the way psychologists speak about how women and men think and act. In *This Changes Everything: The Relational Revolution in Psychology*, Pulitzer Prize–winning journalist Christina Robb details how the work of Carol Gilligan, Jean Baker Miller, Judith Lewis Herman, and their colleagues brought the democratic insights of the civil rights movement and the women's movement to bear on psychology. I credit a great deal of my own growth in relationship and in the language for speaking about relationship and connection to the work of these women and the women and men with whom they worked. Carol Gilligan began her work by questioning Lawrence Kohlberg's scale of moral development because she uncovered a significant paradox in his theory: "The very traits that have traditionally defined the 'goodness' of women, their care for and sensitivity to the needs of others, are those that mark them as deficient in moral judgment."[9] This led Gilligan to posit that the way women paid attention to relationships, cared for and about others, and both thought and felt at the same time constituted not a "developmental deficiency," as she wrote, but was the result of "a different social and moral understanding."

As Gilligan researched the way women talked about making moral decisions, she began to hear a new and *different voice*.[10] The dominant "male" voice, which Gilligan heard in about 80 percent of the men she studied, speaks about *rights*, *fairness*, doing the *just* thing, whether or not it hurts someone, because *universal principles* are most important to them. The different "female" voice, which Gilligan heard in about 80 percent of the women she studied, speaks about *caring* about others, being *responsible*, wanting to know who might get hurt by a particular decision and how to avoid hurting others as much as possible. Gilligan did not value one of these voices as better than the other but "described them as complements that integrate mercy and justice when women and men work together."[11] However, when she began her speaking and writing (1976), only the "male" voice had any standing in the worlds of business, politics, and psychology, hence Gilligan's terminology of *dominant voice* and *different voice*.

Gilligan went a step beyond saying that most women made moral decisions differently from most men. She gave a political and cultural reason for this difference that relates to what I have said in previous chapters about power and oppression. As Robb summarizes Gilligan's reasoning, "Because women were taught to rate themselves as less valuable and because they had less power to make decisions, they made different kinds of decisions, decisions that were much more alert to the risk of inflicting pain."[12] These different decisions, made in the different voice that Gilligan was hearing, pointed to a major problem. In psychology, white men had been studying white men and boys and drawing conclusions about all humanity. They *literally* were not listening to the voices of half the population (women) and were trying to understand them based on conclusions they had formed from studying a small segment (middle-class white men and boys) of the population.

And when female graduate students, and later female psychologists and psychiatrists, reported discrepancies between what they were taught in traditional psychology programs and what they were hearing from their female clients, their reports were dismissed as irrelevant or aberrant. In fact, many female therapists in training reported that they did not dare discuss what they were hearing or learning from their female clients and how they were working with them for fear of ridicule or not being licensed. Fortunately, supported by the women's movement, some female psychologists, psychiatrists, and researchers began to take seriously what they were hearing from women and began talking to one another about what they were hearing and what they themselves knew from their own experience. One such group met at the home of Jean Baker Miller, the psychiatrist whose 1976 classic *Toward a New Psychology of Women* earned her the title of grandmother of the relational psychology movement.[13]

Irene Stiver, Janet Surrey, Judith Jordan, and Alexandra Kaplan met weekly for fifteen years with Miller at her home and discussed how they were *actually* working with private clients, in corporate settings, and in psychiatric facilities. They supported one another in developing a new language and theory centered around connection. They gave lectures and published papers through the Stone Center at Wellesley College.[14] Like Gilligan, these relational theorists asserted that labeling women as inferior, abnormal (men are normal), or deviant was not only unhelpful but also biased and wrong. Furthermore, as Robb writes, the labels "dependent," "enmeshed," and "merged" did not "fit the reality they encountered in women patients, students, experimental subjects, and themselves. And not only the words but the molds and models of what women were or should optimally or normally be were wrong."[15] These women decided to shift the paradigm for understanding human growth and development. Rather than focus on *individuals* or *selves*, they decided to assume that human beings are fundamentally connected and that the connections between and among people are at least as important as the people they connect. We are all, always, in relationships. We change and are changed in relationships. Healthy people don't outgrow relationships to become autonomous, as traditional psychologists and psychiatrists taught. Healthy people always engage in strong, growing, lasting relationships. The theoretical perspective on what constitutes the basic human motive also shifted from having one's needs met, from being gratified, to participating in a mutual connection. As Miller and Stiver later wrote, "It's not a question of *getting*, but of *engaging* with others."[16]

The Five Good Things of Relationships

What characterizes good relationships? According to Miller, five good things flow from healthy relationships.[17] The first good thing can't be described in a word. *Zest* may be the closest, though Miller didn't like the commercial aspects of the word. *Vitality*, *aliveness*, and *energy* also express the sense of spaciousness or, as Robb puts it, "simply turning up the volume of life" that this quality represents.[18] This first good thing is not to be confused with simply being happy. One can have zest or increased vitality in the midst of sadness or pain if one is aware of being connected with someone else in the sorrow or pain. In a good relationship, you feel alive even when you experience painful emotions.

Good relationships are also characterized by *power and effectiveness*. Miller wrote that in a good relationship you feel "empowered to act *right in the immediate relationship—in this interplay, itself*."[19] This empowerment is relational; it is power you share with another person, not power over her. It allows a person who is in need (for example, someone who is about to lose a job or a loved one or someone who is struggling with cancer) to feel heard and gives her the courage and energy to move into the next relationship where she will be heard and be even more able to change or heal. Speaking about the mutuality of such relationships, Janet Surrey writes that as people allow their relationships to deeply change them, "neither person is in control; instead each is enlarged and feels empowered, energized, and more real."[20]

Knowledge is the third characteristic of a good relationship. People in good relationships explore and discover more about how they feel and what they think. They increase their knowledge about themselves and about others through being immersed in relationship.

A *sense of worth* flows from healthy relationships. When you are and feel alive, effective, and aware, you have a greater sense of worth. This sense of worth does not develop until people who are important to us convey to us that they recognize and acknowledge our experience. When I feel free to truly express myself and another person I respect really hears me, sees me, accepts me, and wants to be connected with me, then I feel more worthy.

Miller's final characteristic of a good relationship is the *desire for even more connection*. Because we feel more zest, more effectiveness, deeper knowledge, and increased worth, we desire more connection to the people who bring these things out in us. Miller writes that this desire for more connection is different from being loved or feeling approval. She states:

> It is much more valuable. It is the active, outgoing feeling of caring about another person because that person is so valued in our eyes. It leads to the desire for more and fuller connection with that person and also to a concern for that person's well-being. We cannot will this feeling into existence. It comes along as a concomitant of this kind of interchange. And it leads to wanting more relationship with the person whom we value and care about.[21]

In addition, the momentum of a good relationship pushes us into wanting relationships with people we don't know or don't know well yet. So the idea of being connected becomes more attractive. Even persons who previously experienced isolation as a form of protection begin to believe that connection may offer more protection.

Robb says that each of these five characteristics of good relationships "moves between the people in relationship, moves outward beyond that relationship to other relationships, and moves inward to the most intimate well of self-knowledge in each person."[22] Sometimes one person experiences the most zest;

sometimes the other. Sometimes one has more power or is learning more; sometimes the other. Often another person sees my worth more than I do and calls it forth in me. The desire for more connection may alternately be stronger in one and then the other. Healthy relationships are naturally always changing and allow for growth and expansion. An example of how relational psychologists understand this growth and change *relationally* can be seen in how they talk about adolescence. Traditionally, psychologists talk about the need for an adolescent to *separate* from his parents to become an independent adult. Relational psychologists would talk about the movement in the relationship—the relational changes that the adolescent's new abilities and awareness require of all the parties. Relational psychologists would emphasize preserving the underlying *connection* so that the adolescent and the parents can all make the changes they need to make.

I would add that healthy human relationships also have the potential for deepening one's relationship with God and with the rest of creation. It may be possible to grow into deeper relationship with God *because* one is bereft of healthy human relationships or when one has been deeply hurt in human relationships. However, my experience has been that when healthy human relationships have brought me the gifts of zest, effectiveness, knowledge, worth, and desire for more connection, then my relationship with God has also seemed more alive and I have desired an even deeper connection with the Divine.

But what about bad relationships? How can we say that human growth and even a deeper relationship with God depend on good relationships when so many relationships are destructive and block growth? The relational-cultural theorists say that only *good* relationships can teach us to limit the damage of bad relationships or, if necessary, help us end them. Judith Jordan, director of the Jean Baker Miller Training Institute, puts it this way: "You don't just leave a bad relationship; you need good relationships to help you leave bad relationships."[23] The fact that we participate in destructive relationships does not negate relational theory. One of the factors that contribute to harmful relationships may be rating *self* as the primary category, the numero uno, and valuing separation and individuation over relationship and relational growth.

The significance of this relational approach is best seen in contrast with more traditional psychological approaches, which use autonomy, adaptation, achievement, or, in Maslow's case, self-actualizing peak experiences as the standard of individual health and development. Miller instead began talking about "growth-fostering relationships" as the standard for development in her 1976 groundbreaking book, *Toward a New Psychology of Women*. Twenty-one years later, Miller and her colleague Irene Stiver wrote, "The goal of development is not forming a separated self or finding gratification, but something else altogether—the ability to participate actively in relationships that foster the well-being of everyone involved."[24] Both Miller and Gilligan, along with their colleagues, point to a different standard of development based on their research on and with women. Put most simply, the male researchers—based on their work with men—talked about *autonomy*, *individuality*, and *self*, and these female researchers and clinicians—based on their research on women *and* men—are talking about *relationship* as the primary concept of human understanding and development.

Principles of the Relational Model

Janet Surrey and Stephen Bergman have worked with more than twenty thousand women and men, boys and girls. Based on the relational model or connection model that emerged from their work with Jean Baker Miller, Judith Jordan, and Irene Stiver, they have initiated and studied dialogues between men and women for three decades. They are both on the faculty of Harvard Medical School and the Jean Baker Miller Training Institute (formerly the Stone Center) at Wellesley College. Surrey is a psychologist; Bergman is a psychiatrist and novelist. Together they wrote *We Have to Talk: Healing Dialogues between Women and Men*, as well as a play about the beginning of Alcoholics Anonymous, *Bill W. and Dr. Bob*.[25] "In Western culture," Bergman and Surrey write, "women have 'carried' responsibility for relationships and for fostering the development of others."[26] Boys and men have been encouraged, at a much earlier age than girls, to act as if they were independent not simply of their mothers or parents, but of relationships in general. The female developmental path includes the distortion by dominant mainstream culture of girls' relational voice at adolescence from a voice demanding mutuality and equality to a voice that is subservient, "selfless," "nice and kind" *or* to a voice that is a "selfish" and "mean."[27] Similarly, the dominant culture ignores and suppresses boys' relational voice, at an even earlier age.[28]

Seeing the center of human development in relationships rather than in the development of the self also allows us a more open discussion of the role that power plays in human development. Differences between men and women regarding experiences of connection and disconnection have a great deal to do with who has more power in the culture and how it is exercised. Men historically and today are in a dominant or nontarget position and women are in the subordinated or target position. Discussions of gender differences that do not include the impact of power will do little to bring about serious change in the ways men and women work together.

Relational Practice on the Institutional and Cultural Levels

I have described the benefits of a relational view of human development and how it differs from the traditional focus on the self. I turn next to a discussion of how relational theory applies at the institutional and cultural levels so that in the next chapter we can see how men and women can find ways to work together to create less oppressive organizations and a more equitable and just society.

Joyce Fletcher, a relational theorist and researcher, in her book *Disappearing Acts: Gender, Power, and Relational Practice at Work* describes how emotional intelligence and relational behavior get "disappeared" in the workplace. She identifies essential strategies for successfully and effectively implementing, naming, and acquiring recognition for this way of thinking and interacting within organizations.[29]

Fletcher's book is based on her study of a group of female software design engineers whom she followed as they used relationships both to further a particular project and to enhance their organization as a whole *and* as they were pressured by male leaders of the organization to pretend that their relational work had no value.

Fletcher defines relational practice as "a way of working that reflects a relational logic of effectiveness and requires a number of relational skills such as empathy, mutuality, reciprocity, and a sensitivity to emotional contexts."[30] This way of working is intentional. The workers who use it choose to use it because they believe it is a more effective way of accomplishing goals than leadership methods that stress competition and purely "rational" processes. Fletcher stresses the importance of "highlighting the relational skills, strategic intention, and underlying beliefs of the perspective" in order for the description of this alternative way of working to "retain its full power as a 'subversive story'" that challenges dominant organizational assumptions and accepted corporate norms.[31] The purpose of such a subversive story is not to substitute a new set of values (for instance, regarding how power or knowledge is distributed and exercised) for the old set, but rather to expose hidden assumptions of the prevailing corporate culture and their limitations. This process enables new things to be said and new thinking to emerge. It assumes a *power-with* methodology rather than a *power-over* methodology. This subversive storytelling is a necessary step in aiding men and women to work together for change when male, power-over assumptions about work have governed what is valued as effective work and have disappeared the relational contributions of women.

Fletcher writes about four categories of relational practice: preserving, mutual empowering, self-achieving, and creating team. *Preserving*, which is characterized by a focus on *task*, has to do with "doing what ever it takes" to ensure the life and well-being of the project—even at the cost of one's personal agenda.[32] It includes the willingness to extend what one does beyond one's job description, not as a way of being "nice" but to be effective and get the job done. Preserving includes a willingness to share power and to minimize differences of status. It includes "keeping the project connected to the people and resources" it needs by resolving interpersonal conflict, by appreciating people beyond the immediate team, and by absorbing stress and "acting as a buffer between people."[33] Preserving stresses the open flow of critical information (as distinct from keeping information secret to gain tactical advantage) to prevent unintended consequences. In a church setting, a youth leader exercises preserving behavior when she informs the religious education director that she is planning an outing that might have a bearing on Sunday school attendance for the junior high.

Fletcher unapologetically compares preserving behavior to mothering when she writes, "What differentiates preserving behavior from other categories of relational practice is the focus on task and the relational representation of this focus as one of protection, nurturing and connecting."[34] Finally, preserving means being emotionally literate and affectively competent "in order to recognize and take action when, for example, someone 'might be feeing like they're getting taken advantage of.'"[35] An example of preserving behavior in a congregational setting might be a rector who decides to take the time to make sure everyone's voice is heard, especially the small minority of people who disagree with a majority who want to move ahead quickly now that the direction is clear. Preserving means attending to emotional responses, not simply trying to convince people of the correctness of the reasoning process that is leading to a change.

Mutual empowering, which is characterized by a focus on *other*, is behavior that values and makes possible the contributions and achievements of others. It sees these contributions not as a threat to one's self-advancement but rather as necessary to the overall success of the project. The development and enhancement of others' power and abilities is a goal of leaders and all team members. Mutual empowerment includes *empathic teaching*, where the expressed or perceived needs of the learner are seen as more important than the teacher's need to express dominance by exhibiting superior knowledge. In addition, the outcome of a project is expanded to include increasing the knowledge and competence of team members by encouraging them to learn new skills from one another or from other individuals or teams. Again, sharing information is stressed, as is training in relational skills, so that the strategic benefit of paying attention to repercussions and emotions, for example, is widely distributed in the organization. Mutual empowerment means seeing requests for help *as helpful* to the success of the project and the development of the team rather than as deficiencies of the individual whom the project manager then labels as inferior. It means creating a culture where anyone in any position can ask for help without feeling guilty, inferior, or inadequate. Male clergy may find it hard to ask for help if they expect of themselves or are expected by their congregation to have all the answers. Female clergy may think that asking for help indicates to others that they are not as good as male clergy, that they do not measure up to the standard of omniscience or autonomous leadership that men have been expected to display.

Mutual empowerment values interdependence over independence. It "reflects a concept of power and expertise that is fluid, where dependency on others is assumed to be a natural, but temporary, state."[36] This notion of *fluid expertise* means that "power and expertise shift from one party to the other, not only over time but in the course of one interaction," and it requires the skills of empowering others *and being able to be empowered*—the ability to learn from and be influenced by those above you, beside you, and below you in status or seniority.[37] Mutual empowerment takes places in a congregation when the senior pastor publicly solicits the expertise of the associate pastor regarding worship or seeks expert advice from a lay member of the board regarding strategic planning or dealing with conflict. These examples of fluid expertise are even clearer and more significant in creating an alternative to the dominant power paradigm when the one asking for help is in the nontarget position in regard to race, class, gender, age, and so forth.

Self-achieving, which is characterized by a focus on *self*, uses "relational skills to enhance one's professional growth and effectiveness."[38] The emphasis is on maintaining connections with coworkers because of the belief that relationships are crucial to one's own growth and achievement. In the relational model, people never pull themselves up by their own bootstraps. A person who is self-achieving pays close attention to interpersonal distress in the organization and feels a sense of urgency to repair disconnection, to "make things right" relationally. Here the focus is not on correcting misinformation about concepts or data, but rather on maintaining the potential effectiveness of long-term relationships. For example, a supervisor or coworker may choose not to directly confront someone with whom she disagrees in order to maintain or develop a relationship that is necessary to the outcome of a project. At the same time, Fletcher talks about the need to be authentic and to trust in the other person's commitment to maintaining the relationship. In discussing the central relational paradox, the concept of moving "*out* of relationship for the *sake* of relationship," she states:

> Not speaking your mind, while it might appear to preserve the relationship, is an act of distancing and inauthenticity that undermines mutuality because it assumes unequal investment in the connection. For example, if one party sacrifices voice to preserve connection, it assumes that the other is not up to the task of furthering the relationship through listening, understanding, and responding.[39]

The relational skills in the category of self-achieving include recognizing, taking responsibility for, and working to overcome breaks in relationships, especially by using feelings as data about what has happened or might happen. They also include *relational asking*, requesting help in such a way that the needs of the one being asked and that person's likely response are taken into account. One form of relational asking is "making visible one's 'not knowing'" as a way of inviting others to contribute.[40] For example, one might say, "This is as far as I have been able to go in looking at this problem. What can you contribute?" Self-achieving relational behavior also includes the "skill of staying with contradictory behavior—feeling good about getting recognized, feeling bad about how it was done—until an action that might resolve the contradiction evolves."[41] In a congregational setting, a pastor is exercising self-achieving relational behavior when she does not back down from disagreeing with a member of the congregation whose financial support and community influence are very large. Instead, the pastor trusts her relationship with this person and is confident that speaking her "truth in love" will be met by a similar desire to stay in relationship and work toward the good of the community.

Creating team, which is characterized by a focus on *group life*, involves creating underlying conditions in which the "we" (to borrow Bergman and Surrey's term) can flourish and people can experience their connections emotionally. This relational practice emphasizes understanding and affirming the uniqueness of individuals—their differences—by stressing listening, respecting, and responding to people. For Fletcher this means creating the *experience* of team rather than striving to fabricate a team *identity*. Traditionally, team leaders built teams by "setting boundaries, determining lines of authority, setting goals, or defining tasks."[42] By contrast, Fletcher places emphasis on baseline conditions that are necessary for building relationships. The first condition, created *within* individuals, is attending to individual differences by acknowledging "others' unique preferences, problems, feelings, and circumstances."[43] Once again, Fletcher notes that the behavior of attending to the feelings of individuals should not be considered as merely being "nice"—an added frill—but rather should be seen as intentional, strategic, and necessary for the desired outcome of an efficient and effective team that produces results. She makes this point because men often devalue and disappear the *deliberative* and *effective* work of women by describing it as *simply* nice or sensitive, with no acknowledgment that the behavior is competent and helpful. Focusing on the feelings and unique contributions of others on the team helps to bring about the zest that Miller names as the first quality of good relationships and contributes to the members' experience of being truly known and valued. I dare say this quality is part of what led the 2004 Boston Red Sox to win the World Series for the first time in eighty-six years. Management and every member of the team valued the uniqueness (long-haired, bearded, song-writing ballplayers) of each member of the team. They first *experienced* from one another what Fletcher calls *instrumental affirmation* and the validation of one another's uniqueness prior to and as a precondition of becoming and being a team. Only through the experience of valuing their differences were they able to articulate their team *identity*, expressed in the phrase of the then Red Sox center fielder Johnny Damon—"We're the idiots." Against the more traditional, disciplined baseball culture, their happy-go-lucky, zesty esprit de corps became a subversive story.

Fletcher's second baseline requirement for building team is creating conditions *among* people that enhance working together. Here people are taught skills to absorb stress or tension, such as helping individuals save face in conflict situations, for example, when they are battling over resources. It includes creating a climate where either/or thinking is replaced by both/and thinking and where the goal is to have as many winners as possible rather than one winner (for example, the employee of the month) and many losers. I remember Super Bowl XXXVI (2002) when, according to custom, the starting players of the St. Louis Rams were introduced by name, leaving all the backup players unnamed. The New England Patriots broke with the tradition and were introduced only by their team name. The impact was immediately recognized by the crowd and the announcers. Everyone on this team mattered. They were all part of the starting team. Even those who spent most of their time on the bench were responsible for bringing the team to that championship game—and, as it turned out, to their first Super Bowl victory as well as victory in two of the next three Super Bowls.

The most successful adult education program I experienced in a congregational setting exemplifies for me the value of creating team. At a point when I was looking for something to spark my enthusiasm amid the routine responsibilities of parish life, I invited half a dozen people to work with me in designing and implementing a nine-month education program looking at the congregation's history, revealing its demographic and theological diversity, and dreaming about its future, including drafting a new mission statement. Seventy adults, about 80 percent of the adults in the congregation, met once a month after the main service and engaged in very diverse activities—from listening to a "Viewers Digest" version of the history of the denomination in six monologues delivered in period costumes, then discussing the impact of change, to re-creating parish history on storyboards, to dividing into groups based on professional interests and discussing the role of their faith at work, to playing a game to reveal their theology of church.

Zest characterized those events on Sunday mornings, and attendance was significantly higher than the other Sundays of the month. The energy of the large group was directly proportional to the enthusiasm of the leaders, who met once a month to plan two months ahead and to "test drive" the community experience. Though I was nervous about letting go of my initial dream for this program, I remember inviting the planning group to take major responsibility for imagining, creating, and implementing the program. Our planning process involved practices that enabled us to become a team—mutually cocreating the exercises and events, trusting one another when we were scared, taking individual and corporate risks, playing through the planning, valuing our significant differences, and relying on the various types of expertise within the group. In retrospect, I could see that our *process* of becoming a planning team was as important as any of our desired outcomes, and what we learned *as a team* became the energy and leaven for the larger community events.

In summary, relational practice is an *intentional* set of behaviors or skills that can be taught and learned, *strategically motivated* by the belief that this way of acting is a more effective way of getting the job done, in large part because differences are recognized and valued. In traditional organizations, relational practice is seen as subversive. It challenges underlying assumptions about the distribution of power, about competition and cooperation, about how much attention ought to be paid to feelings, about autonomy and dependence, and about what constitutes success and how to achieve it.

How Relational Practice Is Disappeared on an Institutional Level

One of Fletcher's most significant contributions is her description of how organizations both depend upon relational practice and strive to make relational work invisible, thereby making the contributions of women, who primarily carry out relational work, disappear. She uses the term *disappear* transitively to draw attention to power dynamics and the way nontarget or dominant groups can so devalue target or subordinated groups that the target population and their contributions—in this case, women's relational work—disappear. Historically, the Madres de Plaza de Mayo applied the term *the disappeared* to their children and grandchildren who were kidnapped and murdered in Argentina during the 1970s. The action of the madres in calling the world's attention to these disappearances was a courageous act of refusing to disappear themselves when their public demonstrations put them in great danger. Fletcher's choice of *disappearance* to describe the devaluing of relational practice echoes Gilligan's description of how the voices of girls are simply not heard or are disappeared. In a similar way, in 1976, Miller first described how women's relational strengths are recast as weaknesses or unimportant idiosyncrasies.[44] So what does this disappearance look like, and how can relational practices be implemented or recovered and sustained?

Fletcher describes three factors that contribute to how relational work gets disappeared or constructed as something other than work: misattribution of motive, the limitations of language, and the social construction of gender.[45] Traditional organizations frequently see relational work as motivated by a desire to be liked rather than as an *intentional* strategy of listening, with the possibility of being affected by others in order to bring about effective, growth-enhancing relationships along with good product outcomes. Nonrelational leaders may label those who are attentive to feelings as emotionally dependent, soft, or touchy-feely. They see relational leaders, especially women, who write thank-you notes or speak in corporate meetings about "*our* team" as being nice, polite, or self-effacing—insufficiently concerned with their own advancement and therefore insufficiently concerned about the bottom line or the company's goals. Relational leaders are seen as wimps—a derogatory term. Listening, paying attention to feelings, building trust and team are not seen as real work. In the church, male and female clergy have the experience of receiving negative evaluations for "being too concerned about everyone's feelings and not being enough of a real leader," as though one could truly lead a community without attending to the feelings of the members.

The language used to describe "real work" and a given culture's assumptions about who gets to decide what qualifies as work also contribute to the disappearance of relational work. Fletcher gives the example in a corporate setting where an engineer shares with another team her own team's hard-won solutions to a difficult problem. Her male colleagues see her actions as helping out. She and her team are not credited with doing real work. No value is placed on the fact that they have saved the other team months of time and tens of thousands of dollars. She is simply being nice. The language of nurturing and helping is associated with the home, with the private sphere, with unpaid work, with femininity, and not related to competence and real outcomes or dollar values. These associations make it difficult to put a monetary value on paying attention to feelings or acting in ways that encourage mutuality. Thus in the corporate setting, little or no value tends to be placed on these actions, which should be seen as effective and contributing to the goals of the organization.

Looking at the use of language in church settings is tricky. I believe churches are a hybrid of the domestic sphere (family, the internal world) and the public sphere (business, the external world). A great deal of preaching and teaching in churches deals with equality, mutuality, helping, nurturing, building community, noticing and valuing differences, and even respecting feelings—which tend to correlate with the language and values of the domestic sphere.

Yet in church board meetings and performance evaluations, corporate, public-sphere language still has a dominant place. Clergy and lay employees are evaluated more on whether they are growing budgets and attendance than on how sensitive they are at listening to or incorporating different voices. Small (family- or pastoral-sized) churches complain that most denominational programming is designed for larger (program- or corporate-sized) churches.[46] They assert that regional and national denominational offices assume that bigger is better, as distinguished from closer or friendlier is better. While written resources and programs for small churches are growing, the bias towards large churches, especially in metropolitan areas, means that a language that values the bottom line, hard numbers, measurable outcomes, and "real work" becomes the dominant, defining language for what should be normative and valued for every size church.

The bias toward larger churches and corporate language and values means that it is difficult to exercise relational practices in churches of all sizes, because relational practices are seen as countercultural and inferior to corporate values. Cultural support is missing, and the people who practice these values are often disappeared. Because the corporate sphere is associated with men and male values and the domestic sphere is associated with women and female values, it is not surprising to still find that men are far more frequently the senior pastors at the larger churches and women are far more frequently the pastors (often part time) at smaller churches. This is the case despite the fact that most mainline denominations have ordained women for more than thirty years and women are being ordained in larger numbers than men in many denominations today. The biases toward "real work" and against relational practice correlate with gender in the church as they do in the corporate world, even though the church seems to straddle the domestic/corporate line.

The third aspect that contributes to the disappearing of relational work is the social construction of gender. Fletcher argues that the first two acts of disappearing—the misinterpretation of motive and the limits of language—apply to anyone who works relationally, but "when women enact relational practice, something else happens and a gender dynamic kicks in."[47]

The women engineers in Fletcher's study claimed that they were *expected* to act relationally—to be helpful, to listen to others, to pay attention to feelings, to resolve conflict, to value difference, to express gratitude and affirmation to others—and at the same time they were *devalued* for doing these things. Because women engaged in behaviors that were less valued in the organization, they were regarded psychologically as having greater dependency needs. They were also told that they were "taking things too personally"—in other words, they were deviating from the accepted rational, objective, emotion-blind norm.[48]

Because male leaders in her study associated relational practice with what women are, rather than with an intentional strategy many women chose, the expectation that men would reciprocate was also disappeared. Often when women attempt to act in mutually empowering ways and expect reciprocity, men redefine their actions as mothering, as selfless giving, which requires no reciprocity. Women are responded to not as peers but *as women* in a patriarchal system where men are dominant and women are subservient. Fletcher believes that when women are helping, listening to, and teaching others (especially men) and their activities are considered natural expressions of their gender, patriarchy is unwittingly reinforced—women's role in life is confirmed as giving support and men's role is "to draw on this support in order to act."[49] A double bind results for women who try to set limits and to differentiate the types of helping they are willing to give; they are seen as acting against nature. They are told not that they are unhelpful but that they are unfeminine. Men who set similar limits and qualify their willingness to help are told they have good boundaries and are able to exercise leadership.

As I have already indicated, churches straddle the line between the private and the public sector. In so far as they resemble family and home, which is more the case with smaller churches, they seem to encourage relational values and practices. Even in larger churches, helping, listening, teaching, paying attention to feelings, mutual empowering, and resolving conflict are often highly valued. At the same time, though there are exceptions, women are more likely to pastor small, financially struggling churches—churches that resemble families. Men are more likely to pastor larger, more financially stable churches—churches that are run more like businesses. Though the deployment demographics by gender are changing, male senior pastors more often serve with women as assistant or associate pastors, rather than the reverse. In multiple-staff situations, women are also more likely to be slotted into positions that include oversight of children's religious education, pastoral visitation and training, welcoming of newcomers, and support of volunteers. Others count on female staff members to foster the relational health of the professional staff as well as boards and committees. When this relational work is not stated in the job descriptions of female staff members, their relational work is effectively disappeared and devalued as work.

We also see the effects of the social construction of gender when we look at the role of church secretaries. In many church settings, the staff and the congregation depend on a female church secretary to provide important relational practices for the organization—remembering birthdays and anniversaries of employees, affirming volunteers, and anticipating conflict and working to resolve it before it comes to the pastor's attention. These practices are also frequently attributed to the secretary's wonderful personality rather than being seen as highly competent work that is necessary for the efficient operation of a complex organization and the accomplishment of its goals.

In concluding the discussion of relational theory, I want to return to the discussion of power introduced in chapter 2. Robb calls relational psychology the first democratic psychology. By this she means it is a psychology for political equals. Focusing on self implies other, and the juxtaposition of self and other easily devolves into self-over-other or self-less-than-other. Focusing on the relationship—the we or the "between"—means not seeing one person as inherently *over* or *better than* and another person as *under* or *less than*. On an interpersonal level, this means seeing and naming the imbalances of power in relationships as they play out in terms of gender, race, lay/clergy status, class, and so on and noticing whose values and work are celebrated, honored, and valued and whose values and work go unnoticed or are not valued. On an institutional level, we need to notice how larger, more corporate-style churches often receive more resources and how smaller, more familial churches are often less valued.

The prevalence of this dynamic, especially because it may be unconscious and therefore not discussed, invites us to revisit the behaviors of oppression and internalized oppression discussed in chapter 2. Because larger churches have more financial power and greater professional staff resources, leaders of larger churches and denominational leaders may see larger churches as better than smaller churches. As a result, such leaders may have a tendency to offer help that is not helpful to smaller churches (dysfunctional rescuing) and blame the smaller churches when the "help" is rejected as not useful. They may also neglect smaller churches (avoiding contact) and fail to notice the differences and the significance of the differences in churches of different sizes regarding their gifts, internal resources, and needs.

On the other hand, because of their lesser power and influence, smaller churches may act out of internalized oppression, even if they are no longer in a survival mode and even when denominational leaders are making personal and program resources available that are better suited to their needs. The most common internalized oppression behaviors for small churches are blaming the system (the denominational headquarters) and reactively avoiding contact with denominational leaders who are perceived as uninformed or unresponsive regarding their situation. Often people behave in these ways unconsciously. Calling attention to these behaviors and discussing how power, church size, and the distribution of resources are related is a way to ensure that smaller churches (which employ a more relational model of leadership than larger churches) are not disappeared.

In summary, relational theory is a clear and specific challenge to theories and behaviors that favor some individuals and groups over others. It is also a way of recognizing, understanding, and celebrating the differences within our communities and among our communities. Relational theory allows us to honor not only individual differences but also differences *in relationships* and in communities. Celebrating the relationship differences truly transforms congregations. At the same time, relational theory articulates criteria and goals *for relationships.* Healthy relationships are zesty and empowering, increase our knowledge and the knowledge of others, enhance our self-worth, and are desirous of deeper relationship. Relational theory, unlike some theories of human behavior and development, assumes that human beings are made to be in good relationships. The good news is that people in power have sometimes decided they would rather have good relationships or love than power, or that the people they have dominated have tried to create a resistance that works to make things equal again. Relational theory can thus be seen as an ally to the story of Christianity and other faiths that believe human beings are created as equals and called to resist oppression.

Reflection Questions

1. What relational practices does your community (local church or regional church structure) depend upon? Who performs these practices? Are these practices regarded as intentional actions to increase the effectiveness of the organization?
2. Whose work in the organization is labeled "nice"? Who is called "sensitive"? Who is called "competent"?
3. How might relational competence be articulated as a criterion of selecting leaders?
4. What relational skills are most needed in your faith community?
5. In what ways is training provided for committee or board chairs to develop their relational skills?
6. Whose voice is most likely to be heard on the church board? on the staff? from the pews? Whose voice do you think is least likely to be heard?

7. When your voice is not being heard, to whom do you turn for support? When your work is not seen and valued, to whom do you go for affirmation? What would need to change for that work to be valued in the organization?

6

Transforming the Way Women and Men Work Together

The difference between women's and men's inclination to turn to the social group in times of stress ranks with "giving birth" as among the most reliable sex differences there are.

—*Shelley E. Taylor*[1]

It becomes clear that men themselves are fashioned by an event that is profoundly different from that fashioning women: the disconnection from the relationship with mother, in the name of becoming a man.

—*Stephen J. Bergman*[2]

What would our congregations look like if the relationships between men and women were characterized by equality, mutuality, creativity, and the desire for deeper connection? How would board and committee meetings be different if men were less competitive, if the desire for closer connection were as significant as power or authority? What if the central organizing principle of our mission and ministry were simply the *deepening of relationships*—with God and with each person we met?

From the first chapter of Genesis, we might conclude that God intended difference in gender:

> So God created humankind in his image,
> in the image of God he created them;
> male and female he created them.
>
> —Genesis 1:27

And even those of us who know very little French may understand and agree, "*Vive la difference!*" But what is the significance of that difference? And how will seeing, recognizing, celebrating, and utilizing the differences between men and women transform congregations? Before we talk about some significant differences, I want to make two important points.

Naming the Historical Power Imbalance

The first point harkens back to chapter 2 and has to do with power. In the category of gender, throughout modern history and in our own time, men as a group have had more power, privilege, and access to resources than women as a group have had. Men still often earn more for the same jobs. Men are generally promoted faster than women. They can buy cars more cheaply. Until recently, medical and psychological researchers have taken men as the norm and have seen women as deviant when they don't fit the predicted outcomes.

In the language of chapter 2, men are the nontargets and women are the targets of gender oppression. So if we were to look at the chart of behaviors of modern oppression and internalized oppression in chapter 2 (figure 2.3), men's behaviors fall in the left column and women's behaviors in the right column. For example, a man might *dysfunctionally rescue* a woman by offering her help that she doesn't need and in fact may resent. A man is *blaming the victim* when he is tries to justify illegal or inappropriate sexual advances by saying that the woman was asking for it because of how she was dressed. In both cases, the man is acting as though he is better than the woman, knows more about her than she does, and has a right to do as he chooses and to define her desires and needs. He is acting from a power-over position.

On the other hand, a woman who takes advantages of shortcuts or special treatment because she is a woman may be attempting to *beat the system*, a form of internalized oppression, if she is assuming that taking the normal course would be too difficult or beyond her ability. There may have been a time when women could only function or advance in a particular system by such indirect means—when beating the system was a survival behavior. If the system is open and equitable, however, such behavior becomes counterproductive. Even though she may make a momentary advance, she colludes in allowing herself to be thought of as less than the men around her because she behaves as though she lacks the ability to take a more direct route to her goals. In the long run, beating the system gives the message to others that she sees herself as less than and she may then be treated as less than. Or a woman may *blame the system*, saying, "The good jobs always go to the men," when she applies for a promotion for which she is clearly not qualified and when, in fact, she has not taken advantage of training opportunities that were available to her to prepare for that position. In both cases, her behavior can be called internalized oppression, because the woman has internalized a sense of being inferior.

Not all men act in dominant and oppressive ways based on a conscious or unconscious attitude of superiority. Nor do all women act from internalized oppression based on a conscious or unconscious attitude of inferiority. But historically, in society and in the church, there has been a power imbalance, an inequity that predisposes men and women to engage in a dance of oppression and internalized oppression. And in this dance, men *as a group* are the privileged ones, the nontargets, and women *as a group* are the targets of oppression. If we are to transform our congregations, we are going to have to admit to these historical power dynamics and learn new dance steps.

Gender: It's Not Binary

My second introductory comment has to do with the fact that sociological and psychological research indicates that gender is not binary. The attitudes, skills, and behaviors we have attributed to men as a group and to women as a group don't fit the experience of many individual men and women. Many men possess attitudes and skills that are often characterized as female, and many women possess attitudes and skills that are often characterized as male. This awareness of not fitting the gender stereotype that many of us feel about ourselves and observe about others often becomes more obvious as gay, lesbian, bisexual, and transgendered people come to feel more at home in our communities and in our churches. They often bring the gift of challenging common assumptions about gender roles, thus freeing everyone to look at how we limit our thinking about what are "normal" or appropriate behaviors or roles for girls and boys, men and women. Rarely are women's and men's actual behaviors this *or* that, masculine *or* feminine. Instead, they show a spectrum of behaviors, just as skin pigmentation shows a spectrum of colors. The dissonance between male and female stereotypes and the attitudes, skills, and behaviors of individual people lead some scholars to conclude that gender is socially constructed in much the same way that race is socially constructed.[3]

This is a huge, emerging topic, and it is scary for some people because it seems to go against tradition, common sense, or everything they have experienced *personally* about gendered behavior or appearance. While television, movies, and the Internet make it possible for people to view a variety of differences that challenge gender stereotypes, people who live relatively isolated lives by choice or circumstance may not have personally witnessed these unconventional differences. The point here is that when we speak about differences regarding gender, those differences do not neatly divide into two completely distinct categories. It would be more useful to think of gender as a continuum than as a binary category. One of the reasons for viewing gender as a continuum is that many people experience the binary categories of "men" and "women" as oppressive. Individuals feel that they do not fit into those neatly labeled boxes, or they resist the binary *power* differences that go along with gender differences by crossing the line or moving outside the boxes as a way of attacking the societal assumption that two sizes fit all. In a similar way, people of mixed racial and cultural heritage have insisted that new categories—biracial, triracial, multiracial—be created because someone who has grandparents who are white, black, Latino/a, and Native American cannot check one box *or* another—white or black or Latino/a or Native American.

What makes categories such as race and gender oppressive is not simply an individual's discomfort with being placed in a limiting or incorrect box. The oppression is about the individual's loss of power that the dominant culture awards in an either/or way. Men have it; women don't. Whites have it; blacks (and other people of color) don't. To believe that gender is binary and fixed or settled by fate easily leads to gender and sexual identity hierarchies (men are *better*; women are *worse*; and heterosexuals are *better*; gay, lesbian, bisexual, or transgendered are *worse*) that can be used to create power imbalances. For nontarget groups, the fear of losing power or of knowing one's "rightful" place in the system, in part, makes it hard to give up a binary understanding of gender, as well as other binary concepts.

Hierarchical or oppressive thinking will not disappear if we merely introduce more categories into our thinking about race or if we see gender as a continuum. Reasonably self-aware people might still admit to believing in hierarchies based on their own experience with multiple groups. For example, they might say lesbians aren't as scary or confusing as transgendered people or Asian Americans are easier to accommodate than African Americans. And so on. Ultimately at stake is the belief that there is *one best way* to be in any category (race, gender, sexual identity) and other ways of being are *better* to the degree that they approach that ideal. Regarding race, the ideal in the United States is projected as "white." To the degree that someone is or appears "white" or acknowledges the power and privilege attributed to being "white" and therefore "acts white," that one is better than others who are further from being or acting "white."[4] The end of oppressive racial, gender, and sexual oppression requires *both* replacing binary or categorical models with continuum thinking *and* replacing better-than thinking with understanding, valuing, and celebrating all differences.

Classifying gender into two categories (masculine and feminine) doesn't do justice to the reality of gender, which is experienced by many people more as a continuum. For this reason, it seems more helpful to speak about male and female tendencies, with the understanding that individual men and women (be they gay, lesbian, straight, bisexual, or transgendered) may exhibit a variety of attitudes, knowledge, feelings, and skills. Even when I use the common terms *men* and *women*, you as reader should be aware that these terms are to be seen as describing socially constructed continuums. So dropping the binary categories is not enough to bring about gender equality. We must acknowledge the historical and current power imbalances between men and women and work to correct that the power inequity on the institutional and cultural levels. Historically, men have had a vested interest in maintaining power; for example, men did not allow women to vote in the United States until the Nineteenth Amendment was ratified in 1920. Women were neither ordained nor seated with voice and vote in many national church legislative assemblies until relatively recently.[5] Recognizing these institutional- and cultural-level histories and the ways in which they still play out today is critical to the task of transforming how men and women work together.

How We Got This Way

Bergman and others believe the value that women and men place on relationship and autonomy, respectively, are the result of early socialization. Traditionally, girls are taught to value relationships and not to express the autonomy, assertiveness, and adventurousness that work for boys. Boys, on the other hand, are encouraged to become independent and autonomous. "Men," writes Bergman, "are fashioned by an event that is profoundly different from that fashioning women: the disconnection from the *relationship* with mother, in the name of becoming a man."[6] At a very early age, boys start to lose relational qualities—empathy, tenderness, curiosity in relationships, the ability to cry. Bergman writes: "Prompted by father and the male image in the culture, the boy is heavily pressured to disconnect, to achieve maleness. Not only is he expected to turn away from mother to do this, and not only is mother told she has to support this, but it is bigger than merely mother: It is a turning away from *the process of connection*. A boy is taught to become an agent of disconnection."[7]

In this process, boys learn to devalue relational skills. They are told that independence and autonomy are what is of value. Over time, because men are supposed to devalue relational skills, and refrain from practicing them, men's relational skills atrophy; being less skilled relationally, they begin to dread the call to deeper relationship as they experience it from women who love them and who have been encouraged to practice and develop relational skills. The "we" of relationship may become scary and stifling to men. Terrence Real, therapist, author, and founder of the Relational Life Institute, articulates three stages in early male development. The first stage is the traumatic loss of connection. Then the loss of expressiveness. Finally, the dissociative loss of knowing what they feel—all in the interests of becoming a man! Real calls this process "the toxic legacy of masculinity."[8]

Girls are socialized differently. Girls are not faced with the same social pressure to disconnect from their mothers and *from connection itself* between ages three and five as boys are. For girls the crisis of connection and disconnection occurs as adolescence approaches. Carol Gilligan, Mary Pipher, and Catherine Steiner-Adair have been the pioneers in describing the transition for girls to adulthood.[9] For the first decade of their lives, girls develop creativity, perceptiveness, sensitivity, and intellectual acumen *in the context of relationships*. Relationships, not separation or autonomy, are central to their growth and health. According to Judith Jordan of the Jean Baker Miller Training Institute, empathy—being aware, attuned, resonant, and responsive to the feelings of others—is a central feature of female development.[10] Empathy takes the form of learning to listen and is culturally supported for girls. It involves being present with others, seeing the other person, and knowing that one is seen. Empathy is two-directional, mutual. It develops in relationship. Note the contrast with boys, who are encouraged to be independent nearly to the extent of not listening to others.

During adolescence, a shift takes place for most girls. Due in large part to cultural pressure, girls begin to sacrifice their needs and desires *in order to be in connection* in a culturally acceptable way with others who have more power than they have and don't care what they need or desire. This shaping of a girl's self emotionally, intellectually, and bodily to conform to external cultural norms is referred to as the *central relational paradox*—"keeping your true feelings out of relationship to maintain some semblance or remnant of relationship."[11]

Gilligan speaks about this as a loss of *voice*. Gilligan is not speaking metaphorically. She is referring to how we sound to ourselves and to others.[12] Voice is relational. A voice is heard, listened to, by speaker and listener. Relationship and empathy are built into it. *Voice* is different from *self*. The concept of self does not require a listener and gives the illusion that it is possible to live without relationships. Drawing on an interview, Robb quotes Gilligan, "What you get when you take yourself out of relationship is 'the self.' And 'the self,' is the culturally sanctioned strategy for maintaining yourself outside of relationship."[13] On the other hand, how we speak depends on who is listening and on the mutuality or differential in power between speaker and listener. When the power is unequal, girls begin to lose their voice and go out of authentic relationship with their values, their ideals, and their history, but they keep trying to maintain the semblance of mutuality in relationships where the other or the culture is bullying them, and of course it doesn't work. Sacrificing one's true voice for the appearance of relationship where you have to act less-than results is a plummeting of self-worth and confidence in adolescent girls, a loss of Miller's five good things (zest, empowerment, knowledge, self-worth, and desire for more connection). The last loss is very important. If the dominant culture is pressuring a girl to be inauthentic in her feelings, thoughts, bodily presentation, if this is what is required to have a relationship, why bother?

In the end, saying that the culture organizes male and female developmental paths to lead in opposite directions is only somewhat oversimplified. Starting at about age three, boys are socialized to give up relationships to become powerful, autonomous individuals—differentiated selves. At adolescence, girls are socialized to give up power *and* carry all responsibility for relationships because of the external pressure of dominant groups—men, parents, teachers. Girls are socialized to be nice in a way that allows them to maintain some semblance of relationship when political equality is denied. But because all humans are wired for connection and long for mutuality, they find these attenuated relationships depressing and unsatisfying.

Relational Impasses: Different Ways that Men and Women Get Stuck

The power of Bergman and Surrey's work lies in their descriptions of three relational impasses that they have observed during thirty years of work with couples in workshops and private therapy: dread/yearning, product/process, and power over/power with. "An impasse occurs," they write, "when a relationship is stuck, static, unmoving and there is a sense that it may never move again."[14] Such impasses occur in all relationships, between people who live together and between people who work together, between people of different genders and people of the same gender. None of us is perfect, so minor disconnections occur frequently. In a healthy, mutual relationship, these disconnections are an opportunity to reconnect—to look at the relationship, discuss it, and form deeper, better connections. In a nonmutual, growth-hindering relationship, minor disconnections are not healed but multiply, build up, and lead to greater disconnections. Given a lack of mutuality or a power imbalance, when two people begin to disconnect, the movement of disconnection increases the power distance between them and makes it harder and harder for them to reconnect. They begin to fall into a life-draining spiral.

In domestic situations, minor disconnections can be triggered by one partner strewing clothes or towels on the floor, leaving lights turned on throughout the house, or not putting the newspaper sections back in order—or by one partner constantly tidying up the other's belongings or putting the newspaper in the recycling bin before the other has had a chance to read it. Or a major disconnection may arise out of differences in setting limits or disciplining children. In any of these situations, either or both parties may sense that these incidents will begin a series of reactions that regularly lead to spiraling argumentation, isolation, blame, shame, and the sense that I/we can't get out of this mess. Over time, the disconnections can form patterns. If these patterns are not interrupted and changed, they lead to significant impasses that constrict the relationship so that there is less and less room for honesty, tolerance, movement, growth, or genuine connection. The impasses may even begin to characterize or determine the relationship as a whole.

In congregational settings, disconnections between women and men can also lead to impasses in the way women and men work together. For example, a disconnection may occur when a female pastor asks a male assistant what he is feeling about his work at the church and about their relationship on the staff, when a woman suggests that a work group spend time getting to know one another before beginning their assigned task, or when a man is chosen as a committee head in spite of the longer service on the committee and greater expertise of a woman member. These examples correspond to the three types of relational impasses identified and described by Bergman and Surrey.

The Dread/Yearning Impasse

Susan and John are having their monthly lunch following a particularly tense staff planning meeting. Susan is forty years old and has been senior pastor of Emmanuel Church for five years. The congregation hired John ten months ago, shortly after he graduated from seminary. He is her age and went to seminary after working for a number of years in an international organic foods company. John has brought fresh ideas and new energy to the congregation, and their working relationship has been good from Susan's perspective, but recently she has begun to be aware of some tension between them.

SUSAN (curious, happy she hired John, interested in understanding what she perceives as a change in him, wants to work more closely together and feel better about how they work together): So, John, how are you feeling about your work at Emmanuel? It has been nearly a year now.

JOHN (puzzled at this question and feeling a little tense, doesn't know what she's getting at and decides to play it safe): Fine. I think things are generally pretty good. I like the people here a lot.

SUSAN (notices he is withdrawing, tries to reassure him, switches from asking about his feelings to inquiring about what he thinks, but continues to pursue her yearning for a deeper knowledge about the relationship and hopefully a deeper working relationship): I know the personnel committee is about to meet with you as we begin to review your first year. You've made some great contributions here. The new members committee really has some direction under your leadership, as does the social justice task force. Your skills from your former career and your passion for engendering healthy people and a healthy planet are really evident in your work there. But I'd like to know what you think about how we work together?

JOHN (pausing, recalling similar questions from her before, feels frightened about where this may be going and how it will end—if it ever will): I don't know. (Pausing again, feels a need to make something up to make it all go away.) Fine, I guess. What do you mean?

SUSAN (senses even more urgency to open up this discussion and turn it around): Surely, you know what I'm talking about.

JOHN (numb, paralyzed, and convinced that nothing good will come out of this, speaks slowly and deliberately): No, I don't.

SUSAN (nearly losing the positive larger picture, focuses more narrowly on the personal disconnection—fear of her own potential loss in this relationship—and responds with real

> exasperation): This is just like the meeting we just came from! When you are working alone or with one person from the congregation, everything seems fine. But when I'm looking for a response from you about something I've said or about some way we could work together, you retreat, you act as though you don't know what I am saying. You pull away. What is it with you?

If this dialogue sounds at all familiar, you have undoubtedly walked in the land of the yearning/dread impasse. In this impasse, the male participant generally feels in his gut and in his heart an overwhelming sense of dread—fear that he will lose his independence and autonomy, that things will get out of control. Invitation to connection from the female participant is experienced as a demand for his soul. Curiosity about what he thinks *and feels* is experienced as a criticism of his competence and style of interaction.

At the same time, the female participant becomes increasingly angry when her desire to achieve mutual connection (her yearning) is misunderstood and rebuffed.[15] She is aware of her history with him of being misread and having her need for information and connection denied. Bergman and Surrey recall a female participant from one of their workshops who said, "Men don't give women enough information to keep us from going crazy." To which a male participant responded, "That's because you're always asking for more."[16]

From their work with couples, Bergman and Surrey are convinced that men do have feelings, that they do listen—at least until dread immobilizes them—and that they desire connection, even if they have deep needs to protect their sense of worth, and that they have been taught not to value connections. Part of the problem in the yearning/dread impasse is a difference between men and women regarding the amount of time needed to process feelings. Most men need time to sort out their feelings. They even need time to realize and say they need time to sort out their feelings. If pushed to respond too quickly, the pressure leads to dread, and the melange of other unprocessed feelings together with this dread gels into an overwhelming desire to escape. At this point, further listening by men becomes nearly impossible. In addition, women are generally more willing to process their feelings relationally, while thinking out loud with others, rather than wait until they have done the processing independently before speaking.

In the yearning/dread impasse, most women start out feeling a desire for connection, a yearning to be closer. When the male partner begins to withhold his feelings or to withdraw, without saying why, her yearning is frustrated and initially increases. As he responds to her yearning with ignorance (I don't know what you want or need—which he indeed may not know, because he is socially conditioned not to know or not want to know) or dread, she is faced with a dilemma: to continue to pursue him and take care of her needs in the relationship or to withdraw as he is withdrawing. His disconnecting leads to the *central relational paradox* for the woman. She must let go of her yearning for deeper relationship for the sake of the attenuated relationship she experiences. She must stifle her yearning—a significant part of who she is and what she brings to the relationship—in order to maintain some semblance of relationship with him. Or she must disconnect as he is disconnecting. As Bergman and Surrey put it: "Disconnection leads to further disconnection. He leaves, and she is left alone."[17]

The Product/Process Impasse

Kay and Tom are officers on the church administrative board. They have both been members of the congregation for about twelve years and served in several different leadership capacities with great success. The congregation's pastor of fifteen years, Malcolm, has just announced to them at the bimonthly officers meeting that he will be leaving the congregation in two months, taking early retirement and doing some part-time teaching at a nearby graduate school. While they are surprised by the nearness of his departure, they are aware that he has dropped several hints that a change might be coming, since his children are now both married and established in their careers and his wife has retired from her job to spend more time with their grandchildren. They leave the pastor's office and walk to the parking lot.

KAY (feels a need to connect with Tom by processing her feelings about her connection with Malcolm, who is leaving): Let's go get a cup of coffee. I think we need to talk about what just happened.

TOM (overwhelmed by the amount of work he sees ahead, wants to get right to it and interprets Kay's coffee invitation as an opportunity to get down to work): I know he has been dropping hints about moving on, but I wasn't expecting anything so soon. I sure didn't sign on for finding a new pastor when I agreed to serve as a board officer five months ago. That's a much bigger commitment than I planned on. We'll have to meet with someone from the judicatory office, form a search committee, deal with who knows what kind of interim, and . . .

KAY (shocked by Tom's focus on the tasks needing to be done as a result of Malcolm's imminent departure, attempts again to connect with Malcolm by naming the first task as a relational one—needing to acknowledge the connection she and others have had with Malcolm. Hoping this may connect her to Tom at this difficult time and connect Tom to his own feelings, she cuts him off): I can't believe you're already thinking about all that stuff. Malcolm is the only pastor my kids have ever known. He married Rick and me and baptized our kids. I probably wouldn't even be in church if he hadn't taken such an interest in Rick and me when we went to the church asking about having our wedding there. I'm sure a lot of other people are going to be devastated too.

TOM (acknowledging that others will have feelings about Tom's departure—which means he and Kay will need to work faster—begins to sense his own feeling of anger that he overcommitted himself. Trying to change the topic away from Kay's, others', and his own feelings of loss, he cuts Kay off): Yeah, you are right there. People will be stunned, and given that summer's only about a month away, some folks will be gone soon. We'll need to do some sort of farewell celebration—and what will this mean for the handicapped access project we were supposed to kick off in the fall? I knew I shouldn't have agreed to chair that. Now we'll have to . . .

KAY (aware of differences in how she and Tom approach some situations, names his production mode, acknowledging who he is and trying desperately to connect to him even in his production mode, while also offering him a chance to process his own feelings. Allowing him to see her confusion and irritation at his difficulty processing his feelings, she interrupts again): Gee, you really are in production mode aren't you? Malcolm just buried your father three months ago. You said you couldn't have gotten through the past six months without his help, and now all you can think about is his replacement and how much work you'll have to do! Can't you forget that for a minute and say something about how you're feeling about all of this?

TOM (no longer feeling competent to get the job done—whatever that means now—begrudgingly admits that he feels overwhelmed): I'm feeling like it's more than I want to deal with right now—or any time, frankly.

KAY (not sure where it will lead, decides to gamble that having coffee together, as they have many times before, may offer the possibility of talking about feelings and what needs to be done): Yeah, it does feel pretty overwhelming. How about that coffee?

This second impasse also results from the way women and men are socially conditioned. Women are socialized to notice and foster relationships, in which they and others can work toward a goal, though, as I discussed in the previous chapter, women are often not given credit for their relational work. Men are socialized to get things done, to fix things, to get to the bottom line, to be competent at creating a product or getting results. Bergman and Surrey talk about how you can almost see the little boy or the little girl acting out when you look at male and female dialogues. The little boy needs above all else to be seen by himself and others as competent. He needs to produce things, mostly by and for himself. For men, this product orientation comes with a cost, as Bergman and Surrey point out: "Connection is sacrificed for competence, for being a doer, a producer. Connection is sensed as a hindrance to getting things done, things *you* want or have to do."[18] The little girl, who has always valued relationships to the point of changing rules to make sure others will stay in the game, believes the goal or product is less important than the connections—which always involve processing feelings. Meanwhile, women's (relational) competence is not seen or valued, while men expect their (nonrelational, autonomous, get-the-job-done) competence to be seen and defined as competence. *Dread* of intimacy, along with the imagined loss of autonomy, and *yearning* for connection, even at the expense of personal accomplishments, are the fuel that drives the product/process impasse.

Kay and Tom's dialogue points to one other significant component of the way in which women are socially conditioned. Generally, because women are encouraged to practice fostering the growth of others, and the growth of relationships, they have more confidence in their ability to sustain and develop relationships. This teaches them to value the *continuity of connection* over time for all relationships. To support long-term relationships, women, more than men, remember the details, the feelings, and the history of interactions. Not coincidental is that Kay is the one to refer to the ways in which Malcolm has touched not only her own life, marriage, and children but also Tom's life. Her part of the dialogue frequently refers to the continuity of Malcolm's connections with people. Bergman and Surrey point out that what "happened earlier in the day or yesterday or last week or month or year is important to and part of what is happening right now."[19] Furthermore, they believe women are more likely to notice this continuity and its significance for the present interaction. Often men fail to notice the continuity of connection or want to wipe the slate clean, saying, "Let's just move on. There's work to do. We can't live in the past." Such an attitude places the onus of responsibility on women to carry the connection by themselves, which can lead to anger, disconnection, and isolation.

The difference in social conditioning is evident in the dialogue between Kay and Tom. Their dialogue borders on being stereotypical and would be humorous if it were not so common. The fact that their differences do not escalate and lead them to write one another off is most likely due to a recognition and understanding, on each of their parts, of their differences. *Because of their connection* to one another, they have likely learned over time to place a positive value on their different ways of looking at *what* needs to be done and *how* to do it. The impasse comes when the two people don't notice their differences or when they begin to judge the other's way of being and relating as inferior or wrong.

The Power-Over/Power-With Impasse

Kevin is a recently ordained, twenty-six-year-old associate minister whom the congregation hired four months ago, in part, to work with the youth group. Lois is a thirty-year-old seminary student who was employed for five years as minister for youth and young adults in a large, suburban parish before she went to seminary. She was also part of the leadership team for four annual statewide youth retreats. Lois is doing her internship at Emmanuel Church under the supervision of the senior pastor. Lois was directly involved in planning the youth retreat with the young people and the youth group advisors, Jill and Frank Maynard. Kevin's primary responsibility on the retreat is worship, which he greatly enjoys. At the beginning of the retreat as the adult leaders are introducing themselves, Kevin announces that he expects each of the young people to meet with him privately sometime during the weekend for a spiritual check-in. This announcement takes the other leaders by surprise. Jill and Lois look at each other with raised eyebrows. Frank kind of shrugs. None of them says anything about Kevin's announcement. The group continues with the planned introductory community-building exercise and then breaks for dinner. Lois asks Jill if one of them should talk to Kevin now or wait until the team meeting at the end of the evening. Jill says that she and Frank need to start the cooking, and that she thinks it would be a good idea to speak with Kevin right away, given that he was in the process of posting a sign-up list and might start meeting with individuals before they gather at the team meeting. Lois catches Kevin at a moment when the young people are distracted by some clowning around.

LOIS (a bit apprehensive, because of her history of interactions with Kevin, wanting to really connect with Kevin and make this a mutual exploration, feels a bit alone without Frank and Lois): Kevin, I think we need to talk.

KEVIN (fairly nonchalant, responds with a hint of suspicion): Yeah. What about?

LOIS (wanting more privacy in order not to be distracted or interrupted, tries to buy a little more time to read Kevin's reaction): Let's step outside for a minute. The kids seem to be having fun. And Jill is starting to organize them into helping with dinner and setting things up.

KEVIN (excited about his idea for connecting with individual young people, feels a familiar sense of dread about conversing with Lois and wants to withdraw from her): Well, I'd like to join them. They may have questions about the check-in. I know some of them were starting to talk about it.

LOIS (relieved because of the segue): Yeah, I heard that, too. That's what I want to talk to you about.

KEVIN (beginning to get defensive, thinks, "I can see it coming. She's about to criticize me"): Oh, really? Why?

LOIS (sensing the issue is about safety, both for the youth and for Kevin, and about working as a team): Jill and Frank and I didn't know anything about it. We need to talk about it at the team meeting tonight. I don't think it's a good idea.

KEVIN (becoming more assertive, thinks, "She can't stand it when I have a good idea that didn't occur to her"): I thought you were the one all in favor of spiritual direction.

This is a great opportunity for me to meet get to know these kids a little better individually and for them to begin to think about how God is acting in their lives.

LOIS (feeling the connection slipping away, tries to affirm his overall good intentions and invites him to reflect on the wisdom of the one-to-one meetings—or at least to buy time until tonight's team meeting): Certainly, that's what this retreat is about, but I'm not so sure that it's a good idea to set up one-to-one meetings. It's pretty much common practice these days to have two adults present when dealing with young people. In my experience . . .

KEVIN (getting angry and thinking, "I'm a minister, after all, and she's not," cuts her off): I'm tired of hearing about your experience. What do you think I am? Some kind of pervert? I'm talking about twenty minutes with each kid. I want to listen to them and pray with them about what's important to them. Twenty minutes is hardly enough time. . . . Besides, they don't get many chances to talk to clergy. They're always so busy. This is a great opportunity for them to see that someone cares about their unique relationship to God and will walk with them on their journey. Maybe after you've finished seminary you'll understand that better.

LOIS (sensing the complete loss of connection and unable to process that loss with Kevin, is really ticked): It's not about seminary. And it's not about you, Kevin! We spent months planning this retreat and you decided, without consulting anyone, that you could introduce this "spiritual check-in" idea. (She makes quotation marks in the air.) We need to discuss this with Jill and Frank before you start meeting with anyone or urging them to sign up.

FRANK (opening the door and calling to them): Lois, Kevin, dinner's ready. Kevin, we need you to say the grace.

If we look at the context in which Lois and Kevin interact, we can see that the power-over/power-with impasse they encounter is influenced by the culture and institutions they inhabit. Lois has probably learned informally through a series of rewards and retributions that her success depends on paying attention to the thoughts and feelings of others, even at times to the neglect of her own preferences. In speaking with Kevin, she talks about the process of planning with Jill and Frank. She is concerned about the welfare of the youth and of Kevin, whose reputation could be damaged by even the appearance of impropriety regarding private meetings with individual young people. Like members of other target groups, she as a woman is more tuned in to the power dynamics exercised by members of dominant groups.

Kevin, as a man and a member of the clergy, appears less aware of the impact of his power in suggesting that each of the young people is to meet with him. His intention may be noble—the spiritual growth of the youth—but he ignores power. The young people may experience him as a presumptuous meddler or autocrat intruding into their lives. The impact of his (and only his) desire to meet with the youth alone may be that they see him as more hierarchical or patriarchal than the other members of the leadership team. While intending to get closer to the youth, he may in fact create a greater distance between himself and them by claiming the role of *the* spiritual leader. Clearly, his impact on Lois, and likely on Jill and Frank, is a disconnection or rupture in their relationship and their sense of sharing leadership. Kevin likely learned much of his behavior in the institutions he was part of growing up (school, church, possibly scouting, perhaps his family) and in a culture that encourages boys to be men by thinking for themselves, being decisive, and taking action—frequently independently of others around them.

The way power operates on an *interpersonal* level is strongly influenced by how power functions on *institutional* and *cultural* levels. Those with more power institutionally (within particular churches, businesses, schools, and so on) and culturally (in the press, advertising, the arts, and legislative and judicial systems) tend to want to reserve power for themselves and to protect their privileges. One of the ways they do this is by valuing differences in terms of *better than* or *less than*. And they use their power to convince others that these judgments conform to reality, to the way things are. They do not understand their judgments as opinions. In general, the power-over/power-with impasse unfolds along nontarget/target lines. When we look at gender, men most often assume a power-over stance toward women. Women are often more comfortable with power as something to be shared.[20] The power-over/power-with impasse is most intractable where gender is seen as binary. I have found that this impasse is less common in communities where a greater openness to the full spectrum of gender identities and roles exists, where gay, lesbian, bisexual, and transgendered individuals are valued for their differences rather than being treated as less than others. In such communities, straight men and women experience less stereotyping and greater opportunity to discuss power frankly, share it, and move flexibly in dealing with the power-over/power-with impasse when it occurs.

Nevertheless, many people who identify as male often unconsciously accept and rely on societal rules that favor them, that give them more power and unearned privilege, and see those who identify as female as less than themselves. Though corporate and church employment practices are changing, men (and women) can generally expect to have male supervisors, and men can expect to be paid more than women for the same job and have greater access to promotions. Women cannot as easily expect to be supervised by someone of their own gender, and women experience more resistance from men (and sometimes women) they supervise than male supervisors in similar positions.

Though some women clearly identify with and function according to the male model in power-over structures, those who identify as female are more likely to attempt to share power, ensure that everyone's voice is heard, be comfortable with ambiguous situations, and avoid unilateral stands that lead to win/lose conflicts. They are more likely to initiate and sustain processes that involve dialogue rather than debate.

Deborah Tannen, author of *You Just Don't Understand: Women and Men in Conversation*, also talks about gender differences regarding the use of language and its relationship to power. She makes a distinction between (masculine) *report-talk* and (feminine) *rapport-talk*. "For most men," she writes, "talk is primarily a means to preserve independence and negotiate and maintain status in a hierarchical social order. This is done by exhibiting knowledge and skill, and by holding center stage through verbal performance such as storytelling, joking, or imparting information." On the other hand, Tannen writes, "For most women, the language of conversation is primarily a language of rapport: a way of establishing connection and negotiating relationships."[21]

Institutional power-with models are rare. Twelve-step programs, such as Alcoholics Anonymous, are among the few examples of less hierarchically structured organizations. While some members exert more influence, the goal is to empower even newcomers to speak out and bring about change through peer relationships. Quaker meetings, some cooperative counseling centers, and the peer counseling movement also express the goal of functioning on a power-with model.[22]

Most institutional structures, by contrast, operate from a power-over, hierarchical model that affects both men and women and shapes the context for interactions on an interpersonal level. For women, the cost of these institutional structures is that they are treated as less than and their contributions are trivialized. For men, there is also a cost in terms of health (high blood pressure and alcoholism) and relationships. Energy spent acquiring and protecting power and privilege leaves less energy for engaging in mutual, empathic relationships. Miller's five good things (zest, empowerment to act, knowledge of self and others, self-worth, and the desire for more connection) cannot be obtained in a power-over model.

Learning New Dance Steps

What is the way forward through the three impasses (dread/yearning, product/process, and power-over/power-with)? Clearly, enhanced communication is required. For communication to be successful, the participants in the dance must have a common choreography, a common language and theory about relational development. They need to hear all parts of the music and be aware of all the steps and styles available to them and their partner. Their discussion needs to take into account how power is distributed in the relationship. They benefit when they can look at all four levels of interaction:

- What each is thinking and feeling and how judgments of superiority and inferiority may be attributed to differences (personal level);
- How their behaviors are affecting others, keeping in mind both oppressive and internalized oppression behaviors discussed in chapter 2 (interpersonal level);
- What corporate (written and unwritten) rules, practices, and customs are in place that reinforce the benefits, privileges, access to resources, and odds of success for some people at the cost of others (institutional level); and
- Who gets to decide the rules and define what is regarded as good, true, beautiful, competent, and, we might add, godly and spiritual (cultural level).

Reflection Questions

As with many of the other reflection questions, these can be answered individually as you read this book or as part of a group that answers and then discusses them. They are based on a series of questions Bergman and Surrey used in their dialogues with women and men to unmask the differences between male and female participants and the values they placed on these differences.[23]

In your gender group:

1. Name three strengths that characterize the gender group you identify with. They do not have to be unique to your gender group.
2. What do you most want the other gender group to understand about your group?

3. What does your gender group fear most about the other gender group?

About the other gender group:

1. Name three strengths that characterize the other gender group. They do not have to be unique to that gender group.
2. What do you most want to understand about the other gender group? What questions do you have for the other gender group?
3. What do you think the other gender group fears most about your group?

When a group does this exercise, female and male participants should meet in separate rooms to answer the questions before coming together. A facilitator of the same gender should be in each room to observe the process and answer any questions and to offer observations when the groups reassemble. During the processing of the questions, participants should note who speaks first, length of responses, feelings that are expressed, and humor. Paying attention to these dynamics gives further information about how the impasses are being enacted in real time among members of the group.

Valuing Relational Practices: Women and Men Working Together

Joyce Fletcher advocates a profound change in the way organizations are run. She envisions workplaces where relational practices are widely distributed on all levels of the organization and among women and men. Organizational theorists like Peter Senge,[24] Chris Argyris, Donald Schon,[25] David Bradford, and Allan Cohen[26] have pointed to the difficulty of changing obsolete organizational paradigms or conceptual models. While Fletcher agrees that the leadership assumptions and models are outdated, she articulates a further problem: the gendered nature of the assumptions.[27] Fletcher points to the ways that male managers disappear relational work within organizations, which is usually done by women. Uncovering this disappearing dynamic enables us to see the "powerful, gender-linked forces that silence and suppress relational challenges to organizational norms."[28] Not only are these relational practices stifled, they "are coded as private-sphere (feminine) activities that stand outside the public-sphere (masculine) definition of work and competence."[29] Traditional, dominant organizational assumptions, practices, and structures have determined what is valued within the organization; and those assumptions, practices, and structures prevent change. The changes required are neither simple nor gender-neutral. The necessary changes go to the heart of what constitutes *real work* (developing *relationships* that lead to increased production, not magically increasing production), who does that work, and how it is valued.

Fletcher offers four strategies for introducing relational values and practices into organizations: naming, norming, negotiating, and networking. *Naming* calls attention to relational practice *as work*—as intentional action designed to increase the effectiveness of the organization. Naming includes using the language of competence to redefine and value connecting with others (interfacing) and thanking people (rewarding positive outcomes or continuous teaching), because the language of competence is valued within the organizational systems. Naming calls attention to the intended outcomes of relational practices. When a female leader talks about what "we" have done, the effectiveness of her team-building activities can be trivialized as "nice" because male leaders generally understand leadership as exercised by *one* individual. Fletcher suggests that the female leader continue to use *we* and specify that she is making an intentional reference to the fact that she made sure all the talent of the group was used and together they added value to the project. This naming vividly contrasts relational practice with the current norms and assumptions of the organization and offers an alternative measure of competence—leadership that inspires team achievement, thus maximizing all the human resources. When a female leader refuses to cover over the joint efforts of her coworkers and goes against the norm of claiming their work as her own (by asserting "*I* did this" or "*My* team did this"), and she instead says "*We* did this" and articulates the reason for using the plural, she names the stereotypical assumption that a leader stands alone and claims *sole* credit for all that was done in *his* department.

Naming also includes noticing and calling attention to the hidden work of others. Substituting the word *effective* for *sensitive* and *nice* defines the relational practice of others as intentional and goal oriented. Naming is strategic: using the same language as those in power to claim value for what would otherwise be dismissed. This is not a case of women catering to men's language in order to be subservient. The work the female leader is pointing to *is* effective, not just nice. In fact, in many cases, using the skills and talents of all the team members and naming the fact that that work belongs to all the members results in a more effective outcome. The problem is that male leaders often do not want to look at the more effective outcome of the female leader; they dismiss her description of the joint work ("we") as merely "nice" or "sensitive."

Churches engage in naming in weekly or monthly newsletters by listing the names of volunteers and the number of hours they contributed. Relational practices that are expected of staff can also be written into their job descriptions and become part of their performance evaluations. If the church community depends on these skills, they should be recognized.

Norming exposes the organizational standards concerning effectiveness as well as the potential costs, unintended negative consequences, and the gendered construction of standards and roles. Leadership, decision making, and organizational learning are defined by those with the most power in the system and put into practice in a way that generally favors those who hold power. Fletcher suggests team building, mutual empowerment, and fluid expertise as alternative strategies for leading and learning where power is more widely distributed and mutually shared.[30] Many organizations assume that knowledge and expertise are concentrated in a few people at the top of the organization chart, in positions of power. When the culture of an organization allows people to admit their lack of knowledge and their need for help, greater opportunity for technology transfer, mutual empowerment, and organizational change opens up. Many organizations also show a strong bias toward "rational" thinking, excluding feelings as an empirical source of data about what is happening and needs to happen in an organization. Norming can be a way of integrating emotional literacy and affective competence into the organization's way of operating.

While churches frequently profess to uphold the dignity of every human being or to exercise a preferential option for the poor and marginalized, power is generally concentrated in a few leaders, usually those who are theologically educated at a graduate level and ordained or materially wealthy. This discrepancy between the espoused mutual theory and the hierarchical practice is generally attributed to denominational polity or scriptural precedent. Norming in churches can begin by asking questions. Who gets to make decisions? Who has authority to preach and to lead the community in prayer? Which texts and hymns are held sacred? What language is used to conduct worship? Or what styles of music reflect the cultures of the people? Norming invites the congregation to examine the role of cognition, emotion, and prayer in decision making, as well as the community's understanding of the influence of Scripture and tradition. Because leadership boards, including church governance boards, frequently defer to power as the currency of discussion, norming can include asking, how would our decisions be different if ensuring and deepening connections among members, even those with whom we most disagree, were our primary value?

Negotiating refers to the possibility of saying yes or no to requests for work that the organization may undervalue. When an employee or volunteer agrees to chair a capital funds drive, the results can be easily measured and the person or persons who lead the effort are generally held up as successful when the goals are met or exceeded. Work that happens behind the scenes (such as recruiting and supporting volunteers, anticipating and working to avoid potential conflicts, resolving disputes, and ensuring high quality internal communication) often goes unnoticed and unrewarded. Fletcher suggests that staff members, and I would add volunteers, negotiate the conditions for their acceptance of a job or volunteer assignment so that the work they do is recognized as important to the organization's success. This negotiation would include naming the relational skills involved in the job in the language of competence and perhaps even assigning a monetary value to the work.

Such negotiating is particularly important for women who wish to stay visible in a career track if the position they are being asked to fill is less visible within the organization and not seen as a clear step toward another promotion. Refusing such a position could lead to career suicide because one says no to management. Taking the assignment could render the women invisible on a sidetrack. Negotiating allows a woman's contributions to the organization to be visible. In some church systems, female clergy have found that saying yes to a job in a small, struggling church may lead to being viewed by denominational leaders and larger churches as lacking in skills for work in larger churches or becoming invisible by reason of their isolation. Clearly articulating to the clergy deployment office or the bishop the high level of skills required for work in such a struggling church may be a way for a female clergyperson to stay visible in the system and have her work regarded as beneficial to the denomination. She might be more likely to be viewed as developing skills that will transfer to future jobs in very different settings, rather than being viewed as one who sacrifices herself for work on the margins.

Networking is crucial in a system that does not value relational practice or is changing its norms to a more relational model. In such situations, Fletcher writes, "Relational practitioners who have been made to feel inadequate, naive or ashamed for their efforts to work in a context of mutuality, often find it difficult to 'know what they know.'"[31] The organization will likely tell them they are committing an error or ignore them when they are acting against the norms. Forming connections with allies who can support them is crucial if they are to maintain the energy to remain in the struggle. Networking in itself is a subversive activity in a system that values autonomy and independence. Relational networks assist women within organizations and across departments in the process of finding competency language to describe and "appear" relational work. During the early part of any change process, women may need to find allies among men who value and employ relational work because the system may accord men greater freedom to experiment with new behaviors.

Women in many denominations have formed networks as a strategy for seeking ordination or seeking senior leadership positions. Some of these networks have also included male allies. It may be important for laywomen to form similar networks to examine the extent to which relational practice is valued in their congregation and in regional and national church structures and how relational practices are distributed by gender. If the extent and significance of relational work is not made visible, and women are most likely the ones doing the work, then relational work will most likely continue to be undervalued and those who do it will remain disappeared.

Naming, norming, negotiating, and networking are strategies for bringing about change in the wider culture and in organizations that, by valuing only some forms of work, are unjust and oppressive. In our culture, most institutions, including churches, expect that relational work will be done by women. Institutions frequently do not reward relational work as valuable and often disappear it. Naming, norming, negotiating, and networking make relational work visible and ensure that the most powerful people see it as essential for meeting the goals of organizations by attending to feelings and relationships. These strategies increase the possibility that the contributions of all members of an organization, especially those who are least visible (women and racial and ethnic minorities), will be seen, valued, and rewarded. This work is not about women changing their behavior to satisfy men or to accommodate to their needs or desires. Relational work is about persuading men to see the skilled, proficient, relational work of women *as competent work* rather than dismissing it *as merely nice or sacrificial.* This work is about taking credit where credit is due.

In a power-over system, this means knowing what those in power value and describing what I am doing and why I am doing it in such a way that those in power see the value and reward my work appropriately. Subversively, relational work includes persuading those who believe they should have more power than some others to trade that power for equality, mutuality, authenticity, and respect.

In this and the previous chapter, I have articulated a relational way of understanding leadership, grounded in a theology that views God as fundamentally relational (the doctrine of the Trinity—the plural Elohim of creation) and relational in regard to human beings and the rest of creation (the doctrines of creation and incarnation).[32] I have discussed gender as a continuum and spoken of differences in understanding that can lead to impasses between those who identify more as male or female. I have argued for relationship rather than an autonomous self as the primary category for understanding human beings.

This approach, I believe, acknowledges the historical distribution of power based on gender and other differences and the disappearance of the *work* of women at the same time that organizations, including the church, have depended on women to do that work. Discussing current imbalances in power, who gets to define what is work, and the construction of roles based on gender is a difficult task—partly because those who have power rarely want those discussions to take place. They may fear that their power and privilege will be exposed and people will ask for a more equitable distribution of power, resources, roles, and responsibilities.

Yet we rejoice that we are created by a God who is love. We *all* long for mutuality and equality. Until we are able to have these discussions and bring about greater gender equality, we will be hampered in all our attempts to bring about a deepening of spiritual formation in our churches and meaningful social change in our communities, because half of the people we are (women) and half of the people we wish to serve are seen through dominant male lenses—misunderstood, undervalued, and disappeared. I deeply believe that discussing our differences and similarities, including the role of power in defining who we are and what we are allowed to do, will lead to wonderfully new, exciting, richly resourced faith communities that will attract people who have previously given the church a wide berth. Creating this new community will enable us to engage in effective ministries of justice, compassion, and reconciliation.

Reflection Questions

1. What responsibilities or roles in your church are more likely to be exercised by men? by women? Are these roles valued differently in the community?
2. Name examples of men and women being viewed differently for exercising the same behavior, such as chairing a committee or saying no when asked to provide help.
3. What organizational changes would make the most difference in how women and men work together in your faith community?

7

The Rhythms of Transformation

We need to be the change we wish to see in the world.
—Mohandas Gandhi[1]

God, give us grace to accept with serenity the things that cannot be changed,
courage to change the things which should be changed,
and the wisdom to distinguish the one from the other.
—Reinhold Niebuhr[2]

How do congregations change? Why is change so hard for congregations? What are the resources for transformation? What are the obstacles? If these were simple questions, there would be many more vital congregations. In this chapter I offer an analogy for congregational change that builds upon what most of us know about change from our personal lives.

Change is a fact of daily life, whether we enjoy it or not. Sometimes significant changes are thrust upon us. Sometimes we make conscious decisions that result in significant changes for ourselves and for those around us. Before talking about specific changes, we will consider an image of change that I believe speaks to both the dynamics of change and the feelings that accompany change. Take a look at the illustration below.

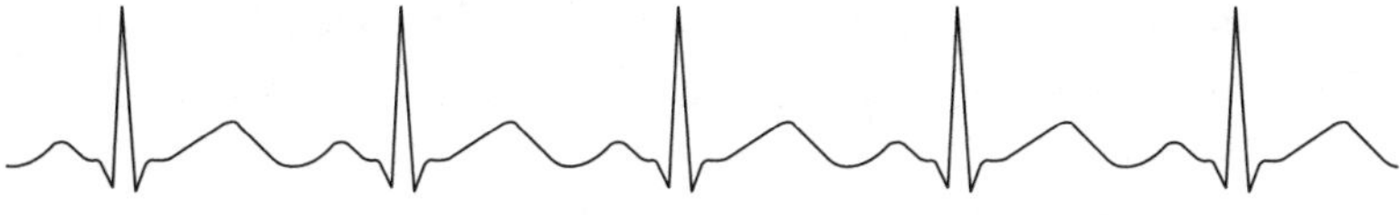

What is this a picture of?
What does it represent?

I suspect you answered that this is an EKG, an electrocardiogram, and that it represents a heart beating. It's a schematic drawing that represents the pattern of contractions and relaxations of the heart muscles. Tension and relaxation. Tension and relaxation. As this pattern recurs, blood is pumped to the lungs, where it picks up oxygen and drops off carbon dioxide. The blood is also pumped through the whole body to carry nutrients to where they are needed and to carry away toxins. Sometimes the heart pumps faster. Sometimes it pumps slower. But as long as we are alive, this rhythm of tension and relaxation takes place within us. In fact, it is the very thing that allows us to go on living. This picture, then, is a picture of *life*.

It is also a picture of *change*—cycles of tension or conflict and relaxation or resolution. On an individual physical level, we understand this picture and accept it as a natural rhythm. Our autonomic nervous system controls our respiration and heartbeat, and we don't think much about it. Perhaps we take this radical alternation between tension and relaxation for granted because it has been going on for our entire life. At any rate, on the most basic level, life requires continual change—tension and relaxation. And this rhythm of tension and relaxation, this change, enables and sustains life.

Now think of the electrocardiogram image as a picture of your life as an individual—with moments of tension or conflict and relaxation or peacefulness. Perhaps you have drawn a personal timeline for yourself at some time—on a retreat or as part of a journaling workshop. A personal timeline allows you to see patterns in your life. It allows you to name the major moments of transition. Understanding and appreciating personal level transformation is a terrific resource for becoming more knowledgeable about the dynamics of organizational or community transformation and more comfortable with the rhythms of change. Before we move on to talk about organizational change and transformation, I invite you to reflect on change in your life as an individual.

Looking at Change on a Personal Level

Take a pencil and paper, and draw your own personal timeline. If you use a standard 8½ x 11 inch unlined piece of paper, you might find it easiest to place the paper sideways in front of you. In computer jargon, this is "landscape" mode, a term I like because it signifies the changing landscape of our lives as opposed to a single snapshot or portrait. On the sheet of paper, draw a line. I usually begin left to right with an arrow on the right to indicate that my lifeline is continuing past this moment.

————————————————————→

Now add the year you were born on the left and the current year on the right. Next, mark some significant moments of change on the timeline wherever they occur. Put the year and a key word, initials, or abbreviations to note what the change is. You can be as detailed as you like. For the purposes of this exercise, it helps to think of some of the more significant changes. These might include the following:

- When a younger sibling was born and you were no longer the center of attention
- When you went away to school
- High school or college graduation
- Falling in love for the first time
- The death of a loved one
- Moving to a new community
- Confirmation; marriage; ordination
- Living abroad
- Events like September 11

Your timeline may look something like this with dates and initials or abbreviations added.

|- - - - -|- - - -|- -|- - - - -|- -|- - - -|- -|-|- - -|- - →

year born **current year**

Reflecting on Your Timeline

When your timeline is complete, if you keep a journal, you might choose to write in it about what you have noticed. Here are some questions to ask yourself while you reflect:

1. What did you notice about the events you placed on your timeline?
2. How many events were the result of choices you made (for example, getting married or ordained; choosing a college)?
3. How many events were initiated from outside or happened *to* you (for example, the death of a loved one; the end of a love relationship; being hospitalized)?
4. How are these events spaced in your life? Are some closer together than others? Are there periods when change is more or less a dominant feature?
5. Are some events the result of earlier decisions or events that happened to you?

When you look at your timeline, you may see a lot of significant changes or only a few. This may depend in part on your age. Life circumstances can also play a significant role. People who grew up in military families may experience many more moves and school changes than others. People with larger and older extended families may experience earlier and more numerous significant deaths. Whether we believe we have experienced many or few significant changes is also quite relative. Each of us has a different set of criteria for determining what a significant change is. If my threshold for change is high, I may only list a few big changes. If my threshold is low, I may list many big changes. An event such as buying my first new car or owning my first home may be significant to me, especially if my parents bought only used cars or always rented their home. For others, these events may be taken for granted and not show up on their list.

Most of us experience a mixture of events where we made choices that influenced or determined a major change along with events that happened to us. As you reflect on this mixture, you might get some insight about whether you see yourself primarily as an initiator of change or primarily as someone who is a victim of external changes. Remembering the discussion of privilege and oppression from chapter 2, it is important to note that our experience of having more or less power to bring about significant changes is not merely a matter of temperament. Our social location and life's circumstances have a lot to do with our ability to influence many changes. Social location also determines to some degree the resources we have to cope with changes that happen to us. When Hurricane Katrina struck the Gulf Coast in August 2005, people with cars and the financial means to relocate or with relatives at a distance who could take them in fared much better than people without cars, savings accounts, job skills, and relatives able to house them.

A clustering of changes can also have a significant effect on a person's resiliency. Less significant changes that occur close together can become overwhelming. The last in a series of changes may not be very significant compared to many of the previous ones, and yet it can be the proverbial straw that breaks your back.[3]

Before discussing a way to process your individual timeline in a group, let's return to the notion that change—tension and relaxation—is the rhythm of life. The picture of the EKG at the beginning of the chapter is a picture of life. If you doubt this, think of what the alternative is. What would your timeline look like without significant moments of change? If your timeline had no tension and all relaxation, it would look like this:

In medical terms, we know this as a "flat line." No tension. No change. No life.

Reflecting on Your Personal Timeline in a Group

Doing the timeline exercise as part of a group of people looking at change and how it affects us can be helpful. In a group, people should be encouraged to share only what they feel comfortable sharing. A particular event, such as a recent death, may feel too delicate to share in a group that is meeting primarily for educational purposes. I have found that when people are encouraged to set their own privacy boundaries, appropriate sharing can take place with each person sharing at the level where they are comfortable. Appreciating difference means appreciating that people have various levels of comfort with this exercise and with sharing personal stories in a group. The reason for looking at how change affects individuals differently is so that participants can learn how to be more intentional as they initiate or participate in transformations that affect many people.

Also paramount is employing the guidelines from chapter 1. If they have not recently been articulated for the group, I would post them or briefly summarize them—especially the guidelines about not shaming and blaming, self-focus, and confidentiality. Regarding confidentiality with this kind of exercise, I compare listening to another person's story to visiting a foreign country.[4] Sharing the timeline exercise is like visiting another person's sacred land or territory. I may be listening to a language that is not my own. To the extent that I am a tourist in another's country, I need to respect areas that are out of bounds. As in the case of many actual countries, there may be areas where photographs and recording devices are not allowed. I may also be prohibited from carrying away indigenous plants or cultural artifacts. In other words, what a person shares is his or hers to share and does not get talked about outside this gathering.

One of the reasons for sharing the individual timeline exercise is to notice that even on a personal level, people differ widely in what they name as significant changes and in how they feel about change in their lives. For example, some of us may be mostly excited about purchasing our first home. Others may feel a lot of fear: How am I going to make the payments? How will I be able to take care of the repairs and upkeep? Some people may experience the sadness that comes with settling down and not being as free to pick up stakes and move. I have found that most people are comfortable with these differences regarding how people understand change in their own lives. We take for granted that we feel differently about significant events in our life stories and that we have different strategies for coping with what we find difficult in the changes we encounter. If we are encouraged to notice this degree of difference on a more conscious level regarding individual changes, then we might be better able to notice, understand, and affirm the different responses people make to corporate changes that affect a large group.

A Timeline of the Church

What would the timeline of the Christian church look like?[5] If we imagined ourselves drawing our corporate timeline, what *significant* moments of change would we include for the church over the ages? I will describe how this process works for a large group, though I encourage you to draw the corporate timeline for yourself as you read. The process of creating the church's timeline takes place after individuals have done their own timelines, shared them with one other person, and processed the general questions on page 188 as a large group. Then the group can look at the rhythm of change in the church's life story, just as they looked at the rhythm of change in their own life stories.

In looking at the church's life timeline, I recommend using sheets of newsprint attached horizontally or a large sheet of butcher paper taped to a long wall. The beginning of the line on the left can be the birth of Jesus or Pentecost. On the far right are an arrow and the current year. Divide the paper in half with the year 1000 near the center. Invite people to name significant events in the history of the church. It is not important to name them in order. The leader places the date or approximate date on the timeline and a word or two to identify the event. It is important to remember that this exercise, like the individual timeline, is not about naming events that are most significant by some objective standard. People from different countries and different denominations will name different events as significant. Even within the same denomination, people will have varying ideas about what events are most significant. A helpful, though not exhaustive, list of significant historical events is provided in appendix D. Some of the most commonly named events are:

- Writing of the four Gospels (60–100)
- Destruction of Jerusalem and the Second Temple (70)
- Council of Jerusalem; Christianity becomes a Gentile religion (90)
- Edict of Milan; Christianity no longer illegal (313)
- Council of Nicea; Nicene Creed (325)
- Life of Muhammed (570–632)
- Charlemagne crowned Roman emperor by Pope Leo III (800)
- Breach between Rome (Catholic) and Constantinople (Orthodox), each side excommunicating the other (1054)
- Jerusalem captured in the Crusades (1099)
- The Inquisition (1232)
- Bible translated into English by John Wycliffe (1320–84)
- West Indies "discovered" by Christopher Columbus (1492)
- John Calvin in Geneva (1504–64)
- Martin Luther's ninety-five theses (1517)
- Ulrich Zwingli's reform in Zurich (1523)
- Act of Supremacy: the pope's authority in England abolished by Henry VIII (1534)
- Jesuits founded by Ignatius Loyola (1534)
- Council of Trent (1545–47; 1551–52; 1562–63)
- King James Version of the Bible (1611)
- *Mayflower* lands at Plymouth with the nucleus of a Pilgrim congregation (1620)
- Society of Friends organized by George Fox (1647)

- Declaration of Independence (1776)
- French Revolution (1789–94)
- *On the Origin of the Species* by Charles Darwin (1859)
- Seizure of Rome by Italian nationalists; fall of papal states; Declaration of Papal Infallibility (1870)
- Conference at Lausanne, which leads to World Council of Churches (1927)
- Second Vatican Council (1962–65)
- Assassination of Martin Luther King Jr. (1968) leading to involvement of churches in civil rights and later Vietnam War protests
- Desmond Tutu becomes archbishop of Cape Town, South Africa; later heads Truth and Reconciliation Commission (1986)
- Bishop Barbara C. Harris, first woman Episcopal bishop (1988)
- Bishop V. Gene Robinson, first openly gay Episcopal bishop (2003)

A simplified timeline of the church might look like the one in figure 7.1.

Figure 7.1. Twenty Centuries of Change

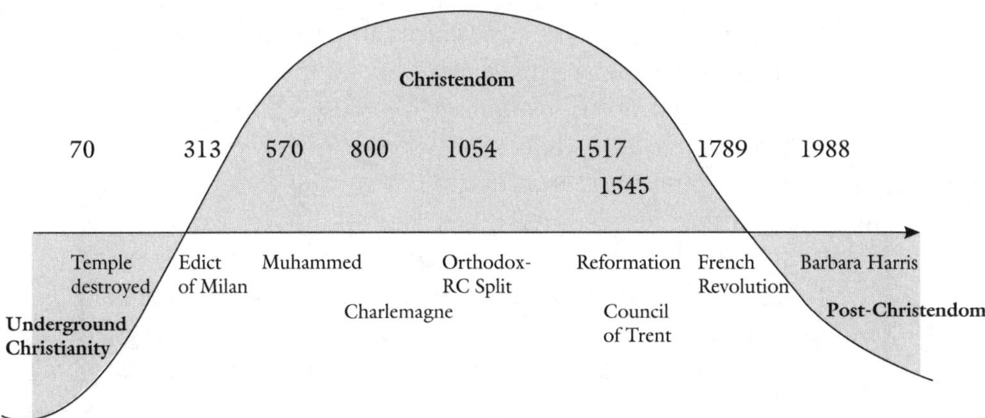

Used by permission

If several more of the events listed above were added to this timeline, we could begin to reflect on the church's timeline in much the same way as we reflected on our own personal timelines. In a group I would begin by asking an open-ended question: what do you notice about the church's timeline?

Generally speaking, people notice that the events are not evenly spaced out. No matter how many events are added, events tend to cluster, such as around the time of the Reformation. These clusters tend to be seen or experienced as times of great tension, conflict, and creativity. There also tend to be times of greater relaxation. For example, generally people name few events between the fifth and tenth centuries.

We might next reflect on how many of the events were the result of choices internal to the church. The Council of Jerusalem is an example where church leaders (Peter and Paul) argue about the direction of mission and evangelism and decide to accept Gentiles into Christianity without circumcision. The split between Eastern (Orthodox) Christianity and Western (Roman Catholic) Christianity is another decision by church leaders. In reflecting on this particular heartbeat, I often point out that this enormous decision with far reaching consequences was focused on one word, *filioque*. Though liturgical and political styles also played a role, many people today find it hard to believe that what are now two major branches of Christianity divided over an argument of whether the Holy Spirit proceeded from the Father or from both the Father and the Son (*filioque*).

As one thinks about the differences among Christians today, even Christians in the same denomination, we might gain perspective by noting that positions that led to major church schisms in the past may seem of little consequence to many people today. It's possible that what seems monumental to us today may seem much less important to future generations. Other examples of significant events on the church timeline that are the result of internal decisions are the adoption of new prayer books and hymnals and the ordination of women. Though it can certainly be argued that both language changes and the decision to ordain women or gay men and lesbians may be influenced by the changing culture, the decisions were still made by church councils and not imposed from outside.

Now look at events that were largely determined outside the church—by governments, political forces, or the society at large. A major change occurred in the beginning of the fourth century. During much of the first three centuries, Christians were persecuted by the civil government. It was against the law to practice Christianity. In 312 the emperor Constantine converted to Christianity. The next year the Edict of Milan was promulgated, making the practice of Christianity legal. This radical change for the Christians was a decision of the government, and Christianity went from being an underground and countercultural religion to a religion tolerated, and later endorsed, by the state. Beginning with the birth of the prophet Muhammed in 570, the rise of Islam (as a religion and as an influence on philosophy) is another example of a significant change that was initiated outside the church. The European "discovery" of new worlds in the late fifteenth century was primarily an economic and political venture that had significant religious consequences when Christian missionaries and theologians began to struggle anew with what salvation meant in lands where the Christian message had not been preached. The French Revolution with its strong anticlerical and antireligious sentiment and the fall of the papal states, which had been nearly one-third of Italy, each signaled a major change in the relationship between civil government and Christianity. These events on the timeline of the church that occurred beyond the control of members and leaders of the faith community are similar to the events on our personal timelines that were not the result of our initiation or choice, such as the loss of a job or relationship or the unexpected inheritance of significant wealth.

The Significance of Christendom in the Church's Timeline

If you look back at the church's timeline, you will notice I have divided it into three periods: Underground Christianity, Christendom, and Post-Christendom. I have already spoken of the early period when Christianity was a countercultural movement without governmental support. By Christendom, I am referring to the period when in much of the Western world there was a presumption that the norms and values of civil society were synonymous with Christian norms and values. I am distinguishing here between Christianity as a religion and Christendom as the blending together of Christian religious values with societal norms and expectations. As we can see in the life of the early church, Christianity as a religion can thrive and grow without societal, political, cultural, and governmental support. Some would even say that Christianity exists in its purest, most vital form when it is free to challenge the culture or stand in opposition to political and governmental powers. As a contrast to the first three hundred years of Christianity when Christian values were counter to cultural norms and values, Christendom assumes it is a good thing for the values of the Christian faith to be the dominant values of the culture and society. In its most blatant form (for example, the Crusades and the Inquisition), Christendom does not tolerate religious difference, thus violating the guidelines "It's okay to disagree" and "both/and."

Let's take a short look at Christendom. Perhaps the height of Christendom is marked by Pope Leo III crowning Charlemagne as Emperor of the Holy Roman Empire on Christmas Day in 800. Also during the era of Christendom, civil and religious leaders united behind the Crusades and the Inquisition. Henry VIII was called the defender of the faith by the pope (before he began divorcing and killing his many wives). New land was conquered by sword and cross simultaneously in the name of nation and church. The pope divided the globe between Portugal and Spain. The pervasiveness of the overlap of everyday Christian beliefs and norms with civil society is exemplified for me by cooking instructions from the fourteenth century that called for boiling an egg "during the length of time wherein you can say a Miserere."[6] The assumption was that everyone who would want to cook an egg knew this Christian prayer in Latin and could recite it from memory!

If these examples of the pervasiveness of Christian values seem strange today, it is because we live in a post-Christendom world. The rise of nation-states, of humanism, and the discovery of the so-called New World in the fifteenth century all begin to chip away at Christendom. Beginning with these events, the overlap of Christian values with culture became less obvious and harder to maintain. For example, the scientific discoveries of Galileo (1564–1642) were condemned by the church. Regarding the end of Christendom, one could argue for several dates: the French Revolution (1789–93); the defeat of Napoleon by Wellington (1815), which officially ended the Holy Roman Empire; or the fall of the papal states (1870). Clearly, the assumption that Christian values were universally accepted as the values of society ended at different times in different places, as did the political overlap of Christian religious power and civil power. Even in the twenty-first century, prominent politicians have referred to the United States as a Christian country, though most religious leaders would disagree, both because they doubt the truth of this assertion and because they value the diversity of religions practiced in the United States.

The point of recognizing the three phases of the church's timeline is that Christian faith has thrived during all three periods. Furthermore, the post-Christendom period is more like the first three hundred years of the church's existence than any time between the fourth and late eighteenth centuries. The similarity of the current (post-Christendom) period to the early church has important consequences when we begin to reflect both on the feelings of loss that some people experience with the lack of cultural support for their beliefs and when we begin to strategize about change. Post-Christendom might be seen as an opportunity for the church to live an adult life, a time for riding the bike of Christian faith without the training wheels of political favoritism and guaranteed cultural support. Post-Christendom Christians can honor people of other faith traditions even as they begin to more deeply understand their own unique contributions to developing a more just, peaceful, and sustainable world.

Three Generations for Every Heartbeat

Now let's look at one significant change in the life of the church—one particular heartbeat. It could be a single day or a period of a few years, depending on your perspective. We could choose any significant change or heartbeat, but I will choose the election of the Right Reverend Barbara C. Harris on September 24, 1988, as the first woman bishop in the Episcopal Church and thus in the worldwide Anglican Communion. I choose her election and subsequent consecration as bishop because it was the first bishop election in which I was able to vote as a clergy delegate and because I have a story that illustrates how one change affects three generations differently.

Barbara Clementine Harris was born in Philadelphia in 1930. She worked in the community relations department of Sun Oil Company. On July 29, 1974, she served as crucifer when the first eleven women priests were ordained in the Episcopal Church at the Church of the Advocate, Philadelphia. She herself was ordained as an Episcopal priest on October 18, 1980. After being elected by clergy and laity to become a suffragan (or assisting) bishop in the Diocese of Massachusetts in September 1988, she was confirmed over the next several months by the required majority of both Episcopal bishops and diocesan standing committees in the United States. She was consecrated Bishop Suffragan of Massachusetts on February 11, 1989, where she served until 2003. Her election and consecration as bishop caused great turmoil in the Episcopal Church in the United States and in the worldwide Anglican Communion. Traditionalists argued that none of Jesus's apostles were women and therefore women could not be ordained to the priesthood, much less elected and consecrated as bishops. Some also argued that her consecration would further damage relationships with the Roman Catholic Church, which were already strained by the ordination of women as priests. Still others argued that her ordination as bishop would not be accepted by the other twenty-six provinces within the Anglican Communion.[7] The fact that she was an African American and divorced and very liberal on social issues may also have contributed to the discomfort some people felt over her consecration as bishop. Suffice it to say, this event caused a major disruption in the Episcopal/Anglican branch of Christianity and other denominations that value the role of bishops in the church.

Now let's look at how this change affects three different generations of people who experience it from different perspectives. The first generation consists of those people who lived most of their lives before the change. Relative to this change, they had been in a period of relaxation. I call this generation the "grandparents." They may not necessarily have been older people, but they have a sense that the way the church has been will likely continue pretty much the same way. They perceive this time of relaxation or equilibrium as a given.

The second generation is made up of those people who are in the middle of their life during the change—those people who experience this change almost entirely as a time of tension, flux, uncertainty. I call this generation the "parents." They may or may not like the change that they are in the midst of, but this change is for them as much a given reality as equilibrium is a given for the grandparents' generation. They do not have the luxury of thinking that life will be pretty much as they have experienced it up to this point.

The third generation includes those people who live most of their life after this change. They are the generation living in the new time of relaxation, during the new period of equilibrium after the change has happened. For them, the new situation is a given. As far as they are concerned, the changed state of affairs is the norm. They have little or no sense of things ever being any different. The "new" equilibrium is not new to them; it's just the way things are. I call this generation the "children." The terms *grandparents*, *parents*, and *children* are not meant to indicate levels of maturity or even necessarily value judgments about the change. They simply indicate the relationship of the various generations to the timing of the change and where they are relative to the rhythm of relaxation-tension-relaxation or old equilibrium-disruption-new equilibrium.

Now let's look at a picture of this change, at one heartbeat on the EKG of the church's timeline.

Figure 7.2. Three Generations of Change

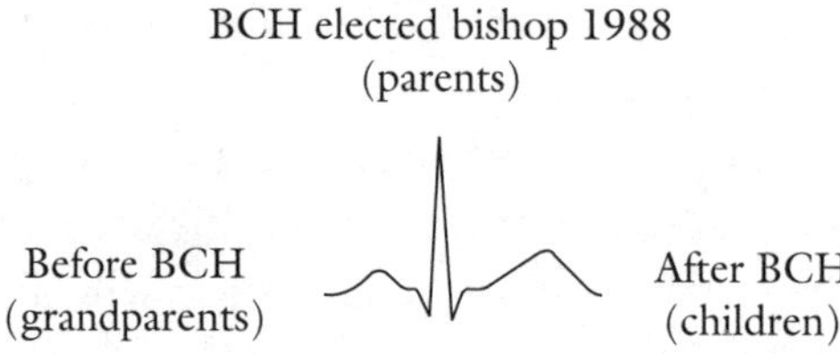

Think of life before Barbara Harris was elected and consecrated as bishop. For many generations, most people never even imagined that women could be priests, much less bishops. This is the grandparents' generation. Then there is the group of people who live through the time of change, the turmoil, the conflict. They are the parents. Last, there is the generation, after the change has taken place, that thinks life has always included women bishops. This is the generation of children.

At the conclusion of one of the first rites of confirmation at which Bishop Barbara Harris presided, a small boy, sitting near the front of the church, leaned over to his mother to ask an important question. He was quite young and had never been to a confirmation before. In fact, he had never seen a bishop before. He was very impressed by the beautiful satiny blue robe the bishop wore. Bishop Harris has a great sense of humor, and she sometimes says she looks like a peacock when she is dressed in her Episcopal vestments. At the conclusion of the ceremony, as the congregation was singing robustly and the trumpets were playing, the boy, greatly impressed with all the pageantry, leaned over to his mother and said, "Mommy, when I grow up, can I be a bishop?" "Sure," his mother replied. The boy was a bit confused at the reply. "No, Mommy, can *I* be a bishop?" "Well, I guess so if you really want to be," his mother responded. He was obviously delighted, and said, "You mean *boys* can be bishops, too?"

This is what it is like to grow up *after* a significant change has taken place. If you don't know the history, you think it has always been that way. Your sense of the norm is different from your ancestors'! It is different from both your "grandparents'," who never imagined the change could happen, and different from your "parents'," who lived through the unsettling struggle of the change, not knowing the ultimate outcome of the disruption.

Different Strokes for Different Folks

Now let's take a look at one significant change, one heartbeat, from another perspective and ask what sort of influence we can have on how people respond to the change.

"The Change Curve" (figure 7.3) is a picture of what takes place when a significant transition occurs. It is basically a movement from one state of equilibrium (a ⟶ b) to a new equilibrium (d ⟶ e). The curve predicts that in an organization experiencing significant change, the movement always passes through a period of disequilibrium or unease. In fact, it says you cannot avoid this unease.[8] The theory holds that there can be no *significant change* when a group moves from a ⟶ b to d ⟶ e *without* going through point c, c', or c." (These low points represent different individuals' or groups' experiences of disequilibrium.) The mythical path b ⟶ d simply does not exist. The phase of disequilibrium is a time when values are being reexamined, when goals are being readjusted. For many people, disequilibrium is also accompanied by strong emotions.

Figure 7.3. The Change Curve

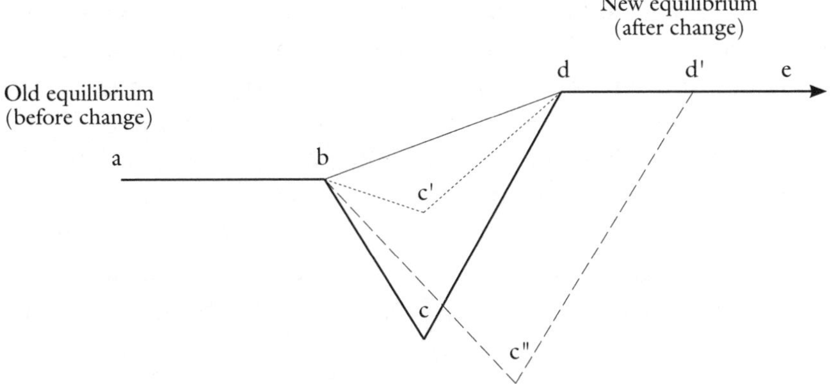

Feelings and Change

Let's return to the notion of feelings as messengers and look at the ordination of Barbara Harris as bishop. Many people felt joyful about her ordination. Both women and men who had fought for equality of women in positions of church leadership rejoiced at this momentous change. They had a sense that what it meant to be a bishop had somehow changed. Their excitement inspired them to "keep on keeping on." That is, they were eager to ensure that Barbara Harris was only the first of many women to become bishop, both in the United States and in the rest of the world, as other provinces felt culturally ready to make such a change. They thought it was important that Bishop Harris have other women colleagues so that she would not be the only woman's voice in the House of Bishops, because they knew she could not represent all women. Their joyful feeling was a message to keep up the struggle.

Many women felt powerful for the first time in the church. They realized they finally had a seat at the table where important decisions that affected them were being made. Some women sensed in a new way that they too might be called to priesthood or service as a bishop. These women and their male colleagues and allies also knew they needed to continue (to keep on keeping on) the work of supporting women as priests and bishops.

Some people were angry that a woman had been consecrated bishop. They were enraged because an important boundary had been violated, biblically or doctrinally. They argued that this ordination was against Scripture and the church's tradition and therefore not valid. Some bishops and dioceses drew a boundary by refusing to acknowledge the validity of priests ordained by Bishop Harris. They would not allow her to preach or to celebrate Communion within their dioceses. They aligned themselves with Anglican bishops in other provinces who also believed women could not be bishops or even priests in many cases. Some members of the Episcopal Church even left the denomination because they considered the violation of boundaries was too great. In various ways, anger led people to reestablish or draw new boundaries, new alliances.

Some people felt sad that the church as they had known it had changed radically. Many of these people found ways to grieve their loss and stay part of the church. If they found people who could understand their feelings of sadness at the loss they experienced, even if these other people did not themselves feel that loss, they felt they still belonged within this particular community of faith. They had a sense of inclusion—the both/and guideline lived on a grand scale. Others, perhaps overwhelmed by this loss, or an accumulation of losses (new prayer books and hymnals, changing ideas about sexuality, church leaders' involvement in political issues), left the church, perhaps for another denomination where they assumed they could be comforted.

Others felt scared. They needed support also. Like those who were sad, most of the frightened found support inside the Episcopal Church; some needed to leave to find that support. Some people were afraid that women bishops would change the church they knew; they needed to have the experience of meeting a woman bishop before they could decide if their fear was justified. Even many of those who supported the consecration of Barbara Harris as bishop were scared. They were afraid that the church would be divided, and they did not want division, so they made a concerted effort to dialogue with others who held different views about women in leadership. Some also feared a backlash against women priests and women lay leaders; so they looked for ways to support all women in their ministries.

Managing Disequilibrium

I always feel nervous when people talk about *managing* conflict. It makes conflict sound bad, and it deceives people into thinking that they should avoid conflict or control it at all costs if it arises. If my belief is not already obvious, let me say plainly that I believe conflict is part of life. Within limits, it is healthy. Tension is part of the rhythm of life. It brings energy into the system. Ronald Heifetz and Marty Linsky, professors at the John F. Kennedy School of Government at Harvard University, talk about the need to apply enough heat to keep tension at a boil in order to bring about needed change—without allowing the tension to boil over and completely disable people.[9] More realistic is to say that conflict is inevitable in living organisms and systems and that conflict is normal.[10]

The Pattern, Duration, and Rate of Disequilibrium

Change-curve theory says individuals and organizations live through rhythms of relative equilibrium ⟶ disequilibrium ⟶ new equilibrium over and over again. The theory also says that people cannot change this overall pattern, and yet they can influence the depth and width of the disequilibrium (b ⟶ c ⟶ d) part of the diagram. That is to say, leaders can have an effect on the degree to which most people experience disruption or conflict—the depth of c or c' or c". Leaders can also influence, to some extent, the *rate* at which people experience the unease (b ⟶ c' or b ⟶ c or b ⟶ c") and the *rate* at which people experience a return to a new equilibrium (c' ⟶ d or c ⟶ d or c" ⟶ d"). This also means that the *duration of disruption* can be influenced to some degree.

I have used the terms *disequilibrium*, *disruption*, *system unease*, and *conflict* somewhat interchangeably. One might argue that they are part of a spectrum of reactions to change. The question then is not how to avoid unease in the system. Instead, the question is how to find the path to the new equilibrium that allows emotions to be expressed, values to be discussed, and goals to be reevaluated and reestablished if necessary.

While this is a great oversimplification, three things affect the duration of disruption and the rates at which people experience unease and a return to a new equilibrium. The first is adequate information combined with feedback and a process of mutuality. The second is sufficient opportunity to process feelings. The third is ample occasion for reconsidering underlying values and for establishing new goals. These three factors can overlap or work in combination.

I have a story that I frequently tell that illustrates the difficulty of change in a community and the necessity of listening to the "talk back" of people in order to adjust the rate of change.

One of the most difficult places to make change is a congregation where clergy have engaged in sexual or financial misconduct. In such after-pastor congregations, mistrust and suspicion of clergy runs high.[11] Under the previous clergy, loyalty rather than accountability was the primary value. In most cases, many parishioners are still loyal to the former pastor, even when there is enormous evidence or admission of the misconduct. Such loyalists frequently blame the victim of the misconduct. Even with the arrival of a new pastor, the loyalty/accountability continuum remains out of balance, tipped toward the loyalty end. People not formerly loyal to the previous pastor become intensely loyal to the new one. While this attention may be flattering to the new pastor, it sets up or deepens factions and works against change. Meanwhile, many people simply want to return to the good old days before any of the mess occurred. In sum, introducing any change into such situations is extremely difficult.

Jacking Up the Ol' House

Rev. Edward G. Rice has been a priest for more than thirty years and worked in many after-pastor congregations. He tells a wonderful parable about change that is applicable to all congregations, even healthy congregations with high levels of trust and cooperation between laypeople and clergy. It is a real story of Ted's work on his island cottage in coastal Maine.

After spending a summer working on the old house he had purchased for vacation use, Ted thought he was nearly done. He had replaced the roof, done some wiring and plumbing, painted, and made many other minor improvements. Then one day, as he was looking under the house for something, he noticed that some of the wooden stilts on one side of the house and the sills along that same side were in terrible shape. As he had done before, Ted called the caretaker, an islander neighbor who had given him sage advise for other repairs. The man walked over to Ted's house.

"Eyah," he said, "ya got a bad case of dry rot. Ya'll have to replace all them rottin' stilts and sills."

Even given all that he had done on the house previously, this task seemed too much for an amateur to undertake. Ted asked his neighbor who he might call to do the work.

"Shucks," he replied, "ya can do this ya'self. It ain't hard. All ya need is some jacks, and I can loan ya them. I'll be back in a bit."

Without another word, the neighbor took off. Ted followed him to a shed where the jacks and some large blocks of wood were stored. They took them back to Ted's cottage and together they measured the foundation to order the new wooden stilts or underpinnings. And then the caretaker explained to Ted how to jack up the house.

"Level out some places and put these blocks under the cross beams. Then put the jacks on them and start jacking away a few inches at a time working your way along where it's rotted out. When she starts talkin' to ya, stop." With that, he walked away.

Ted did as instructed, carefully raising each jack an inch or two at a time and then moving to the next location. When he got it up about twelve inches, he heard some spine-jarring moans and groans coming from the old house. Worn out and a bit concerned, he called his friend and described what he had done and the sounds he had heard.

"Eyah, she's talking to ya alright."

"What do I do now?" Ted asked.

"Nuttin'," came the response.

"Nothing?" Ted asked. He'd learned to be as economical with his words as his friend.

"Eyah, just wait three days and jack her up some more until she talks to ya agin."

Ted did as instructed. This time after six more inches, the house started groaning again. He stopped and called his friend. "Six more inches," he reported.

"Eyah. Wait three days, and try 'er again."

Three days and three inches later, Ted called to report the progress and to say that he could more or less comfortably crawl under the house now and that the new beams had arrived. But before he started tearing out the old beams and putting in the new ones, he had a question.

"Eyah," came the reply.

"I did what you said and got the house jacked up twenty-one inches, but it took a week. Why couldn't I have just jacked it up all the way to begin with?" Ted asked.

"Well, ya coulda done that alright, but ya woulda broke every window in the house, and nonna the doors woulda closed right agin." And the phone clicked off.

Information, Feedback, and a Process of Mutuality

Few people like to be surprised by a major life-changing event. While we have discussed events that *happen to* us, at this point I am speaking about change that leaders are initiating. Giving good information and plenty of it is crucial if we want to slow the rate at which people experience disequilibrium and increase the rate at which they return to a new equilibrium. In churches that are planning changes, such as a new building project, or implementing a national change, such as a new prayer book or hymnal, information needs to be offered before the change. People also need an opportunity to respond to the information and, their leaders hope, to be part of the process of determining how much change will take place and how fast. While newsletters and postings on Web sites are good places to give information, they do not function well as places for receiving feedback and for establishing a mutual process. Many church leaders have had very unpleasant experiences with discussion boards and electronic mailing lists where people often vent their anger about an anticipated change.

I believe the problems with using electronic media for sharing information arises for two reasons. First, adequate guidelines for using the media have not been established or adhered to. Second, electronic media are inadequate to the task of processing deep feelings. Despite these cautions, most churches could still greatly increase their written and electronic communication without running the risk of alienating their congregants. Effectively using these resources to distribute information is possible, and an in-depth community meeting where people process the information about anticipated major changes is also necessary.

Face-to-face meetings are much better for conveying complex information to people who will be asking questions with varying levels of familiarity and understanding about the change. Such gatherings also build a community of support as people become engaged in discussing their resistance and opposition. Informational community meetings also *produce new information.* In some cases, such meetings indicate that the time is not ripe for the anticipated change, even if people are given quality information about the proposed change. And so the rate of change needs to be greatly slowed down. Such meetings are not just *about* change, however; they are *part of* change, because face-to-face meetings allow for feedback and the processing of feelings. They may make clear that the community has not had adequate opportunity to constructively surface and process feelings. When feelings have not been adequately attended to, all the information in the world will not slow the rate of disruption. In fact, pouring out more information without processing feelings may actually aggravate the situation. I think of the process of sharing information without attending to people's emotional reactions as a situation of *impacted feelings*, similar to having an impacted wisdom tooth. Unless the pain is dealt with, more information about good tooth care will be useless.

Processing Feelings

In chapter 3 I explained how feelings can be messengers of what is needed in a situation and the importance of not substituting feelings based on early life patterns. When people substitute a familiar or culturally sanctioned feeling for one they have been conditioned to suppress, they give off the wrong message and their needs are not met. We have also looked at some of the feelings evoked around the consecration of Barbara Harris as bishop as an example of messages about what people needed. At this point I want to talk about the relationship between the processing of feelings and the length of time a community experiences disequilibrium.

The duration of disequilibrium is inversely proportional to the degree to which feelings are processed. As people process their feelings, they can move through disequilibrium to a new equilibrium. Sometimes reaching that new equilibrium means that they remain in their current community of faith. Sometimes people need to move to another community of faith, or leave church altogether, in order to deal with the disequilibrium. If they do move and the feelings are not adequately processed in the new community of faith, the person can still feel a certain internal disequilibrium.

Pastors are familiar with this phenomenon when an individual or a family leaves a congregation to join another one. They may bring their unprocessed anger, fear, or sadness with them, and before long they are in conflict in their new congregation over some issue. Some folks become "serial offenders"—continually moving from one congregation to another. This pattern is more likely to occur when people have substituted one feeling for another. For instance, the person who only expresses *anger* about women bishops and leaves the Episcopal Church for the Roman Catholic Church may have a great deal of *sadness* around leaving a congregation where his family has worshiped for generations and where as a layperson he had a great deal of influence on decisions. If he continues to express only anger, members of his new community of faith may not want to draw close to him and listen to his feelings of loss. So, his need for consolation will not be met because he has substituted anger for sadness or because his anger is so overwhelming that people cannot see and respond to his sadness.

On the other hand, when people are encouraged to self-focus and express and process their true feelings, they are likely to get their emotional needs met even, at times, without moving to another congregation. They may find that while they do not like all that is taking place, they can live with the change because there are others who feel as they do. They have colleagues. As they express their feelings, leaders can respond and perhaps change the pace of transition to assist them.

Reconsidering Underlying Values and Reestablishing Goals

Moving from an old equilibrium to a new equilibrium usually involves bringing underlying values to the surface. Often the essential values remain mostly the same. The changing community does not usually see itself as an entirely new creation. When members of the community look at themselves in the mirror after the change, they usually recognize themselves.

Frequently, though, some values have shifted or gained ascendancy. In the case of those who advocated and supported ordaining women as priests or bishops, the value that the advocates placed on their particular worship tradition and governance style did not change. What changed for those advocating women's ordination was the emphasis they placed on inclusiveness with regard to the exercise of ordained leadership roles. Those advocating the ordination of women valued the potential contribution of women as priests and bishops more than they valued the tradition of an exclusively male priesthood. They were willing to experience disruption within the community and even loss of some members because they believed God called women, as well as men, to ordained ministry. As women began to exercise leadership as priests and bishops, the meaning of priesthood and the episcopacy began to alter. Certainly some advocates of women's ordination valued the inclusion of women in those leadership positions more than the traditional understanding of priesthood and episcopacy.

The greater the change, the more there is a need to openly and fully discuss values and to formally reestablish goals and boundaries. Sometimes changes happen first, and the official alignment of policies follows. The Episcopal Church debated the ordination of women as priests for decades. On July 29, 1974, three bishops ordained eleven women in Philadelphia. This was a case of practical change occurring ahead of policy change. Two years later, the General Convention of the Episcopal Church decided to change its official policy and rewrote canons to allow the ordination of women. They decided that the "Philadelphia Eleven" were validly, but not licitly, ordained. The ordinations were not licit; that is, they were not permitted according to the church laws in force at the time of the ordinations. However, the General Convention, the ruling body of the Episcopal Church, determined, after the fact, that the ordinations fulfilled all the requirements necessary to make them real or valid; therefore the women did not need to be reordained after the Convention changed the policy to *permit* women's ordination in the future.

The Slinky Effect: Differing Rates of Transition

Finally, various individuals and groups in an organization start the cycle of change at different times depending on their proximity to information and their degree of involvement in the decision-making process. The rate at which individuals and groups process their feelings is also different. In a typical congregation, the staff may begin moving through the cycle of change first, then the vestry or governing board or the committee initiating the change. They are followed by those people who regularly attend church and are close to the center of things, followed by the infrequent attendees and more peripheral folks, and finally the folks who come primarily on holidays. The change affects all these people but not at the same rate or to the same degree. Just as one group is beginning to experience a new equilibrium (moving up the c—d incline), another group may be starting to experience the disruption or unease (moving down the b—c decline). The pattern looks like figure 7.4, only with many more overlapping change curves.

Figure 7.4. Overlapping Disruption

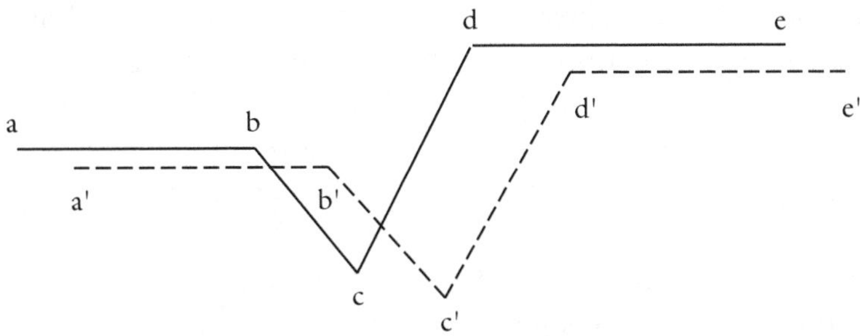

Figure 7.5. The Slinky Effect

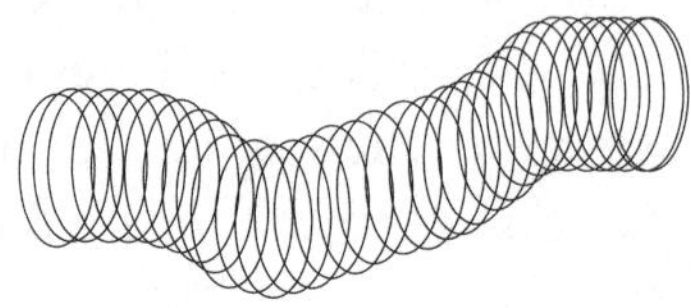

Because the community as a whole experiences this overlapping of disruption and new equilibrium as a dizzying disturbance, a more adequate diagram would be like a spiral or a Slinky toy.

In the midst of this organic flow, it is important for an individual leader or member to practice self-focus and to remember that every congregation is made up of clotheslines and kite strings, of people who respond differently to events in their lives, especially significant changes. The ability of a congregation to acknowledge their differences, to understand those differences at deeper levels, and to appreciate or celebrate those differences is what makes it possible for them to continue to remain a community.

A Community Transformed by Naming and Valuing Differences

I am reminded of a congregation that was deeply fractured by the decisions of their denomination on a national level. It was a small congregation, and three of the fifty active families, representing more than 10 percent of the pledge income, left because of the national church decision. Two of these members were on the church board, two taught in the Sunday school program. The pastor, the first woman to lead this fairly conservative congregation, had been ordained fewer than four years and had arrived shortly after the national decision had been made. Even though it was summer, she decided to call an all-church meeting. After serving ice cream sundaes to create a more relaxed atmosphere, the pastor began the meeting with prayer and then articulated guidelines for the meeting, which was to last no more than two hours. The guidelines included no personal attacks (no shaming and blaming). The group was told that they would not be making any decisions during this meeting (recognizing the different levels of disruption people experienced and allowing time for processing feelings). Each participant was invited to state how she or he felt about the decision of the national church or to pass (self-focus). People were not to respond to or rebut what someone else said. No one was allowed to dominate the conversation (attention to power factors). All were invited to listen to the comments that mirrored their own thoughts and to those that differed (both/and). A short period of silence was observed after each person spoke.[12]

People spoke in support of the national decision and against it. Some said they had mixed feelings—agreeing that it was an action based on social justice and equality and fearing that it would divide the church nationally and globally (both/and). Some were upset that the change was too long in coming. Some were angry that it was too precipitous (differing rates of disruption and reintegration).

As the people went around the room speaking, something happened that surprised the people and the pastor. Person after person began to say, "I see there are people here who agree with me and people with whom I disagree, but this is my church, my community, and I am not leaving" (both/and). A few people expressed sadness that some members had left the church family. They prayed those who left would find a community of faith where they would feel at home (new equilibrium for them). As the meeting progressed, people had a sense that they would need time to further understand their differences. In retrospect, the pastor believed that they had raised up a value at that meeting—that they were all committed to being part of "their church," even though they differed on a very important issue, perhaps on many issues. She felt glad that they had reestablished a basic goal—to stay in relationship. Before the meeting, the pastor had believed that the congregation had a conservative majority and a liberal minority. After everyone had spoken, it became clear to her that there was a *huge* range of opinion and no one group was dominant.

Because some members could not be at the meeting, the pastor sent out notes of the meeting (without identifying individuals) in the next newsletter and posted them on the church's Web site. Six months later, when the church board reversed a decision, made during the prior pastor's tenure, and decided to withdraw from an organization opposed to the national church's decision, the pastor visited the individuals whom she believed were committed to the earlier decision to answer any questions they had (sharing information) and to help them process their feelings. Since the summer congregational meeting took place, many people have talked about the change in their congregation. People with different ideas and theologies engage one another (it's okay to disagree). People are willing to welcome folks into the congregation who are different from them (making contact across difference).

While this story is not unique, it is rare, in terms of both the positive outcome and the significance this one meeting held for the congregation's transition. Such change often takes much longer. Nevertheless, it does show how a congregation can be transformed through using guidelines, processing feelings, and understanding and celebrating differences. Such communities of faith and transformation give us all a glimpse of the multicultural tapestries that God would have our congregations become!

Reflection Questions

According to the change-curve theory, leaders can have some influence on the degree of disruption and the time it takes to move from one phase of equilibrium through disruption to a new phase of equilibrium.

Think of a situation of significant change in a congregation in which you have been involved (introducing a new prayer book or hymnal; changing the chancel furniture, such as moving the altar or pulpit; changing clergyperson or key lay leader; and the like).

1. What was done, or could have been done, to diminish the degree and duration of the disequilibrium? Be specific.
2. What was done, perhaps without awareness, to increase the degree and duration of the disequilibrium? Be specific.

3. What interventions might you suggest to others in a similar situation? Be specific.

Appendix A

Kite Strings and Clotheslines Exercise

I learned this exercise in 1979 as a member of the Paulist Leadership and Renewal Project and have used it ever since in classrooms and on board retreats. The purpose of the exercise is to help people understand some of the dynamics of how individuals make choices in a group—how their behavior is influenced by the assumptions they make and how it may be influenced by what other people say. The exercise is also a wonderful way to bring about greater multicultural awareness within a congregation. The exercise works best with groups of eight to twenty people. It takes about forty-five minutes to do the exercise and process it. You need a room large enough for people to comfortably move from end to end without furniture in the middle. I have often asked a group to move into another room (parish hall) or a hallway if moving the furniture aside for the exercise is too difficult.

Begin by gathering everyone in the center of the room. Tell the group:

"This is an exercise about making decisions and noticing the decisions of others. In this exercise there are no right or wrong decisions. You will be invited to make a series of choices between two options. Choose whichever option makes the most sense to you today. You might make a different choice at another time. When I offer you the choice, I will say, 'How do you see yourself? Are you more like choice A or choice B?' Those who see themselves more like choice A will go to one end of the room. Those who see themselves more like choice B will go to the other end of the room. When I ask you to move, please go in silence to your end of the room. If you are unsure which choice to make, go with your first inclination. I realize sometimes people find it hard to make a forced choice between only two options. Do the best you can. I will offer you five pairs of choices and we will pause after each choice, so you will have a chance to say why you made your choice if you wish to do so. I think you will find this exercise to be fun. Are you ready to begin?"

Assuming that people are ready to begin, continue by asking, "How do you see yourself? Are you more like a kite string or a clothesline?" Pause for a moment to let people think. Repeat the question again if necessary. Then continue, "Kite Strings to this end of the room (point to one end). Clotheslines to that end of the room (point to the other end)."

When people have moved, invite them to remain silent for a moment and to notice the distribution of people by saying, "Notice who is in the same group as you and who is in the other group."

The first time, begin to process the first choice by starting with the larger of the two new groups. This avoids putting people from the minority group on the spot at the beginning of the exercise. Start with a general question. For example, if the kite strings are the larger group, say, "Let's hear from the kite strings. Does anyone want to say why you see yourself as a kite string?" If you have a very talkative group, you might invite them to keep their answers brief, a sentence or two. Follow each response with a "Thank you" or "I see" or "That's great"—some positive response that let's people know their choice and their reasoning about it are okay.

Not everyone needs to explain his or her choice each time. The number of responses will depend on how many people are involved in the exercise and how much time you have allowed for it. With twelve or fewer people doing the exercise, it is possible for everyone to speak, especially if the two groups are about the same size for a particular choice. If the groups are very lopsided, hearing from everyone in the larger group is less important. Three or four responses from each side are usually sufficient to allow for some diversity of responses. Further responses often become repetitious. It is important, however, not to cut anyone off and to be sure that people who are shy or introverted have a chance to speak. As the exercise progresses, you can ask if there is anyone who has not spoken earlier. This is particularly important when a large number of people are involved in the exercise.

After you have heard from the first group (assuming they are the kite strings), invite people from the second group to respond by saying, "Now let's hear from the clotheslines. Will someone tell us why you see yourself as a clothesline?" I often move near the group I am questioning, especially if the group has only one person or a small number of people. Follow the same process of affirming the responses. As the leader, do not to encourage competition between the groups. Competition frequently arises, and there will be an opportunity to discuss it, but it is best not to invite it. If the groups begin by being competitive, remind everyone that there are no right or wrong answers.

After everyone who wishes to speak has been given an opportunity to do so, call the entire group back to the middle of the room and offer the next choice, for example, "palm tree or Christmas tree." Always repeat the introductory words, "How do you see yourself? Are you more like *choice A* or like *choice B*?" (Substitute from the pairs below for *choice A* and *choice B*.) Then point to the end of the room to which participants should move in silence. Give people the opportunity to speak about their choice after everyone has chosen. Begin with the smaller group sometimes so that as leader you are not implying that those in the majority should always be heard from first—thereby subtly indicating that they are *better than* the smaller group. If several people seem ready to speak at once, the leader should be careful not to set a pattern of calling on men (or women) first, white people before persons of color, older people before younger people, and so on.

The paired choices are:

kite strings	clotheslines
palm tree	Christmas tree (evergreen tree)
picture window	screened porch
quill pen	laptop (or computer)
automobile	carousel

I prefer to use Christmas tree with groups that I know to be all Christian because of the incredible diversity of assumptions and associations that people make around a Christmas tree. In my experience, members of this group often articulate the greatest, and often contradictory variations, for their choice. With religiously diverse groups, the leader should use palm tree and evergreen tree.

This example raises the frequently asked question about using other pairs of choices. I have always used these pairs because they seem to work so well. If other pairs are chosen, each choice should be seen as positive. The members of the pair should have something in common. Neither choice in the pair should be an overwhelmingly clear "better" choice. Some updating of choices may be necessary over time. The quill pen/laptop choice began as quill pen/typewriter!

Processing the Experience

When the group has completed all five choices, I invite them into a reflection about the exercise as a whole. At times this reflecting takes place in the same space with the participants still standing. Responding while standing in place tends to keep the individual responses short and the overall processing brief. At times the group pulls up chairs or moves back to the space where they were meeting before the exercise. Then they tend to settle into longer responses and processing.

The purpose of the processing is to help people see how complex decision making is: how assumptions influence our choices, how people make the same choice for different reasons, how people can make opposite choices for similar reasons, how my "allies" on one choice may be opposite me on another choice, and so forth. Pedagogically, it is best to allow these insights to emerge from the group, by beginning with general questions. Begin by asking people what they observed, then invite them to comment on their insights and the meanings of what took place. Processing questions might include:

- What did you observe when we were doing this exercise?
- Where did you find yourself relative to other people?
- Were there any people who were always together in the five choices?
- What did you notice about the reasons people gave for their choices?
- Did competition enter into the choices or the explanation of the choices?
- Were people consistent in their choices?
- What did you learn about yourself and how you make decisions?
- Were you aware of making choices cognitively or affectively—with your head or with your heart?
- Did your emotions play a larger role in some decisions than in others?
- What was it like being in the majority? in the minority?
- Did you rethink any decision when you heard someone speak from your side?
- Did you rethink any decision when you heard someone speak from the other side?
- What have you learned from this exercise that might affect your participation in a group that makes important decisions, such as a church board?
- How might this exercise help you to recognize, understand, value, and celebrate differences?

I have probably led this exercise more than a hundred times. Each time I learn something new about how people interact around decision making. I am aware that the learning for the group varies somewhat depending on the goal I name in introducing the exercise and when I decide to employ it in a weeklong, intensive course or on a weekend board retreat. Over the years, I have tended to use this exercise early in the time a group spends together.

I am increasingly conscious of this exercise's power to help people learn to recognize differences and to understand those differences at deeper levels, steps toward valuing and celebrating differences. I am amazed how such a simple exercise exposes people to their assumptions about differences and helps them get in touch with the common tendency to judge differences as better than or less than. The exercise also allows people to experience their emotional responses to differences and to reflect on them, which is a key component in the journey toward multiculturalism. When the exercise is carefully led so that competition is not encouraged, people often have a corrective experience that allows them to see the benefits of exploring differences. That exploration often offers people a model for valuing and celebrating differences at a later time when the stakes are much higher than telling others whether they see themselves as a kite string or a clothesline. It serves as a practice session for developing a repertoire of multicultural skills. The exercise is almost like learning to play the scales on a piano in order to perform more complicated music. And just as a good musician frequently warms up by playing the scales, groups that wish to attain multicultural competence can warm up with this exercise.

Appendix B

Institutional and Cultural Oppression in the United States

A Selective Legal Timeline Focusing Primarily on Race

Lord, we ain't what we want to be;
we ain't what we ought to be;
we ain't what we gonna be;
but thank God we ain't what we was.

—Response of an African American preacher and slave in 1865, upon hearing the Emancipation Proclamation read for the first time[1]

To combat oppression on a personal and interpersonal level is not enough. To fully comprehend and combat all forms of oppression we need to see how they are woven into the very fabric of our lives through our legislative and judicial processes. This is true whether we are looking at racism, sexism, heterosexism, or any other form of oppression. For the purpose of understanding the political, social, economic, psychological, and educational impact of *institutional* level decisions on a target group, here I am focusing primarily on racial oppression because it is so clear in our society. Using the outline provided below as an example, high school and adult education groups can draw up similar timelines for examining institutional and cultural level oppression regarding class, gender, sexual identity, and so on. Groups might begin by talking about what they already knew about the items on this list, what they had been taught, what was missing from their education, and what they found most surprising. They might also notice whether there are any differences in the answers to these questions based on the age, race, culture, or class of the people responding to the questions—that is, have different people selectively been taught or learned different parts of this history?

What I present here is a list, admittedly incomplete, of significant judicial decisions and legislation dealing with issues of race in the United States. Most of the court decisions presented here are those of the Supreme Court overturning (and sometimes supporting) state laws or lower-court rulings. You will note that many of these laws or court decisions are positive steps toward freedom and equality. Often they are followed by legislation or judicial rulings that take back the very freedom and rights that had been gained, including rights put forth in constitutional amendments.

Perhaps because I am *not* a legal scholar, I present this rather lengthy timeline to help others like myself, especially white people, understand the significance of racial differences on the institutional and cultural levels. I hope this list of laws and court decisions will be a wake-up call to anyone who has been able to avoid facing the appalling inequality of our courts and schools regarding race and color, in much the same way as my visit to the Apartheid Museum in Johannesburg awakened me to the calculated, evolving legal framework for racism in that country. For those of us who do not need such a wake-up call, I hope it serves as a handy reference for some, not all, of the more important laws and court cases regarding discrimination, primarily with regard to race. A few significant historical events and some statistical data are included for context and perspective, as well as a few cases having to do with gender and sexual discrimination.

All the information and quotations for this timeline are taken from *Teaching Tolerance* (Spring 2004), a special issue celebrating the fiftieth anniversary of *Brown v. Board of Education*, published by the Southern Law Poverty Center,[2] and from F. Michael Higginbotham, *Race Law: Cases, Commentary, and Questions*, 2nd ed.,[3] or from online government and university sites that post the cases. All the court cases presented are U.S. Supreme Court cases unless otherwise indicated. The quotations are from opinions handed down in the cases themselves.

1619 The first slaves arrive in Jamestown, Virginia. They are characterized as property and afforded no personal rights.

1787 The Constitution of the United States includes four key racist provisions:

Article 1, §2, Clause 3: "Representatives and direct taxes shall be apportioned among the several States which may be included within this Union, according to their respective Numbers, which shall be determined by adding to the whole Number of free Persons, including those bound to service for a Term of Years, and excluding Indians not taxed, three-fifths of all other persons." The clause is sometimes referred to as the "three-fifths compromise."

Article 1, §9, Clause 1: "The Migration or Importation of such Persons as any of the States now existing shall think proper to admit, shall not be prohibited by the Congress prior to the Year one thousand eight hundred and eight, but a Tax or duty may be imposed on such Importation, not exceeding ten dollars for each Person." This clause is referred to as the "international slave trade provision."

Article 4, §2, Clause 3: "No Person held to Service or Labour in one state under the Laws thereof, escaping into another, shall in Consequence of any Law or Regulation therein, be discharged from such Service or Labour; but shall be delivered up, on Claim of the Party to whom such Service or Labour may be due." This clause is referred to as the "fugitive slave clause."

Article 5: This article prohibits the amendment of the first and fourth clauses of Article 1, §9 of the Constitution before 1808, thus ensuring slavery at least until that date. Many of the framers of the Constitution did not believe slavery would continue past 1808.

In each case above, "persons" meant "slaves." Together the above clauses are often referred to as the 1787 Compromise on Slavery. Because of this compromise, the abolitionist William Lloyd Garrison termed the Constitution "a covenant with death and an agreement with hell."[4]

1789 The Northwest Ordinance for the government of the territory of the United States northwest of the Ohio River prohibits slavery.

1790 The Naturalization Act of 1790 permits only "free white persons" to become naturalized citizens in accord with Article 1, Section 8, of the Constitution. Indentured servants, slaves, free African Americans, and later Asian Americans are left out. These racial restrictions are not fully lifted until 1952.

1793 Fugitive Slave Act. This act allows runaway slaves to be captured without warrant and returned to their owners.

1801 *State v. Boon.* The North Carolina Supreme Court holds that it is *not* a crime for a white owner to kill a slave.

1806 *Hudgins v. Wrights.* Judge Tucker presents the opinion for the Virginia Court that slavery depends on the status of one's mother at the time of birth, and that the law presumes that if one is white or a "copper-colored person with long jetty black hair" (referring to Native Americans), he is a free person, and if one is black, he is a slave. At the time Virginia has twenty-thousand free blacks. According to the ruling, judges can also decide the race of a person based on visual characteristics, given that many blacks and Native Americans do not have birth certificates.

1820 The Missouri Compromise authorizes the Missouri Territory to be admitted into the Union as a slave state, provided that for each slave state admitted to the Union, a corresponding free state also be admitted.

1830 The Indian Removal Act of 1830 allows the president to relocate Native Americans from any states or territories in the East to land west of the Mississippi River.

1831 *The Cherokee Nation v. The State of Georgia*. Justice John Marshall delivers the opinion that Native Americans do not constitute a foreign nation and are not entitled to the rights and privileges thereof. Thus they cannot appeal to the Supreme Court in their dispute with the state of Georgia, which has passed a law making all Cherokees and Cherokee land subject to Georgia state laws (1828). President Andrew Jackson later orders the Cherokees to relocate to Oklahoma during the coldest months of winter. More than four thousand Cherokees die during this one-thousand-mile trek known as the "Trail of Tears."

1841 *The United States v. The Libellants and Claimants of the Schooner Amistad*. Justice Story delivers the opinion that according to the act of March 3, 1819, the blacks, who were born in Africa and mutinied against their Spanish captors, are declared to be free.

1842 *Prigg v. The Commonwealth of Pennsylvania*. During the 1820s in Pennsylvania, alleged fugitive slaves can be detained only by judicial officers. The state requires extensive proof of ownership and criminalized private seizure of a black person—all in an attempt to balance the state's obligation under the 1793 Fugitive Slave Act guaranteeing due process, especially for blacks, who are the most vulnerable. Justice Story, a long-time critic of slavery, nevertheless authors the Supreme Court *Prigg* decision, which invalidates the Pennsylvania law on the grounds that it violates the Fugitive Slave Act of 1793 and the Constitution. The decision voids state legislation that would "interfere with or . . . obstruct the rights of the owner to reclaim his slave." While this decision is in the short-term interest of Southern slave owners, its effect is to make slavery a *federal* issue. Chief Justice Taney sees that if the federal government supports slavery, it could also work against slavery, so he writes a separate opinion suggesting that states are not only prohibited from interfering with the rights of slave owners but must also protect those rights. In the eyes of radical abolitionists, the *Prigg* ruling validates the reading of the Constitution as a proslavery document. Free blacks in Northern states are at grave risk. *Prigg* presumes that *all* blacks, even those found in free states, are slaves. This decision leads abolitionists to develop increased private initiatives such as the Underground Railroad. This decision raises the awareness of slavery as a federal issue that can no longer be ducked by Northern states.

1849–50 *Roberts v. City of Boston*. The Massachusetts Supreme Judicial Court rules that segregated schools are permissible under the state's constitution. The U.S. Supreme Court later uses this case to support the "separate but equal" doctrine. Sarah Roberts walks by five schools to get to her "colored" school. The city ordinance requires that students attend the nearest school. The judge, Lemuel Shaw, has served on the Boston School Committee that had ruled in 1846 that "the continuance of the separate schools for colored children, and the regular attendance of all such children upon the schools, is not only legal and just but is best adapted to promote the education of that class of our population."

1850 The Fugitive Slave Act (1850) amends the first Fugitive Slave Act (1793), making it easier to return runaway slaves.

1851 *Souther v. The Commonwealth* (of Virginia). Justice Field delivers the opinion that Simeon Souther is guilty of second-degree murder for the whipping death of his slave. He receives a sentence of five years in prison. The Sessions Acts of 1847–48 provided that murder committed by "*willful* and *excessive whipping* [or] *cruel treatment*" is murder in the first degree and punishable by death. Had the slave, Sam, not died, there would be no crime and no punishment.

1857 *Scott v. Sanford.* The famous Dred Scott case is actually a series of cases beginning in 1847. The Supreme Court in 1857 upholds the denial of citizenship to African Americans and rules that descendants of slaves are "so far inferior that they had no rights which the white man was bound to respect." From 1834 to 1836 Dred Scott lived with his owner, Dr. John Emerson, in the state of Illinois, in which slavery is prohibited by the Northwest Ordinance of 1787. Illinois law holds that if you claim your freedom in this free state, you are free. From 1836 to 1838 Scott lived in the territory of the Louisiana Purchase and north of the latitude of 36 degrees 30 minutes, where slavery is prohibited by act of Congress in 1820. In 1838 Scott and his family moved with Emerson to Missouri where slavery is permitted. Seven of the nine Supreme Court justices own slaves, including Chief Justice Roger Taney, who holds that Congress cannot pass laws to say that blacks are free. He thereby throws out the 1850 Compromise in which the federal government determined free territories.

1859 *George v. State.* Mississippi's highest court rules that it is *not* a crime to rape a woman who is a slave.

1861 The Civil War begins as the Southern states secede from the Union.

1863 President Abraham Lincoln issues the Emancipation Proclamation, freeing slaves in Southern states. The proclamation has little effect because the war continues. (Recall that Lincoln is from Illinois where Scott tried to claim his freedom.)

1865 The Civil War ends, and the Thirteenth Amendment abolishing slavery is enacted.

The Freedmen's Bureau Act establishes financial and social assistance for freed slaves.

The *Black Code of Mississippi* impedes the civil rights of freed slaves in Mississippi. Black codes throughout the South are an attempt to reenslave blacks by attacking their rights with regard to property, labor, and criminal justice activities.

1866 The Civil Rights Act declares that all persons born in the United States, including former slaves, are citizens. This act also prohibits racial discrimination in the lease and sale of land, in the issuance and enforcement of contracts, and in presenting lawsuits and gives federal courts jurisdiction over all disputes under the act.

1868 The Fourteenth Amendment is ratified, guaranteeing "equal protection under the law." Citizenship is extended to African Americans. "All persons born or naturalized in the United States, and subject to the jurisdiction thereof, are citizens of the United States and of the State wherein they reside." This overturns the *Dred Scott* decision by making *all persons* born within the United States and subject to its jurisdiction citizens of the United States. Section 1 of the amendment includes three clauses:

Privileges and immunities clause: "No State shall make or enforce any law which shall abridge the privileges or immunities of citizens of the United States, . . ."

Due process clause: "nor shall any State deprive any person of life, liberty, or property, without due process of law, . . ."

Equal protection clause: "nor shall any State deny to any person within its jurisdiction the equal protection of the laws."

The Radical Republicans intend this amendment to punish the South and to centralize in the hands of the federal government large powers, previously exercised (unevenly) by the states.

1870 The Fifteenth Amendment prohibits racial discrimination in voting and gives Congress the authority to enforce this prohibition.

1870 *People v. De La Guerra.* Justice Temple delivers the opinion that Pablo de la Guerra, born in Santa Barbara, California, in 1819, when it was part of Mexico, is a citizen of the United Sates according to the Treaty of Guadalupe Hidalgo (1848), which gave citizenship to Mexicans who chose to stay in the territory that was ceded to the United States after it defeated Mexico.

The Enforcement Act reaffirms the Civil Rights Act of 1866, providing federal courts jurisdiction over all disputes regarding the civil and constitutional rights of blacks. "That all citizens of the United States who are or shall be otherwise qualified by law to vote at any election . . . shall be entitled and allowed to vote at all such elections, without distinction of race, color, or previous condition of servitude."

1871 Act of 1871 (the Ku Klux Klan Act) strengthened sanctions against those who impeded black suffrage. It gave the president the right to use federal forces to enforce the law. This act made it a crime for two or more persons to conspire for the purpose of depriving anyone of the equal protection of the laws. This act is invalidated by *United States v. Harris* (1883).

1873–78 *The Slaughterhouse Cases.* The Louisiana state legislature gives a twenty-five-year monopoly to a particular slaughterhouse. The plaintiffs, who lose their case, argue that the privileges and immunities clause of the Fourteenth Amendment extends to their right to practice their profession and operate their own separate slaughterhouses. The Supreme Court adopts a structural reading of the Constitution, arguing that the core danger to the Constitution is posed by federal power, and thus the first eleven amendments are directed at confining federal power. The Court suggests that *the state*, not the federal government, is the guarantor of basic civil rights generally. The *Slaughterhouse Cases* drastically circumscribe the privileges and immunities clause, reducing it to a procedural rule that rights should be allocated evenhandedly with regard to citizens of different states. This ruling, led by Justice Miller, completely reverses the movement toward centralization to protect former slaves and swings back toward extreme states' rights views held by the Democratic Party before the Civil War.

1875 *United States v. Cruikshank*. The ruling, delivered by Chief Justice Waite, continues the approach of the Supreme Court in the *Slaughterhouse Cases*, narrowing the scope and coverage of the Reconstruction Amendments (Thirteenth, Fourteenth, and Fifteenth). For blacks in the Southern states, the federal government is the only power likely to enforce their legal rights as citizens, and this case dilutes the Fourteenth Amendment, especially the privileges and immunities clause. "The government of the United States is one of delegated powers alone. Its authority is defined and limited by the Constitution. All powers not granted to it by that instrument are reserved to the States or the people."

Congress passes the Civil Rights Act of 1875, banning racial discrimination in public accommodations.

1876 The end of Reconstruction comes with the very close presidential election of 1876. The results in Florida, Louisiana, Oregon, and South Carolina are disputed. The Democrat Samuel Tilden received more popular votes than Republican Rutherford B. Hayes. There are claims of violent intimidation by whites of black voters in the South. An election commission of eight Republicans and seven Democrats works out a compromise. Hayes is given a one-vote majority in the Electoral College and becomes president in return for the withdrawal of federal troops to their garrisons, and thus an end to Reconstruction, given that federal troops are needed to enforce black civil rights.

1880 *Stauder v. West Virginia.* Justice Strong delivers the opinion that a West Virginia state law barring blacks from jury service violates the equal protection clause of the Fourteenth Amendment.

1882 The Chinese Exclusion Act suspends the immigration of Chinese laborers for ten years. Two years later it is expanded to exclude all Chinese and is eventually extended indefinitely.

1883 *United States v. Harris.* A band of twenty men led by R. G. Harris kidnapped four African Americans from a Crockett County, Tennessee, jail. The four African American men were beaten and one was killed. A deputy sheriff tried to prevent the lynching, but failed. Section 2 of the Force Act of 1871 was declared unconstitutional on the theory that an act to enforce the equal protection clause applied only to state action, not to state inaction.

The Civil Rights Cases. The Supreme Court strikes down the Civil Rights Act of 1875, arguing that discrimination *by individuals or private businesses* is constitutional. These cases continued the narrowing of federal protection for blacks. Congress does not have the authority to prohibit discrimination in public accommodations according to the Thirteenth or Fourteenth Amendments.

1884 *Elk v. Wilkins.* John Elk, an American Indian, brings the case against Charles Wilkins, a voter registrar in Omaha, Nebraska, for failing to register him. Justice Gray delivers the opinion that Indians are no more "born in the United States and subject to the jurisdiction thereof" within the meaning of the Fourteenth Amendment than the children of foreign governments. Elk therefore is not a citizen and has no voting rights under the Fifteenth Amendment. Only in 1924 does Congress pass legislation granting citizenship to all American Indians.

1889 *Chae Chan Ping v. United States.* Justice Field delivers the opinion that, under the Constitution, Congress holds power to exclude aliens and that Congress can exercise that power for any reason it chooses, including race.

1890 Louisiana passes the first Jim Crow law, requiring separate accommodations for blacks and whites.

1896 *Plessy v. Ferguson.* The Supreme Court authorizes segregation, finding Louisiana's "separate but equal" law constitutional. This law is the institutionalization of white supremacy and black inferiority and becomes the legal justification for Jim Crow laws. Homer Plessy, who was of one-eighth African heritage, intentionally rides in a whites-only railroad car. He is arrested and comes before Justice John Howard Ferguson, a carpetbagger from Massachusetts. Justice Henry Billings Brown delivers the Court's opinion. This landmark case was delivered by a Northerner. Brown was born in Lee, Massachusetts. A graduate of both Yale and Harvard Law Schools, he was a district judge of the United States Court for the Eastern District of Michigan before being appointed to the Supreme Court by President Benjamin Harrison. The Court wrote:

> The object of the [Fourteenth] Amendment was undoubtedly to enforce the absolute equality of the two races before the law, but in the nature of things it could not have been intended to abolish distinctions based upon color, or to enforce social, as distinguished from political, equality, or a commingling of the two races upon terms unsatisfactory to either. Laws permitting, even requiring, their separation in places where they are liable to be brought into contact do not necessarily imply the inferiority of either race to the other, and have been generally, if not universally, recognized as within the competency of the state legislatures in the exercise of their police power.

This case frequently argues from precedents established before the Thirteenth, Fourteenth, and Fifteenth Amendments were passed, thereby largely ignoring them. *Plessy* becomes the precedent in as many as fifty subsequent school cases in which state and federal courts approve discrimination and segregation.

1898 *United States v. Wong Kim Ark.* Justice Gray delivers the opinion that a child of parents who are not American citizens (and the parents are not diplomats of their country of origin) who is born in the United States is a citizen of the United States within the meaning of the Fourteenth Amendment.

1899 *Cumming v. Richmond (GA) County Board of Education.* Justice Harlan finds that a state can levy taxes on black and white citizens alike while providing a public school for white children only.

1908 *Berea College v. The Commonwealth of Kentucky.* Justice Brewer upholds a 1904 Kentucky law that prohibits a private college from teaching white and black pupils in the same institution. Berea was founded in 1854 by a small group of Christians. Its charter begins with the words "God hath made of one blood all nations that dwell upon the face of the earth." After the Civil War, it admitted students without discrimination. In 1904 it had 753 white students and 174 black students. It receives no state assistance. Justice Harlan dissents from this opinion.

1917 *Buchanan v. Warley.* Justice Day delivers the opinion that begins to dismantle state-sanctioned segregation, by striking down racial residential-segregation ordinances as violations of the due process clause of the Fourteenth Amendment.

Congress creates "an Asiatic barred zone"—excluding all Asian immigration.

1920 The Nineteenth Amendment gives women the right to vote.

1921 Emergency Quota Act. Congress establishes a temporary quota system meant "to confine immigration as much as possible to western and northern European stock."

1922 *Ozawa v. United States.* Justice Sutherland delivers the opinion that Japanese people are not considered white for the purposes of immigration and naturalization.

1924 Indian Citizenship Act of 1924 grants citizenship to all American Indians.

Immigration Act of 1924, also called the Johnson-Reed Act, limits the number of immigrants who can be admitted from any country to 2 percent of the number of people from that country who were already living in the United States in 1890. The law restricts southern and eastern European immigrants who had begun to enter the country in large numbers beginning in the 1880s and entirely prohibits East Asians and Asian Indians from immigrating. It sets no limits on immigration from Latin America.

1927 *Gong Lum v. Rice.* Justice Taft upholds the Supreme Court of Mississippi, which declared that a Chinese student could be defined as nonwhite for the purpose of segregating public schools. *Roberts v. City of Boston, Plessy,* and *Berea College* are all cited as precedents.

1934 Congress passes the Indian Reorganization Act, abandoning the policy of assimilation, now protecting American Indian culture, and encouraging tribal self-government.

1936 *Missouri ex rel. Gaines v. Canada.* Chief Justice Hughes orders Missouri's all-white law school to admit an African American student, stating that the practice of sending black students out of state for legal training when there is a law school for whites within the state does not fulfill the state's "separate but equal" responsibility.

1940 *Alston v. School Board of City of Norfolk.* A federal court requires equal salaries for African American and white teachers.

1941 Executive Order 8802 reaffirms the policy that all persons are part of the national defense program regardless of race, creed, color, or national origin. This order requires all departments of the federal government and defense industry contractors not to discriminate.

1944 *Korematsu v. United States.* The Civilian Exclusion Order No. 34 of the Commanding General of the Western Command, U.S. Army, directs that after May 9, 1942, all persons of Japanese ancestry should be excluded from specific areas. Fred Korematsu, an American citizen of Japanese descent, is convicted in a federal district court of remaining in San Leandro, California, a "Military Area." There is no question of Korematsu's loyalty to the United States. In June 1941, he volunteered for the navy but was rejected for health reasons. At the time of the exclusion order, he is engaged to an American citizen of Italian descent who is not subject to exclusion. Justice Black delivers the opinion for the Supreme Court that his federal court conviction stands. Justice Murphy in dissent writes, "This exclusion of 'all persons of Japanese ancestry, both alien and non-alien,' from the Pacific Coast area on a plea of military necessity in the absence of martial law ought not to be approved. Such exclusion goes over 'the brink of constitutional power,' and falls into the ugly abyss of racism. . . . I dissent, therefore, from this legalization of racism." Though the Court states that rigid scrutiny would be applied regarding racial exclusions, it sanctions the forcible internment of thousands of Americans of Japanese descent. Though the United States is at war with Germany, Italy, and Japan, Americans of German and Italian descent are not subject to internment. The Supreme Court accepts California's rationale that Japanese Americans have a different sense of patriotism.

1946 Congress passes the Indian Claims Commission Act of 1946, which removes the barrier to tribal money claims against the federal government.

Morgan v. Commonwealth of Virginia. Irene Morgan is arrested and convicted for refusing to move to the "colored section" of a Greyhound bus. NAACP attorneys William Hastie, Thurgood Marshall, and Leon Ransom argue that having been victorious in a "death struggle against the apostles of racism" (the Nazis), the United States cannot sanction racism at home. Justice Reed delivers the opinion that racial segregation on *interstate* buses and trains violates the commerce clause of the U.S. Constitution (rather than relying on the Reconstruction amendments).

1947 *Westminster School District v. Mendez.* A federal appeals court strikes down segregated schooling for Mexican American and white students. California Governor Earl Warren repeals a state law segregating Asian American and Native American students.

1948 *Sipuel v. Board of Regents of the University of Oklahoma.* The Supreme Court orders the admission of Ada Lois Sipuel, a black student, to the whites-only University of Oklahoma School of Law, because Oklahoma has no school of law for blacks. Thurgood Marshall and Amos Hall argue on behalf of Sipuel.

Shelley v. Kraemer. Justice Vinson delivers the opinion that *judicial enforcement* of racially restrictive covenants violates the equal protection clause of the Fourteenth Amendment. Such clauses, implemented by whites, prevent the few racial minorities who can afford to own property in more desirable areas from moving in. This case is the culmination of more than thirty years of court battle. Attorneys George Vaughn, Herman Willer, and Thurgood Marshall argue on behalf of the petitioners.

1950 *Sweatt v. Painter.* Black World War II veteran Herman Sweatt applies to the University of Texas Law School. In response, the university, committed to segregation, opens a law school for blacks in the basement of a nearby building. W. J. Durham of Dallas and Thurgood Marshall of New York City, attorneys for the petitioner, convince the Supreme Court that underfunded Jim Crow graduate schools are not the constitutional equivalent of the well-endowed, long-established, esteemed schools that have been open to all other races for decades. Though this ruling does not overturn *Plessy*, it represents the first time the Court has looked at the substance of education by considering not merely the types of facilities but the opportunities they afford. Chief Justice Vinson rules that learning in law schools "cannot be effective in isolation from the individuals and institutions with which the law interacts"—a victory against legalized *avoidance of contact*.

McLaurin v. Oklahoma State Regents for Higher Education. Chief Justice Vinson rules that the Fourteenth Amendment precludes differences in treatment by the state based on race. While admitted to the University of Oklahoma to pursue a Doctor of Education, G. W. McLaurin had been required by the university to sit at a designated desk in a room adjoining the classroom; to sit at a designated desk, set apart, in the library; and to eat at a designated table and at a different time from other students. Again *Plessy* was not overturned: blacks would be admitted to whites-only institutions *only if* the state failed to provide a separate institution for blacks.

1952 The Supreme Court hears oral arguments in *Brown v. Board of Education (of Topeka)*. Thurgood Marshall is the lead counsel for the black school children. The cases come from Kansas, South Carolina, Virginia, and Delaware, all seeking admission of black minors to public schools in their communities on a nonsegregated basis. The argument is made based on equal protection under the Fourteenth Amendment. It is a direct attack on *Plessy*. The court goes beyond the consideration of "tangible" factors, such as buildings, curricula, qualifications and salaries of teachers, to consider the *effect of segregation itself* on public education.

Immigration and Nationality Act (or McCarran-Walter Act) repeals the blanket exclusion laws against the immigration and naturalization of Asians, although it establishes only token quotas for Asian immigration and is clearly biased towards Europeans.

1953 Chief Justice Vinson dies during Supreme Court recess, and Republican California Governor Earl Warren is appointed Chief Justice of the Supreme Court by President Eisenhower, whom Warren supported for president after withdrawing from the race himself. Eisenhower later calls his appointment of Warren "the biggest damn-fool mistake I ever made." Second round of arguments on *Brown*.

1954 *Brown v. Board of Education (Brown I).* Chief Justice Earl Warren leads a unanimous ruling that overturns *Plessy* after nearly sixty years. "We conclude that in the field of public education the doctrine of 'separate but equal' has no place. Separate educational facilities are inherently unequal." The Court delays deciding how to implement the decision and asks for another round of arguments.

Bolling v. Sharpe. The Warren Court rules that the federal government must desegregate the Washington, DC, schools.

Attorney General Herbert Brownell Jr. launches "Operation Wetback," indiscriminately deporting more than one million citizens and noncitizens to Mexico in 1954 alone. (Five hundred thousand people had been forcibly returned to Mexico during the Depression.)

1955 *Brown v. Board of Education (Brown II).* The Warren Court orders the lower federal courts to require desegregation "with all deliberate speed," setting off a backlash across the country (see below). Federal judges hold more than two hundred school desegregation hearings between 1955 and 1960.

1956 Tennessee Governor Frank Clement calls in the National Guard after a white mob attempts to block the desegregation of a high school.

The University of Alabama, under court order, admits Autherine Lucy, its first black student. White riots follow. Lucy is later suspended and then expelled for criticizing the university.

The Virginia legislature calls for "massive resistance" to school desegregation and threatens to close schools that have been ordered to desegregate.

1957 More than one thousand paratroopers from the 101st Airborne Division and a federalized Arkansas National Guard are called in to protect nine black students who are integrating Central High School in Little Rock, Arkansas.

1959 Prince Edward County, Virginia, officials close their public schools rather than integrate them. Whites attend private academies. Black students do not go back to class until 1963, when the Ford Foundation funds private black schools. In 1964, the Supreme Court orders the county to reopen its schools on a desegregated basis.

1960 Federal marshals in New Orleans shield six-year-old Ruby Bridges from an angry mob as she attempts to enroll in school.

1962 James Meredith, a black student, is admitted to the University of Mississippi under a federal appeals court order. More than two thousand white people riot.

1963 Vivian Malone and James A. Hood, black students, successfully register at the University of Alabama, despite Governor George Wallace's "stand in the schoolhouse door" after President Kennedy federalizes the Alabama National Guard. President Kennedy is assassinated on November 22.

1964 President Lyndon B. Johnson signs the Civil Rights Act of 1964.

Title II provides for the desegregation of all public places of accommodation.

Title IV provides that the federal government is authorized to file school desegregation cases.

Title VI prevents discrimination in activities or programs receiving federal financial assistance.

Title VII prohibits employment discrimination based on race, color, religion, sex, or national origin.

1965 The Voting Rights Act enforces the Fifteenth Amendment by preventing states from imposing prerequisites or qualifications based on race or color.

The Immigration and Nationality Act amendments of 1965 abolish "national origins" as a basis for allocating immigration quotas that had been in place since the Immigration Act of 1924. Asian countries are now on equal footing.

1966 *Loving v. Virginia.* Justice Warren delivers the opinion that state law barring interracial marriage violates the equal protection clause of the Fourteenth Amendment. Virginia has prohibited interracial sex and marriage for more than three hundred years. Such marriage is a felony in Virginia until *Loving.*

1968 *Green v. County School Board of New Kent County.* Chief Justice Brennan, for a unanimous court, orders states to dismantle segregated school systems "root and branch," identifying five factors—facilities, staff, faculty, extracurricular activities, and transportation—to be employed as a gauge of compliance with *Brown.* "The time for mere 'deliberate speed' has run out. . . . The burden on a school today is to come forward with a plan that promises realistically to work, and promises realistically to work now. . . . The Board must be required to formulate a new plan . . . which promise[s] realistically to convert promptly to a system without a 'white' school and a 'Negro' school, but just schools."

Fair Housing Act of 1968. "It is the policy of the United States to provide, within constitutional limitations, for fair housing throughout the United States." It is unlawful to deny "a dwelling to any person because of race, color, religion, sex, familial status, or national origin."

1969 *Alexander v. Holmes County Board of Education.* Justice Black delivers the opinion for the Supreme Court ordering the immediate desegregation of Mississippi schools, declaring the "all deliberate speed" standard no longer constitutionally permissible.

1971 *Swann v. Charlotte-Mecklenburg Board of Education.* Chief Justice Burger, after five edits, delivers the unanimous opinion approving busing, compulsory education, and magnate schools as appropriate means to overcome the role of residential segregation in preserving racially segregated schools.

Title IX of the Educational Amendments of 1972 extends *Brown* to gender, prohibiting discrimination in any educational program receiving federal funding.

1973 *Keyes v. School District No. 1, Denver.* Justice Brennan rules that the constitutional responsibility to desegregate rests on the demonstration of officially discriminatory action, making "the differentiating factor between *de jure* segregation and so-called *de facto* segregation . . . *purpose or intent* to segregate." This distinction is mostly technical. In reality, segregated housing, in many communities, is the result of legally enforced restrictive covenants. The Federal Housing Administration's lending policies take into account "adverse influences" that include the mixing of "inharmonious racial groups." Thus racially separated neighborhoods are not simply *de facto* segregated, but are so as the result of state and national policy (*de jure*). The Court finds that the Denver school board has intentionally segregated blacks and Mexican Americans from whites.

San Antonio Independent School District v. Rodriguez. Justice Powell rules that education is not a "fundamental right" and the Constitution does not require equal expenditures on education within a state. This ruling locks minorities and whites who live in poor areas into inferior schools.

1974 *Milliken v. Bradley.* Chief Justice Burger delivers the opinion that federal remedial powers regarding desegregation stop at the school district line unless the nearby district or the state have contributed to the constitutional violation. The decision brings to an end two decades of successful desegregation litigation and means that *Brown* will have limited impact on many racially isolated urban districts. Justice Thurgood Marshall in his dissent wrote:

> After 20 years of small, often difficult steps toward that great end, the Court today takes a giant step backwards. Notwithstanding a record showing widespread and pervasive racial segregation in the educational system provided by the State of Michigan for the children of Detroit, this Court holds that the District Court was powerless to require the State to remedy its constitutional violation in any meaningful fashion. Ironically purporting to base its result on the principle that the scope of the remedy in a desegregation case should be determined by the nature and the extent of the constitutional violation, the Court's answer is to provide no remedy at all for the violation proved in this case, thereby guaranteeing that Negro children in Detroit will receive the same separate and inherently unequal education in the future as they have been unconstitutionally afforded in the past.

Lau v. Nichols. The Burger Court rules that Chinese students with limited English proficiency in the San Francisco Unified School District are to be provided with instruction under Title VI, which prohibits schools from receiving federal funds if they discriminate based national origin, race, or color.

1978 *Regents of the University of California v. Bakke.* A fractured Supreme Court (5-4) led by Justice Powell rules that race can be a factor, but not the deciding factor, in a university admission policy. The University of California, Davis, medical school's admissions program, which set aside sixteen out of one hundred seats for certain minorities, is declared unconstitutional because it sets aside a specific number of seats for black and Latino students. Regarding *compelling interest,* Powell rejects "reducing the historic deficit of traditionally disfavored minorities in medical school and in the medical profession," remedying societal discrimination, and "increasing the number of physicians who will practice in communities currently underserved." He accepts the use of race as serving one compelling interest: "the attainment of a diverse student body," as long as "constitutional limitations protecting individual rights may not be disregarded." He states that the "nation's future depends upon leaders trained through wide exposure to the ideas and mores of students as diverse as this Nation of many people."

1982 *Bob Jones University v. U.S.* and *Goldsboro Christian Schools, Inc. v. U.S.* Justice Burger rejects tax exemptions for private religious schools that discriminate.

1986 *Riddick v. School Board of the City of Norfolk, Virginia.* A federal court finds, for the first time, that once a school district meets the *Green* (1968) criteria, it can be released from its desegregation plan and returned to local control.

1987 *McCleskey v. Kemp.* Justice Powell delivers the opinion that the equal protection clause has not been violated, even though a disproportionately high number of blacks have received death sentences in Georgia.

1988 Restitution for World War II Internment of Japanese Americans and Aleuts. The Civil Liberties Act of 1988 states:

> The Congress recognizes that . . . a grave injustice was done to both citizens and permanent resident aliens of Japanese ancestry by the evacuation, relocation, and internment of civilians during World War II. . . . These actions were carried out without adequate security reasons and without any acts of espionage or sabotage documented by the Commission, and were motivated largely by racial prejudice, wartime hysteria, and a failure of political leadership. The excluded individuals of Japanese ancestry suffered enormous damages, both material and intangible, and there were incalculable losses in education and job training, all of which resulted in significant human suffering for which appropriate compensation has not been made. For these fundamental violations of the basic civil liberties and constitutional rights of these individuals of Japanese ancestry, the Congress apologizes on behalf of the nation.

A symbolic amount of twenty thousand dollars was paid to each surviving internee.

School integration reaches a historic high. Nearly 45 percent of black students in the United States are attending majority-white schools.

1991 *Board of Education of Oklahoma City v. Dowell.* Justice Rehnquist relaxes the obligations of desegregation, saying that court orders are not meant "to operate in perpetuity." The Oklahoma City school system returns to neighborhood schools, abandoning its desegregation efforts after being released from a court order.

1992 *Freeman v. Pitts.* Justice Kennedy delivers the opinion that school systems can fulfill their integration obligations in an incremental fashion.

United States v. Fordice. Justice White delivers the 8-1 opinion that adoption of race-neutral measures, by itself, does not fulfill the constitutional requirement to desegregate colleges and universities that were segregated by law.

1993 *Shaw v. Reno.* Justice O'Connor delivers the opinion that the equal protection clause prevents states from drawing political districts based on racial considerations unless there is a *compelling government interest.*

1995 *Missouri v. Jenkins.* Chief Justice Rehnquist delivers the opinion that judicial remedies were intended to be "limited in time and extent." The new goal for desegregation is to return schools to local control.

Adarand Constructors, Inc. v. Peña. Justice O'Connor delivers the opinion that federal racial classifications for affirmative action in business, like those of a state, must meet three conditions: be subject to the most *strict judicial scrutiny*, serve a *compelling governmental interest*, and be *narrowly tailored to serve that interest.* This case makes it much more difficult for women and racial minorities to achieve significant economic power relative to men and whites.

1996 *Hopwood v. Texas.* A federal appeals court prohibits the use of race in university and college admissions, ending affirmative action in Louisiana, Texas, and Mississippi.

2002 United States schools are resegregating, according to a report from Harvard University's Civil Rights Project.

2003 *Grutter v. Bollinger.* Justice O'Connor delivers the opinion (5-4) that the Constitution "does not prohibit the [University of Michigan] law school's narrowly tailored use of race in admissions decisions to further a compelling interest in obtaining the educational benefits that flow from a diverse student body."

Gratz v. Bollinger. On the same day as *Grutter*, Chief Justice Rehnquist delivers the opinion (6-3) that invalidates the University of Michigan's undergraduate admissions program, which awards points to applicants for various factors, including race.

2003 *Goodridge v. Department of Public Health* (Massachusetts Supreme Judicial Court). Chief Justice Margaret Marshall, in a 4-3 ruling, finds that Massachusetts may not "deny the protections, benefits and obligations conferred by civil marriage to two individuals of the same sex who wish to marry." In a clarification issued on February 4, 2004, the four-justice majority states that "the history of our nation has demonstrated that separate is seldom, if ever, equal" and that nothing short of equal marriage (that is, civil unions) would be constitutional.

2007 *Ledbetter v. Goodyear Tire & Rubber Co.* Chief Justice John Roberts, in a 5-4 decision, upholds the Eleventh Circuit's decision, finding that the limitations period for a disparate pay claim cannot be extended or disregarded. According to the ruling, Lilly Ledbetter cannot receive back pay from Goodyear Tire Company even though she was being paid less than men with her same position because she had not filed for discrimination within the one-hundred-eighty-day limitation period for each of her unequal paychecks. This appears to roll back the equal pay provisions of Title VII of the Civil Rights Act of 1964.

2007 *Parents Involved in Community Schools v. Seattle School District #1, et al.* and *Meredith v. Jefferson County (Kentucky) Board of Education.* Chief Justice John Roberts, in a 5-4 opinion, strikes down Seattle and Louisville racial balancing plans, stating that the school districts had not shown that the interest they seek to achieve (diverse student bodies) justifies the extreme they have chosen (relying upon racial classification of individual students in making school assignments). He further states that accepting racial balancing as a compelling state interest would justify the imposition of racial proportionality throughout American society. In effect, race cannot now be a factor in assigning students to high schools.

Appendix C

The Feeling Wheel

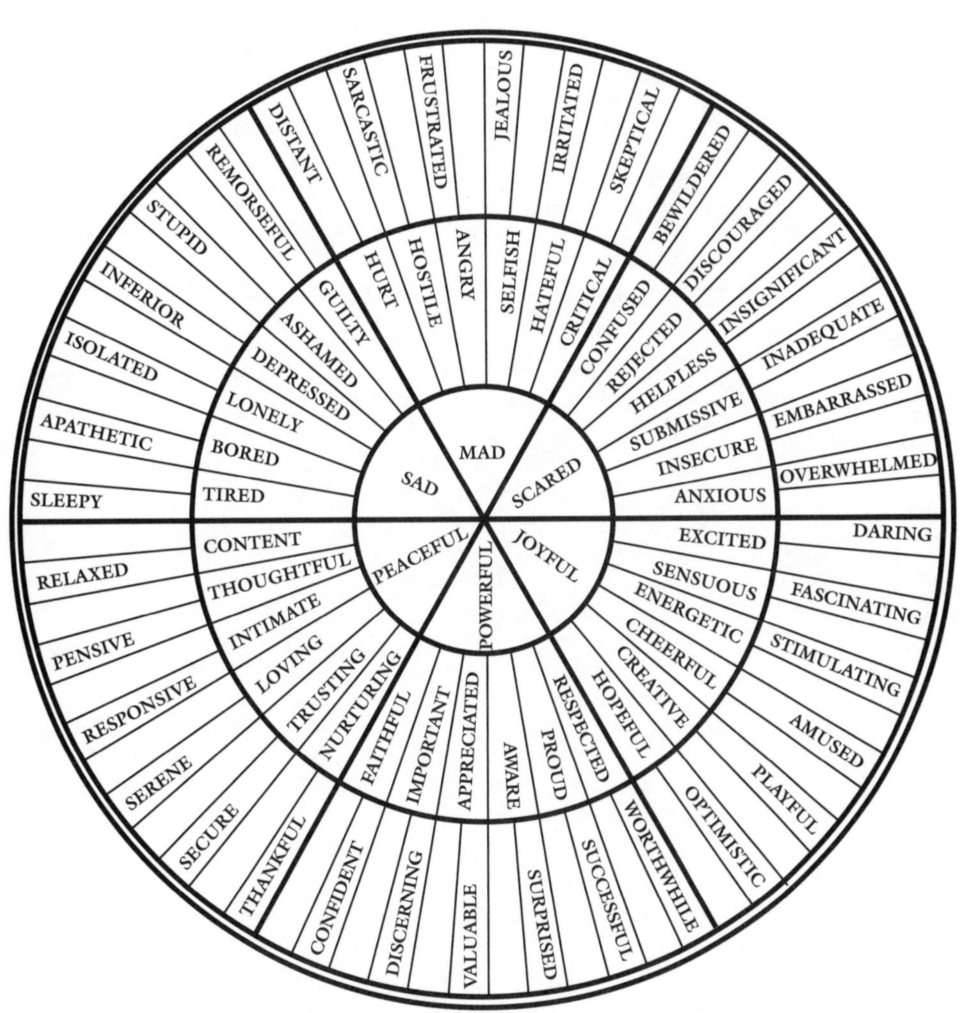

Appendix D

Some Important Dates for a Christian Church Timeline[1]

60–100 The four Gospels are written.

70 Jerusalem (and the Second Temple) is destroyed.

90 Council of Jerusalem is held. Christianity admits Gentiles without requiring them to become Jews first.

140–200 The church slowly agrees on the canon—which books constitute the New Testament.

144 Marcion is excluded from the church in Rome because he wants to eliminate the Hebrew Scriptures and distance Christianity from its Jewish roots.

313 Constantine and the Eastern Emperor Licinius issue the Edict of Milan, formally extending toleration to Christians.

324 Constantine wins control of all the Roman Empire.

325 Council of Nicea (later called First Ecumenical Council) is held, and the first draft of the Nicene Creed is created.

451 Council of Chalcedon argues over the understanding of Christ's divinity and humanity: one person and one nature or one person and two natures.

527–65 Justinian I recaptures most of Italy and North Africa.

529 Code of Justinian, the basis for bodies of law for Christian Europe, is developed.

632 Muhammed (b. 570) makes his last pilgrimage to Mecca with forty thousand followers.

638–56 The Arabs conquer Palestine, Iraq, Syria, and Egypt.

711–16 Arabs conquer Spain.

800–840 The Donation of Constantine, giving wide secular powers to the pope, is forged in France.

800 On Christmas Day in Rome, Pope Leo III crowns Charlemagne Roman emperor, "restoring" the empire in the West.

1054 Relationship between Rome (Catholic) and Constantinople (Orthodox) is breached, each side excommunicating the other.

1073–85 Pope Gregory VII (Hildebrand) makes powerful effort to reform the church and rid it of lay control. He forbade the investiture of bishops and abbots by lay princes and tried to change the rules to require that priests be celibate.

1099 The crusaders take Jerusalem.

1232 The Inquisition is made systematic, partly because of the Albigensians.

1320–84 John Wycliffe translates the Bible into English.

1400–1500 In this century of discovery, the church confronts the machine age, modern science, humanism, the rise of nation-states, and the "new world."

1492 Christopher Columbus lands in the West Indies.

1517 Martin Luther presents his ninety-five theses (1530 Augsburg Confession).

1523 Ulrich Zwingli begins to lead reform in Zurich.

1532 John Calvin publishes the *Institutes of the Christian Religion* in Geneva.

1534 Henry VIII abolishes the pope's authority in England (Act of Supremacy). Ignatius Loyola founds the Jesuits in Paris.

1545–47 First session of the Council of Trent is held, followed by sessions in 1551–52 and 1562–63.

1549 First Prayer Book of Edward VI is prepared.

1552 Second English Prayer Book changes words for administration of Communion to more "Protestant" understanding.

1559 Elizabethan Prayer Book combines sentences of administration from first two Prayer Books.

1611 King James Version of the Bible is completed.

1620 *Mayflower* carries the nucleus of a Pilgrim congregation to the American colonies.

1647 George Fox begins to organize what would become Quakers or Society of Friends.

1682 Quaker William Penn organizes Pennsylvania on a foundation of religious toleration.

1722–50 Johann Sebastian Bach becomes organist at St. Thomas's church in Leipzig.

1726 The Great Awakening evangelical renewal begins in America.

1776 Declaration of Independence is signed.

1789–94 French Revolution is fought, and the "Terror" of 1792–93 attempts to de-Christianize France.

1807 Britain prohibits the slave trade (though not yet slavery) after the campaign of William Wilberforce.

1815 Napoleon is defeated at Waterloo, marking the end of the Holy Roman Empire.

1833 J. H. Newman and John Keble begin Oxford Movement.

1840 David Livingston begins his missionary work in Central and East Africa.

1848 Karl Marx and Frederick Engels publish the *Communist Manifesto.*

1859 Charles Darwin publishes *On the Origin of the Species.*

1870 Rome is seized by Italian nationalists and the papal states fall. First Vatican Council declares pope infallible.

1894–96 Armenian Christians are massacred in Turkey.

1900	Boxer Rebellion occurs in China, and Christians massacred.
1900–1907	Modernist controversy arises, and historical criticism is applied to the Bible.
1927	Conference at Lausanne that leads to World Council of Churches is held.
1933	Hitler takes over Germany. In 1934, Synod of Barmen, German Christians opposed to Hitler found the Confessing Church.
1939–45	World War II and Holocaust (1941–45) take place. Taize is founded to help European Jews (1940).
1947	The Church of South India is founded as a union of Anglican, Methodist, Congregational, Presbyterian, and Reformed churches.
1958–63	Pope John XXIII leads the Roman Catholic Church and calls the Second Vatican Council (1962–65).
1961	Orthodox Churches join the World Council of Churches in New Delhi.
1968	Martin Luther King Jr. is assassinated. Many church leaders are involved in civil rights movement and later in Vietnam War protests.
1980	Archbishop Oscar Romero is assassinated in El Salvador.
1986	Desmond Tutu becomes archbishop of Cape Town, South Africa. He later heads the Truth and Reconciliation Commission (1995).
1988	Barbara C. Harris is elected bishop suffragan in Massachusetts, the first woman bishop in the Anglican Communion.
1989–90	Communist regimes fall in Eastern Europe and Russia, resulting in less religious persecution.
2003	V. Gene Robinson, partnered gay Episcopal priest, is elected bishop of New Hampshire.

Notes

Preface

1. I learned the Kite Strings and Clotheslines exercise as a member of the Paulist Leadership and Renewal Project, a consulting and training organization founded in 1976 and partially funding by a Lilly Endowment grant. The instructions for using this exercise and the pair choices can be found in appendix A. The tool is based on an exercise in Sidney B. Simon, Leland W. Howe, and Howard Kirschenbaum, *Values Clarification: The Classic Guide to Discovering Your Truest Feelings, Beliefs, and Goals* (New York: Hart Publishing Co., 1972), 94–97. Three of the paired choices I have offered come from that exercise; however, the purpose of the exercise and the processing, which I suggest be done in the whole group, are much different as I have outlined them.

2. Chris Argyris and Donald A. Schon talk about the difference between espoused theory and theory-in-action in *Theory and Practice: Increasing Professional Effectiveness* (San Francisco: Jossey-Bass, 1974). For an application of their work to church settings, see Anita Farber-Robertson, *Learning While Leading: Increasing Your Effectiveness in Ministry* (Herndon, VA: Alban Institute, 2000).

3. Jonathan Myrick Daniels (March 20, 1939–August 20, 1965), a seminarian at Episcopal Theological School (ETS), was killed for his work in the American civil rights movement. He was shot by a store owner when he stepped in front of a young black girl, Ruby Sales. His death helped galvanize support for the civil rights. In the late 1990s, Ruby Sales received a Master of Divinity degree at Episcopal Divinity School, which was formed in 1974 as the result of a merger of ETS and Philadelphia Divinity School.

4. VISIONS, which stands for Vigorous InterventionS In Ongoing Natural Settings, was founded by three African American women who grew up together in North Carolina and who integrated their schools in the early sixties. These women and their allies began multicultural training and consulting in the early 1980s. The organization currently numbers about fifty consultants working in corporations, nonprofit agencies, schools, churches, and the public sector. The consultants represent many backgrounds and work in multicultural teams. Further information can be found at www.visions-inc.org.

5. Information about Ecclesia Ministries can be found at www.ecclesia-ministries.org.

6. The terms *common cathedral* and *common cinema* are intentionally lowercase to emphasize a different understanding of power and privilege within the community. The lowercase sometimes challenges computer spell checkers, but not nearly as much as common cathedral challenges traditional denominational church structures. Both word processors and denominational structures have to reset their defaults!

7. Michael Battle, *Reconciliation: The Ubuntu Theology of Desmond Tutu* (Cleveland: Pilgrim Press, 1997).

Chapter 1

1. Ruth Fulton Benedict, chapter 1, *The Chrysanthemum and the Sword: Patterns of Japanese Culture* (Boston: Houghton Mifflin Co., 1946), as found in John Bartlett, *Familiar Quotations*, 15th ed., ed. Emily Morison Beck (Boston: Little Brown and Company, 1980), 796.

2. Hans Bohr quoting his father as published in Stefan Rozental, ed., *Niels Bohr: His Life and Work as Seen by His Friends and Colleagues* (New York: John Wiley & Sons, 1967), 328.

3. VISIONS, Inc. materials are copyrighted and have been used with permission. For information on the use of their materials or for consulting or training, visit www.visions-inc.org.

4. REI (Recreational Equipment Inc.), "How to Choose Cycling Shoes," REI, http://www.rei.com/rei/learn/noDetail.jsp?storeId=8000&langId=-1&catalogId=40000008000&URL=rei/learn/cycle/howshoesf.jsp#ORIG.

5. Charles R. Foster, a white professor of religion and education at the Candler School of Theology at Emory University, applies the concept of being "in time" to the operation of a multicultural Sunday school, where people "work with the assumption that class begins for each child as she or he arrives." Teachers plan many points of entry, knowing that children arrive at various times so that "there is no such thing as 'arriving early' or 'coming late.' Time begins when someone arrives." Charles R. Foster, *Embracing Diversity: Leadership in Multicultural Congregations* (Herndon, VA: Alban Institute, 1997), 80.

6. Ronald A. Heifetz and Marty Linsky, *Leadership on the Line: Staying Alive through the Dangers of Leading* (Boston: Harvard Business School Press, 2003), 14.

7. There are churches with great cultural diversity in terms of demographics that set the times of their services and expect that everyone will show up "on time." In some of these churches the on-time attendance is as high as in a homogeneous white church. By "truly multicultural" I am referring to culturally diverse congregations where different cultural views of time, music, relationship, responsibility for children, and so forth are in tension with one another—where there is likely no one right way to do most things. My point is that a demographically diverse congregation may be operating on a monocultural set of assumptions dictated by the group with the most power. This will become clear in the chapter on power and difference.

8. For a thoughtful discussion of multicultural congregations, see Charles R. Foster, *Embracing Diversity*, especially chapter 2, "Negotiating Differences."

9. Eugene H. Maly, "Introduction to the Pentateuch," *The Jerome Biblical Commentary* (Englewood Cliffs, NJ: Prentice-Hall, 1968), 3–4.

10. E. A. Speiser, *Genesis: Introduction, Translation, and Notes*, The Anchor Bible (Garden City, NY: Doubleday & Co., 1985), xxviii.

11. Jiddu Krishnamurti, *Freedom from the Known* (New York: HarperCollins Publishers, 1969), 15.

12. Either/or thinking has its roots in the ancient world of the Greek philosophers. I grew up thinking in discrete categories with a linear notion of cause and effect. I grew up interpreting life through the lens of categories such as right or wrong, individual identity, and time as measured on a clock. Christianity came to me in Sunday school

with similar distinctions between body and soul. When I studied philosophy in college, I realized that this categorical way of thinking came from the ancient Greek philosophers. Later as I studied the Bible, I had to learn that this way of thinking was foreign to most of the biblical world, including the authors of the biblical texts. They thought in a more organic, holistic, both/and manner. In their worldview, the cause-and-effect relationship between things was much more mutual because of the way things are enfolded in reality. Identity begins with the group, not the individual. We are, therefore, I am. Time has more to do with relationships than with discrete units measured by a clock. This worldview predominates in Africa, Asia, and the Middle East.

13. See David W. Augsburger, *Conflict Mediation across Cultures: Pathways and Patterns* (Louisville, KY: Westminster/John Knox Press, 1992), 52, for a comparison of both/and and either/or conflict.

14. Hans Bohr quoting his father as published in Stefan Rozental, ed., *Niels Bohr: His Life and Work as Seen by His Friends and Colleagues* (New York: John Wiley & Sons, 1967), 328.

15. Once the feelings are named, the speaker can return to the content and ask from a place of curiosity, "Is there any grain of truth in what I have said?" The discussion that follows is referred to as checking out a fantasy and is part of the cooperative process used in transactional analysis.

16. The theory-in-action analysis of Chris Argyris and Donald Schon, *Theory in Practice*, focuses on learning from the unintended consequences of one's actions.

17. The traditional examination of conscience is a spiritual discipline by which a person reviews her thoughts, words, and actions of the day for conformity or lack of conformity with moral law, usually the Ten Commandments.

18. Ronald A. Heifetz, *Leadership without Easy Answers* (Cambridge, MA: Belknap Press of Harvard University Press, 1994); and Ronald A. Heifetz and Marty Linsky, *Leadership on the Line*, 9–20, 51–74.

Chapter 2

1. Nelson Mandela, *Long Walk to Freedom: The Autobiography of Nelson Mandela* (Boston: Little, Brown and Company, 1994), 544.

2. For a further discussion of power, see Jean Baker Miller, "Women and Power," in Judith Jordan, ed., *Women's Growth in Connection* (New York: The Guilford Press, 1991) 197–205.

3. Privilege comes from the Latin *privus* and *lex* meaning private law. *The Oxford English Dictionary, Second Edition* (Oxford: Oxford University Press, 1994) defines privilege as "A right, advantage or immunity granted to or enjoyed by a person, or a body or class of persons, beyond the common advantages of others; an exemption in a particular case from certain burdens or liabilities." See Peggy McIntosh, "White Privilege and Male Privilege: A Personal Account of Coming to See Correspondences through Work in Women's Studies" (Working Paper No. 189, Wellesley Centers for Women, Wellesley, MA, 1988). A version of this article, entitled "White Privilege: Unpacking the Invisible Knapsack" and excerpted from the Winter 1990 issue of Independent School, can be found at http://seamonkey.ed.asu.edu/~mcisaac/emc598ge/Unpacking.html#top.

4. I am speaking here of the U.S. context. While I have found that the principles in this chapter apply in other countries, learning this model is easier if focusing on one context.

5. This diagram is slightly altered from Valerie Batts's chapter, "Is Reconciliation Possible: Lessons from Combating 'Modern Racism,'" in *Waging Reconciliation: God's Mission in a Time of Globalization and Crisis,* ed. Ian T. Douglas (New York: Church Publishing, 2002), 38. An earlier version of this material was published as *Modern Racism: New Melody for the Same Old Tunes* (Cambridge, MA: Episcopal Divinity School, 1998).

6. Groups who wish to bring about significant change regarding racism and any of the other forms of oppression using this model are encouraged to use trained outside consultants who have experience with the types of resistance typical of members of both dominant and subordinated groups. Groups are also encouraged to devote large blocks of time—several full days or a series of weekends—to this work. Because most of us have spent a lifetime living in the monocultural world of the old creation, we shouldn't expect to move out of it in a couple of hours or a single afternoon.

7. I still remember the poem in Hungarian. It translates: "One, two, three, four. Little dog, where are you going? Not very far. Just to the end of the world." I find it ironic that my father taught me this

particular nursery rhyme given that my grandparents, at ages sixteen and eighteen, traveled across the Atlantic and, by assimilating into the United States society, brought about the end of their native cultural world.

8. While if would be easier to use *American* than "people from the United States," I find the latter phrase more accurate and less culturally imperialistic. People who live in South America, Central America, and Canada identify themselves by their country of birth or residence rather than referring to themselves as "American," though they have as much claim to the term as people who live in the United States. Most often when people from the United States speak of themselves as Americans, they are ignoring, rather than including, the other peoples who also live in the Americas. I will avoid the use of the term *American* unless I am quoting someone or allowing for the fact that the overtones of cultural imperialism are indeed present.

9. The definition of oppression is taken from Valerie A. Batts and Joycelyn Landrum Brown, "Assumptions and Definitions," in an internal publication of VISIONS, Inc. (Roxbury, MA: VISIONS, Inc., 1990), revised 7/2003.

10. Ibid.

11. Joe Kraus, "How *The Melting Pot* Stirred America: The Reception of Zangwill's Play and Theater's Role in the American Assimilation Experience," *MELUS* (Fall 1999): 5, http://www.findarticles.com/p/articles/mi_m2278/is_3_24/ai_62350897.

12. Ibid.

13. Israel Zangwill, *The Melting Pot* (New York: Macmillan, 1926), 33.

14. Kraus, 8.

15. I am reminded of the following joke: What do you call a person who speaks three languages? Answer: Trilingual. What do you call a person who speaks two languages? Answer: Bilingual. What do you call a person who speaks only one language? Answer: American.

16. "The House We Live In," *Race: The Power of an Illusion,* episode 3, film, written, produced, and directed by Llewellyn M. Smith (California Newsreel, 2003).

17. The grid was developed by Valerie A. Batts and Joycelyn Landrum Brown, consultants at VISIONS, Inc. I have slightly modified the "Religious Oppression" row and I have added the "Clericalism" row.

18. Jocelyn Samuels, address to U.S. Senate Committee on Health, Education, Labor and Pensions on "Closing the Gap: Equal Pay for Women Workers," April 12, 2007, National Women's Law Center (April 2007), http://www.nwlc.org/display.cfm?section=employment. Samuels went on to say that there "is not a single state in which women have gained economic equality with men, and gender-based wage gaps persist across every educational level" even though the Equal Pay Act was passed in 1963.

In Fiscal Year 2006, the Equal Employment Opportunity Commission (EEOC) received 23,247 charges of sex-based discrimination and recovered $99.1 million in monetary benefits for charging parties and other aggrieved individuals (not including monetary benefits obtained through litigation). See *The U.S. Equal Employment Opportunity Commission,* http://eeoc.gov/types/sex.html.

19. Using transactional analysis theory, Valerie Batts says that prejudice is learned and "occurs when an individual presents faulty information as fact based on values, beliefs and/or attitudes which she has incorporated in the Parent ego state without Adult processing." This contamination of the Parent and Adult ego state is maintained by justification and is an example of "old-fashioned" racism. Batts further states that Parent-Adult contamination is frequently accompanied by a contamination of the Adult ego state by the Child ego state, referred to as a phobia or delusion, which is "an unwarranted emotional reaction presented as fact. It is maintained by rationalization, ways of explaining away contradictory data." Valerie Batts, "Modern Racism: A T. A. Perspective," *Transactional Analysis Journal* 12:3 (1983): 207–9. The ego states will be further explained in chapter 4.

20. Batts, "Is Reconciliation Possible?" 52. See also James Jones, "Racism in Black and White," in Phyllis A. Katz and Dalmas A. Taylor, eds., *Eliminating Racism: Profiles in Controversy* (New York: Plenum Press, 1988), 117–135; and Asa G. Hilliard, *The Maroon within Us* (Baltimore: Black Classic Press, 1995).

21. Batts, "Is Reconciliation Possible?" 46. Also, Batts, "Racism: A T. A. Perspective," 207–9. The term *symbolic racism*—"the expression in terms of abstract ideological symbols and symbolic behaviors of the feeling that blacks are violating cherished values and making illegitimate demands for changes in the racial status quo"—was also used to describe

this change from overt racism. See John McConahay and Joseph Hough, "Symbolic Racism," *Journal of Social Issues* 32:2 (1976): 23–45.

22. McIntosh, "White Privilege and Male Privilege."

23. Mary Sonn and Valerie Batts, "Strategies for Changing Personal Attitudes of White Racism," paper delivered at the Annual Convention of the American Psychological Association, Los Angeles, 1985.

24. Batts, "Is Reconciliation Possible?" 59.

25. Ibid.

26. Ibid.

27. The VISIONS model uses either "antagonistic avoidance of contact" or "anti-white avoidance of contact."

28. Batts, "Is Reconciliation Possible?" 60–61.

29. Ibid., 62.

30. This chart is an adaptation of copyrighted VISIONS training materials. See Batts, "Is Reconciliation Possible?" 62.

31. See Noel Ignatiev and John Garvey, *Race Traitor* (New York: Rutledge, 1996).

32. For information about the Apartheid Museum, visit http://www.apartheidmuseum.org.

33. The Workmen's Circle movement is a way working-class Jews keep alive the cultural values of Judaism in a somewhat secularized setting.

34. See the story of First Presbyterian Church, Altadena, California. Several Pasadena churches began a ministry to Japanese immigrants in 1905. In 1913, Pasadena Union Church was founded by twenty-three of these immigrants. The church later became bilingual and joined the Presbyterian denomination. The story is told in Mark Lau Branson's book, *Memories, Hopes, and Conversations: Appreciative Inquiry and Congregational Change* (Herndon, VA: Alban Institute, 2004).

Chapter 3

1. Louisa May Alcott, *My Kingdom*, st. 1, in *Louisa May Alcott: Her Life, Letters, and Journals*, ed. Ednah D. Cheney (Boston: Little, Brown and Company, 1919), 32.

2. In chapter 5 I discuss how women are expected to carry the brunt of relational work and then have their work disappeared in many organizations. Though relational work depends on more than emotional or

affective competence, it cannot be done without significant emotional skills. Women have more cultural support to name their emotions and to respond to the emotions of others, even though the importance and the effectiveness of their resulting work is often belittled.

3. Dr. Isaac Jennings used the term *orthopathy* in 1802 to define a form of alternative medicine, also known as "natural hygiene." Dr. C., "The Physiological Laws of Life," *Orthopathy*, http://members.iimetro.com.au/~hubbca/orthopathy.htm. Kevin T. Bauder, president of Central Baptist Theological Seminary uses the term *orthopathy* to refer to how we are "to love God aright" in "The Importance of Affections in the Christian Faith," Religious Affections, http://religiousaffections.org.

4. The Greek ορθηοσ (orthos) means erect, regular, right, or correct. Παθηοσ (pathos) means what one has experienced or suffered. It can be used to describe a passion or an emotion such as love or hate. Παθητικόσ (pathetikos) means capable of feeling. In modern English, the words *pathos* and *pathetic* connote suffering and a degree of passivity on the part of the subject. *Orthopathy* can have a more active connotation because of its resonance with *sympathy* (first used in 1579) and *empathy* (first used in 1912). Though sympathy indicates the idea of someone having an affinity with another person's feelings, it does not connote a *rightness* of feelings relative to a situation or congruence between a feeling and a stimulus.

5. See Carol Gilligan, *In a Different Voice: Psychological Theory and Women's Development* (Cambridge: Harvard University Press, 1982); Mary Field Belenky, Blythe McVicker Clinchy, Nancy Rule Goldberger, and Jill Mattuck Tarule, *Women's Ways of Knowing: The Development of Self, Voice, and Mind* (New York: Basic Books, 1986); and Judith V. Jordan, Alexandra G. Kaplan, Jean Baker Miller, Irene P. Stiver, and Janet L. Surrey, *Women's Growth in Connection: Writings from the Stone Center* (New York: Guilford, 1991), who all speak of women's decision making from a relational viewpoint, as distinguished from a solely emotional viewpoint. Judith V. Jordan, ed., *Women's Growth in Diversity: More Writings from the Stone Center* (New York: Guilford Press, 1997) includes several essays about relational theory and issues of diversity, especially concerning race, gender, and sexuality.

6. VISIONS consultants developed "Feelings as Messengers" based on transactional analysis theory. A basic summary of transactional analysis

can be found at the International Transactional Analysis Association (ITAA) Web site, www.itaa-net.org/index.htm.

7. Many cultures, including Middle Eastern cultures, do not separate intellect and emotions in the way most Western cultures do. Thus we may conclude that feelings have more value in the Scriptures simply because they are not relegated to a *lesser than* status relative to thoughts.

8. "The Feeling Wheel Poster" and Gloria T. Willcox's book, with Olive Young, *Feelings: Converting Negatives to Positives* (St. Petersburg, FL: Win-Win Team Publishing, 2001), can be ordered from Network of Christian Counseling Centers, Inc., P.O. Box 710, St. Petersburg, FL 33731, or from Willcox by e-mail, gtwillcox@aol.com, or by phone, (727) 347-0832.

9. For further information about substitution of feelings, see Eric Berne, *Structure and Dynamics of Organizations and Groups* (New York: Grove Press, 1959), and Fanita English, "The Substitute Factor: Rackets and Real Feelings—Part I," in *Transactional Analysis Journal* 1:4, 27, and "The Substitute Factor: Rackets and Real Feelings—Part II," in *Transactional Analysis Journal* 2:1, 23–25.

10. I suspect that an unscrupulous leader would have ample opportunities to take advantage of someone using other means. The possibility of the misuse of the theory by devious people should not prevent its beneficial use by properly trained, well-intentioned people.

11. The literature on emotional literacy and emotional intelligence is large and growing. See Claude Steiner, *Emotional Literacy: Intelligence with a Heart* (Fawnskin, CA: Personhood Press, 2003); and Daniel Goleman, *Emotional Intelligence: Why It Can Matter More Than IQ* (New York: Bantam, 2006).

12. I have used masculine references here because in my experience men often have more difficulty identifying their feelings and substitution patterns. For a discussion of "male relational dread," see Samuel Shem and Janet Surrey, *We Have to Talk: Healing Dialogues between Women and Men* (New York: Basic Books, 1998), 16–19. Samuel Shem's novel, *Fine*—about a psychiatrist-in-training (Fine) and his wife who is trying to make it as a stand-up comic—has a wonderfully humorous interchange about the difficulty of men knowing their own feelings (New York: Dell, 1985) 83–85. Samuel Shem is the pen name for Stephen Bergman.

13. Two excellent books on theological reflection are Abigail Johnson, *Reflecting with God: Connecting Faith and Daily Life in Small Groups* (Herndon, VA: Alban Institute, 2004) and Patricia O'Connell Killen and John de Beer, *The Art of Theological Reflection* (New York: Crossroads, 1995).

14. Certainly, God might be speaking in other ways. One might get at these by looking at institutional or cultural levels and asking, for instance, who is benefiting in this situation? Who is left out?

15. Carol S. Robb, ed., *Making the Connections: Essays in Feminist Social Ethics* (Boston, MA: Beacon Press, 1985), 14–15. This essay is an expansion of Harrison's inaugural lecture as professor of Christian ethics at Union Theological Seminary in New York.

16. Ibid., 15. See also two extensive treatments of anger: Carol Tavris, *Anger: The Misunderstood Emotion* (New York: Simon and Schuster, 1982), which deals with the social perspective of anger; and Garret Keizer, *The Enigma of Anger: Essays on a Sometimes Deadly Sin* (San Francisco: Jossey-Bass, 2002). See also Augsburger, *Conflict Mediation across Cultures,* 113–142, for a discussion of cultural differences and the social construction of anger.

17. Because the power imbalance inherent in clergy relationships with laity in their parishes precludes the possibility of a mutual relationship between equal, consenting adults, such relationships are abusive. The fact that the individuals later marry does not mitigate the abuse of power that the pastor exercised over the parishioner. See Marie M. Fortune, *Is Nothing Sacred? When Sex Invades the Pastoral Relationship* (San Francisco: Harper and Row, 1989). At the same time, laypeople have power in congregations because of their baptism, and the health of churches depends on their ability to exercise that power. The both/and principle applies: Laypeople have power and they can be abused.

18. The story of this congregation is also an example of an "afterpastor" situation—one in which there has been a violation of trust by a previous clergyperson or a key lay leader. Noteworthy texts on this topic include: Fortune, *Is Nothing Sacred?*; Beth Ann Gaede, ed., *When a Congregation Is Betrayed: Responding to Clergy Misconduct* (Herndon, VA: Alban Institute, 2006); Nancy Myer Hopkins and Mark Laaser, eds., *Restoring the Soul of a Church: Healing Congregations Wounded by Clergy*

Sexual Misconduct (Collegeville, MN: Liturgical Press, 1995); and Keith Wright, *Religious Abuse: A Pastor Explores the Many Ways Religion Can Hurt as Well as Heal* (Kelowna, BC: Northstone Publishing, 2001). In afterpastor situations, community norms need to be reestablished. Such norms include guidelines for interactions between individuals and, frequently, policies and procedures around handling money, supervision of children, and open meetings and processes (as opposed to secret decision making). The substitution of feelings is common in these situations. In the aftermath of abuse, people may also tend to depend more heavily on cognitive analysis and decision making to the near exclusion of any emotional competence.

19. Making contact is an alternative (positive) behavior. See chapter 2 regarding alternatives to oppressive behaviors, page 61.

Chapter 4

1. Ursula K. Le Guin, "National Book Award Acceptance Speech," *Algol* (November 1973): 14.

2. Eric Berne, MD, *Transactional Analysis in Psychotherapy* (New York: Grove Press, 1961); and *Games People Play: The Psychology of Human Relationships* (New York: Grove Press, 1964). See also Thomas A. Harris, MD, *I'm Okay—You're Okay: A Practical Guide to Transactional Analysis* (New York: Harper and Row, 1967).

3. Berne, *Games People Play*, 23.

4. See Christina Robb, *This Changes Everything: The Relational Revolution in Psychology* (New York: Farrar, Straus, Giroux, 2006) 198–211 for a discussion of Carol Gilligan's use of "voice."

5. Sue Annis Hammond, *The Thin Book of Appreciative Inquiry*, 2nd ed. (Bend, OR: Thin Book Publishing Company, 1998).

6. Mark Lau Branson, *Memories, Hopes, and Conversations: Appreciative Inquiry and Congregational Change* (Herndon, VA: Alban Institute, 2004).

7. Cooperrider and Srivastva first published their ideas about AI as a chapter entitled "Appreciative Inquiry in Organizational Life" in *Research in Organization Change and Development*, vol. 1, ed. William

A. Pasmore and Richard W. Woodman (Greenwich, CT: JAI Press, 1987).

8. David L. Cooperrider and Diana Whitney, *Appreciative Inquiry: A Positive Revolution in Change* (Taos, NM: Corporation for Positive Change, 1999), Appreciative Inquiry Commons, http://appreciativeinquiry.case.edu/intro/whatisai.cfm.

9. Hammond, *Thin Book*, 20, and Branson, *Memories, Hopes, and Conversations*, 139, provide tables of similar assumptions. The summary I offer is based on them. On the last point—how our language creates our reality—Robert Kegan and Lisa Laskow Lahey, who teach at the Harvard Graduate School of Education, talk about how leaders use language to "continuously manufacture nonchange" and how we can develop new "mental machines," grounded in how we talk about what we are doing, to bring about change in *How the Way We Talk Can Change the Way We Work: Seven Languages for Transformation* (San Francisco: Jossey-Bass, 2001), 76.

10. Branson, *Memories, Hopes, and Conversations*, 139.

11. Branson uses "provocative proposals." Hammond uses "provocative propositions."

12. Branson, *Memories, Hopes, and Conversations*, 146–47.

13. These characteristics represent Jean Baker Miller's five good things about healthy relationships, which are explored in chapter 5.

Chapter 5

1. Margaret Bullitt-Jonas, *Holy Hunger: A Memoir of Desire* (New York: Knopf, 1999) 131.

2. Carl Gustav Jung, "Psychology of the Transference," in *The Practice of Psychotherapy,* vol. 16, par. 454, 244, ed. Gerhard Adler et al., *Collected Works*, Bollingen Series 20 (New York: Pantheon, 1954).

3. See Michael Battle, *Reconciliation: The Ubuntu Theology of Desmond Tutu.*

4. Jean Baker Miller and Irene Pierce Stiver, *The Healing Connection: How Women Form Relationships in Therapy and in Life* (Boston: Beacon Press, 1997), 52. The emphasis is the authors'.

5. Ibid., 38.

6. See Leonardo Boff, *Holy Trinity: Perfect Community* (Maryknoll, NY: Orbis Books, 2000).

7. The Hebrew word for the divinity, *Elohim* (literally, "Gods"), is plural in form, yet requires a singular verb—a creative way of treating God as a syntax-busting community.

8. Martin Buber, *The Knowledge of Man: Selected Essays* (New York: Harper & Row, 1965), 75.

9. Carol Gilligan, "In a Different Voice: Women's Conceptions of Self and of Morality," *Harvard Educational Review* 47, no. 4 (November 1977), 484.

10. Gilligan had intended to study men who chose to resist the draft. The military draft ended, therefore she decided to study women who were considering whether to have an abortion.

11. Robb, *This Changes Everything*, 26.

12. Ibid., 31.

13. Jean Baker Miller, *Toward a New Psychology of Women* (Boston: Beacon Press, 1976).

14. See Judith V. Jordan, Alexandra G. Kaplan, Jean Baker Miller, Irene P. Stiver, and Janet L. Surrey, *Women's Growth in Connection: Writings from the Stone Center* (New York: Guilford Press, 1991); Judith V. Jordan, ed., *Women's Growth in Diversity: More Writings from the Stone Center* (New York: Guilford Press, 1997); and Judith V. Jordan, Maureen Walker, and Linda M. Hartling, *The Complexity of Connection: Writings from the Stone Center's Jean Baker Miller Training Institute* (New York: Guilford Press, 2004).

15. Robb, *This Changes Everything*, 153.

16. Miller and Stiver, *The Healing Connection*, 48.

17. Jean Baker Miller, "What Do We Mean by Relationships?" *Work in Progress*, no. 22 (Wellesley, MA: Stone Center, Wellesley College, 1986).

18. Robb, *This Changes Everything*, 154.

19. Miller, "What Do We Mean by Relationships?" 9. The emphasis is Miller's.

20. Janet L. Surrey, "Relationship and Empowerment," in *Women's Growth in Connection: Writings from the Stone Center*, 168.

21. Miller, "What Do We Mean by Relationships?" 11.

22. Robb, *This Changes Everything*, 158.

23. Robb, 161, quoting Jordan speaking at a 1999 colloquium she attended.

24. Miller and Stiver, *The Healing Connection*, 22.

25. Stephen Bergman often writes under the pen name of Samuel Shem. For information on the play, see the Bill W. and Dr. Bob Web site, http://www.billwanddrbob.com/.

26. Shem and Surrey, *We Have to Talk*, 6.

27. See Gilligan, *In a Different Voice*, and Carol Gilligan, Annie G. Rogers, and Deborah L. Tolman, eds., *Women, Girls, and Psychotherapy: Reframing Resistance* (Binghamton, NY: Harrington Park/Haworth Press, 1991.)

28. Stephen J. Bergman, "Men's Psychological Development: A Relational Perspective," *Work in Progress*, no. 48 (Wellesley, MA: Stone Center, Wellesley College, 1991). See also Terrence Real, *I Don't Want to Talk About It: Overcoming the Secret Legacy of Male Depression* (New York: Scribner, 1997).

29. Joyce K. Fletcher, *Disappearing Acts: Gender, Power, and Relational Practice at Work* (Cambridge, MA: The MIT Press, 1999). Fletcher is Professor of Management at the Center for Gender in Organizations at Simmons Graduate School of Management and a Senior Research Scholar of the Jean Baker Miller Training Institute at Wellesley College.

30. Fletcher, *Disappearing Acts*, 84.

31. Ibid.

32. Ibid., 49.

33. Ibid., 51.

34. Ibid., 53.

35. Ibid., 55.

36. Ibid., 64.

37. Ibid.

38. Ibid, 65. I find Fletcher's use of "self" unfortunate. I believe that she is speaking of authenticity or "showing up" as who one is in a relationship rather than an autonomous self apart from relationship. I prefer Gilligan's use of "voice," because voice is a more relational

concept than self and assumes that working to have one's voice heard and valued means working with others who will hear and respond to that voice.

39. Ibid., 67. The emphasis is the author's. Fletcher refers to Lyn Mikel Brown and Carol Gilligan's seminal work *Meeting at the Crossroads* (Boston: Harvard University Press, 1992). See especially page 165 of Brown and Gilligan where they discuss the paradox of women taking "themselves out of relationship for the sake of relationships" (plural).

40. Ibid., 71.

41. Ibid., 68.

42. Ibid., 74.

43. Ibid.

44. Miller, *Toward a New Psychology of Women*. See also Robb, *This Changes Everything*, 325.

45. Fletcher, *Disappearing Acts*, 103.

46. Arlin Rothauge, an Episcopal priest and church consultant, made popular the terms *family*, *pastoral*, *program*, and *corporate* to describe characteristics of different-sized churches. Rothauge studied how congregations of different sizes go about attracting new members. His work was descriptive, not prescriptive or evaluative. The problem that small church leaders describe arises when denominational leaders do not value differences of size and hire staff and promote programs that either benefit larger churches to the exclusion of smaller churches or that assume what works for larger churches will be of benefit for churches of every size. One-size-fits-all programs run contrary to Rothauge's research and subsequent theory. Arlin Rothauge, *Sizing Up a Congregation for New Member Ministry* (New York: The Episcopal Church Center, n.d. [1983]).

47. Fletcher, *Disappearing Acts*, 108.

48. Ibid.

49. Ibid., 109.

Chapter 6

1. Shelley E. Taylor, *The Tending Instinct: How Nurturing Is Essential to Who We Are and How We Live* (New York: Henry Holt and Co.,

2002), 24. Leading up to this quote, Taylor refers to thirty scientific studies that look at what men and women do in response to stress—do they go it alone or turn to others for help? She writes, "Thirty studies show that women draw on their friends, neighbors, and relatives more than men do, whether the stress results from unemployment, cancer, fear of crime, a death in the family, or simple sadness. From a scientific standpoint, this is an amazing consistency. In the social sciences, you rarely see thirty studies all showing the same thing."

2. Stephen J. Bergman, "Men's Psychological Development: A Relational Perspective," 2.

3. Judith Butler, Maxine Elliot Professor in the Departments of Rhetoric and Comparative Literature at the University of California, Berkeley, argues that gender is a reiterated social performance as distinct from the expression of a prior reality. That is, the notion of gender is not essential or natural. She begins by questioning the category "woman" and asks whom it includes and who decides whom it includes. She concludes that notions of "the masculine" and "the feminine" are culturally imposed, not biologically fixed, not binary. See Judith Butler, *Gender Trouble: Feminism and the Subversion of Identity* (New York: Routledge Classics, 1990).

4. My generous use of quotation marks here is to emphasize that race, in this case being white, is socially constructed and to call attention to the fact that no one is actually the color we normally call white. The very use of the term is meant to separate people and to privilege those who are most nearly "white."

5. Antoinette Brown was the first ordained woman minister in the United States on her ordination by the Congregationalist Church on September 15, 1853, but was dismissed in July 1854, evidently by her own wish. She later became a Unitarian. Olympia Brown was ordained by the Universalist denomination in 1863. The Salvation Army ordained both men and women from its founding in 1865. Christian Scientists ordained women beginning in 1876. The Assemblies of God Church was founded and ordained its first woman clergy in 1914. The Northern Baptist Convention ordained women in 1918. AME Zion and Church of the Nazarenes ordained women prior to 1946. More "mainline" Protestant churches ordained female ministers or priests in the following years: United Methodist Church, 1939; Presbyterian Church, 1956 (deacons

in 1923); Episcopalians, 1974 (deacons in 1920); predecessor bodies of the Evangelical Lutheran Church in America, 1970s. See "Chronology of Women's Ordination," World Guide to Women in Leadership, http://www.guide2womenleaders.com/Chronolgy_Ordination.htm.

6. Bergman, "Men's Psychological Development: A Relational Perspective," 2.

7. Ibid., 4. Emphasis is the author's.

8. Terrence Real, *How Can I Get Through to You? Reconnecting Men and Women* (New York: Scribner, 2002), 113.

9. Gilligan, *In a Different Voice*; Mary Pipher, *Reviving Ophelia: Saving the Selves of Adolescent Girls* (New York: Putnam, 1994); Catherine Steiner-Adair, "When the Body Speaks: Girls, Eating Disorders, and Psychotherapy," in Carol Gilligan, Annie G. Rogers, Deborah L. Tolman, eds., *Women, Girls, and Psychotherapy: Reframing Resistance* (Binghamton, NY: The Harrington Park Press, 1991).

10. Judith Jordan, "The Meaning of Mutuality," in Judith V. Jordan, Alexander G. Kaplan, Jean Baker Miller, Irene P. Stiver, Janet L. Surrey, eds., *Women's Growth in Connection: Writings from the Stone Center* (New York: The Guilford Press, 1991), 81–96.

11. Robb, *This Changes Everything*, 307.

12. See Kristin Linklater, *Freeing the Natural Voice* (Drama Book Publishers, 1976). Gilligan's focus on voice was influenced by her study with Linklater, a Scottish-born actress, and Tina Packer, an English-born actress and founder of the American repertory company Shakespeare and Company, based in Lenox, Massachusetts.

13. Robb, *This Changes Everything*, 199.

14. Shem and Surrey, *We Have to Talk*, 63.

15. This desire to preserve the future growth potential of connections is an example of what Fletcher calls "self-achieving" in *Disappearing Acts*, 65.

16. Shem (Bergman) and Surrey, *We Have To Talk*, 66.

17. Ibid.

18. Ibid., 76.

19. Ibid., 80.

20. This is in part what Fletcher refers to as "fluid expertise" in Fletcher, *Disappearing Acts*, 64.

21. Deborah Tannen, *You Just Don't Understand: Women and Men in Conversation* (New York: Ballantine Books, 1990), 77.

22. Though Peer Resources does have an executive team and an advisory board, its purpose is to provide training, resources, and consultation according to a mutual model. See Peer Resources, http://www.peer.ca/peer.html.

23. Shem (Bergman) and Surrey, *We Have To Talk*, 12–37.

24. Peter Senge, *The Fifth Discipline: The Art and Practice of the Learning Organization* (New York: Doubleday, 1990).

25. Chris Argyris and Donald A. Schon, *Organizational Learning: A Theory of Action Perspective* (Reading, MA: Addison-Wesley, 1978).

26. Fletcher (*Disappearing Acts*, 115) quotes Bradford and Cohen, who describe the difficulty of organizational change. "Worker empowerment and participative management programs should have recast the system of leadership and followership, but they have not. They have gotten people to think and experiment, but have not achieved significant reform. Outmoded assumptions about the roles of the leader and the followers block transformation." David Bradford and Allan Cohen, *Power Up: Transforming Organizations through Shared Leadership* (New York: John Wiley and Sons, 1998), xvi.

27. "Gender stereotyping, one of the key barriers to women's advancement in corporate leadership, leaves women with limited, conflicting, and often unfavorable options no matter how they choose to lead," according to a study by Catalyst, a nonprofit organization working to advance opportunities for women and business. The report was based on a survey of 1,231 senior executives from the United States and Europe. One of the key predicaments women face is the too soft/too tough dilemma. "When women act in ways that are consistent with gender stereotypes,"—for example, if they focus on work relationships or express concern for other people's perspectives—"they are viewed as less competent leaders (too soft). When women act in ways that are inconsistent with such stereotypes,"—for example, if they act assertively, focus on work tasks, or display ambition—"they're considered as unfeminine (too tough)." Catalyst, "The Double-Bind Dilemma for Women in Leadership: Damned if You Do, Doomed if You Don't," Catalyst, July 2007, http://www.catalyst.org.

28. Fletcher, *Disappearing Acts*, 116.
29. Ibid.
30. See chapter 5 for further explanations of these terms.
31. Fletcher, *Disappearing Acts*, 130.
32. See 2 Cor. 5:17-19.

Chapter 7

1. Mohandas Gandhi, quoted in Michael W. Potts, "Arun Gandhi Shares the Mahatma's Message," *India-West* 27, no. 13 (February 1, 2002): A34; Arun Gandhi indirectly quoting his grandfather. See also Carmella B'Hahn, "Be the Change You Wish to See: An Interview with Arun Gandhi," *Reclaiming Children and Youth* 10, no. 1 (Spring 2001): 6.

2. Neibuhr wrote this prayer for a service in the Congregational Church of Heath, Massachusetts, where he spent summers. Known as "The Serenity Prayer," it was first printed in a monthly bulletin of the Federal Council of Churches in 1943. John Bartlett, *Familiar Quotations,* 15th ed., ed. Emily Morison Beck (Boston: Little, Brown and Company, 1980), 823.

3. The Holmes-Rahe Scale and other resources for calculating and managing individual stress based on life changes can be found online at Beyond Stretched: Stressed, http://www.geocities.com/beyond_stretched/. See Thomas H. Holmes and Richard Rahe, "The Social Readjustments Rating Scales," *Journal of Psychosomatic Reasearch* 11 (1967): 213–18. See Roy M. Oswald, *Clergy Self-Care: Finding a Balance for Effective Ministry* (Herndon, VA: Alban Institute, 1991), which includes self-assessment tools for looking at stress and burnout.

4. George F. Simons, *Keeping Your Personal Journal* (New York: Paulist Press, 1978), 104–106, includes an exercise called "Soul Country" for private journal use with three conditions for sharing your soul country with a group.

5. This timeline exercise and the EKG (heartbeat) analogy were developed by Bernard F. Swain, with whom I worked at the Paulist Leadership and Renewal Project (Boston) from 1979 to 1982. A similar timeline could be created for Jewish history or the history of any other

religious group. Figure 7.1, "Twenty Centuries of Change," is adapted from Bernard F. Swain © 1980, used with permission.

6. Barbara W. Tuchman, *A Distant Mirror: The Calamitous 14th Century* (New York: Alfred A. Knopf, 1984), 32. *Miserere* is the Latin first word of Psalms 51, 56, and 57 (Hebrew numbering). The reference here is mostly likely to Psalm 51, which had a prominent place in the Divine Office and many ceremonies, including the burial of the dead. It became a popular psalm to set to music, including its earliest known polyphonic setting by Johannes Martini around 1480. The first line of the psalm is, "Have mercy on me, O God, according to your steadfast love; according to your abundant mercy blot out my transgressions."

7. Today there are thirty-seven provinces within the Anglican Communion.

8. See Gil Rendle, "The Roller Coaster of Change," *The Alban Weekly*, January 29, 2007, no. 132, http://www.alban.org/conversation.aspx?id=3670. This short article contains a diagram of a "general sequence of feelings" experienced during a significant change. Though some of the points on the roller coaster are decision options rather than feelings, it is a useful tool for recognizing the importance of processing feelings both individually and as a group during times of significant change.

9. Heifetz and Linsky, *Leadership on the Line*, 107–16. Early in their book, the authors assert that the "hope of leadership lies in the capacity to deliver disturbing news and raise difficult questions in a way that people can absorb, prodding them to take up the message rather than ignore it or kill the messenger" (p. 12). Scientists and those who study the history of ideas talk about the necessary conditions for a revolutionary new idea to emerge. See Thomas S. Kuhn, *The Structure of Scientific Revolutions* (Chicago: University of Chicago Press, 1970); and Christina Robb, *This Changes Everything*, especially chapter 4, "Free Space."

10. I have been dealing primarily with institutional or systemic level change and conflict. See Speed B. Leas, *Discovering Your Conflict Management Style* (Herndon, VA: Alban Institute, 1994), for an excellent resource on personal or individual conflict styles. This booklet allows you to fill out a questionnaire to discover your personal styles of engaging or avoiding conflict. Leas articulates five different styles and their usefulness in different situations.

11. Hopkins and Laaser, eds., *Restoring the Soul of a Church.*

12. As an alternative, after every third or fourth person speaks, a prayer could be said or a hymn could be sung (connecting participants to common underlying values and practices).

Appendix B

1. Cited in Martin Luther King Jr., Address to St. Paul's Church, May 14, 1963, Cleveland Heights, OH.

2. The Southern Poverty Law Center, *Teaching Tolerance* magazine (Spring 2004), http://www.tolerance.org/teach/magazine/features.jsp?p=0&is=34&ar=487.

3. F. Michael Higginbotham, *Race Law: Cases, Commentary, and Questions,* 2nd ed. (Durham, NC: Carolina Academic Press, 2005).

4. William L. Garrison, *Selections from the Writings and Speeches of William Lloyd Garrison* (Boston: R. F. Wallcut, 1852), 140–41.

Appendix D

1. This list is largely selected from a longer list in Owen Chadwick, *A History of Christianity* (London: Weidenfeld & Nicolson, 1995).

Selected Resources

The following is a short list of resources I have found helpful in the work I do consulting and teaching about multiculturalism and transformation. I have emphasized resources on relational theory because I believe they are not well known in faith communities and the potential for transformation from these resources is great.

Antiracism

Authors

Batts, Valerie. "Is Reconciliation Possible: Lessons from Combating 'Modern Racism.'" In *Waging Reconciliation: God's Mission in a Time of Globalization and Crisis*, edited by Ian T. Douglas. New York: Church Publishing, 2002. Offers a model for identifying and changing modern racism and internalized oppression behaviors.

Bowers, Laurene Beth. *Becoming a Multicultural Church* (Cleveland: Pilgrim Press, 2006). Offering stories of moving from a traditional, white church to a multicultural church, the book includes discussions of power and resistance as well as a lengthy multicultural calendar and dates of significance for ethnic and cultural groups. Discusses the struggle of a multiethnic church with GLBT inclusion.

Foster, Charles F. *Embracing Diversity: Leadership in Multicultural Congregations.* Herndon, VA: Alban Institute, 1997. Practical advice for multicultural congregations at all stages of growth.

Higginbotham, F. Michael. *Race Law: Cases, Commentary, and Questions,* 2nd ed. Durham, NC: Carolina Academic Press, 2005. A compendium of cases and commentaries on race, slavery, Reconstruction, segregation, integration. Includes a history timeline and discussions on the nature of race.

Law, Eric A. *The Wolf Shall Dwell with the Lamb: A Spirituality for Leadership in a Multicultural Community.* St. Louis: Chalice Press, 1993. Takes power seriously in looking at multicultural communities.

Kujawa-Holbrook, Sheryl A. *A House of Prayer for All Peoples: Congregations Building Multicultural Community.* Herndon, VA: Alban Institute, 2002. Offers practical suggestions for talking about race and racism in congregations while telling the stories of six multicultural congregations. Includes a forty-six-page annotated bibliography and resource list.

Spellers, Stephanie. *Radical Welcome: Embracing God, The Other, and the Spirit of Transformation* (New York: Church Publishing Incorporated, 2006). A practical theological guide for congregations that want to move from mere inclusivity to welcoming "The Other." Based on two hundred interviews with people in urban, suburban, and rural congregations.

Media and Web Resources

Race: The Power of an Illusion. VHS and DVD, 3 episodes, 56 minutes each. San Francisco: California Newsreel, 2003. An eye-opening series confronting our myths and misconceptions about race through the distinct lenses of science, history, and social institutions.

The Southern Poverty Law Center, *Teaching Tolerance*, Spring 2004. http://www.tolerance.org/teach/magazine/features.jsp?p=0&is=34&ar=487. This issue of the magazine is devoted to the fiftieth anniversary of *Brown v. Board of Education* and the history of school integration in the U.S.

The Tutu Institute for Prayer & Pilgrimage. Supports and enriches spiritual journeys by offering retreats, quiet days, and pilgrimages for people to experience the world as recipients of God's loving grace, and offers stipends for caregivers to provide time for refreshment, reflection, restoration, and renewal. 118 North Washington Street, Alexandria, VA 22314. Phone: (703) 677-5642. E-mail: info@tutuinstitute.org. Web site: www.tutuinstitute.org.

Traces of the Trade: A Story from the Deep North. DVD. Cambridge: Ebb Pod Productions, 2008. A feature documentary in which producer and director Katrina Browne tells the story of her New England ancestors, the largest slave-trading family in U.S. history. Browne and nine fellow descendants retrace the notorious Triangle Trade from Rhode Island to Ghana and Cuba, uncovering the North's hidden complicity in slavery. The film and companion materials are available to congregations and other institutions that wish to engage in the process of truth, repair and reconciliation around the legacy of slavery, with an emphasis on inviting white Americans into this transformative work. Phone: (617) 349-0019. Web site: www.tracesofthetrade.org.

Organizations

California Newsreel. A leading resource center for the advancement of racial justice and diversity, for the study of African American life and history, and for African culture and politics. 500 Third Street, Suite 505, San Francisco, CA 94107. Phone: (415) 284-7800. Web site: www.newsreel.org.

The Kaleidoscope Institute. Directed by Eric Law, the institute offers one-day workshops—"Anti-Racism Orientation Training" and "Basic Skills and Understanding for Leadership in a Diverse Community," as well as workshops that focus more on areas of ministry such as teaching, preaching, intergenerational dialogue, multicultural/multilingual worship, and interfaith engagement. 840 Echo Park Ave., Los Angeles, CA 90026-4209. Phone: (626) 602-5242. Web site: http://www.ladiocese.org/ki.

The Southern Poverty Law Center. An organization internationally known for its tolerance education programs, its legal victories against white supremacists, and its tracking of hate groups. 400 Washington Avenue, Montgomery, AL 36104. Web site: http://www.splcenter.org.

VISIONS, Inc. (Vigorous InterventionS In Ongoing Natural Settings) offers consulting and training for corporations, nonprofit agencies, schools, churches, and the public sector. The consultants represent many backgrounds and work in multicultural teams. 48 Juniper Street, Roxbury, MA 02119. Phone: (617) 541-4100. Web site: www.visions-inc.org.

Transactional Analysis and the Role of Feelings in Transformation

Authors

Berne, Eric. *Transactional Analysis in Psychotherapy.* New York: Grove Press, 1961. The classic text that initiated the study of interpersonal transactions and the role of childhood "scripts" in bringing about personal change.

Harris, Thomas A. *I'm OK—You're Okay: A Practical Guide to Transactional Analysis.* New York: Harper & Row, 1967. A popular approach to TA and game theory.

Willcox, Gloria T. *Feelings: Converting Negatives to Positives.* St. Petersburg, FL: Win-Win Team Publishing, 2001. Her book and "The Feeling Wheel Poster" can be ordered from the publisher at P.O. Box 710, St. Petersburg, FL 33731, or from Willcox by telephone at (727) 347-0832 or by e-mail at gtwillcox@aol.com.

Organization

International Transactional Analysis Association (ITAA). Provides training in transactional analysis. The Web site offers a summary of key TA concepts. 2186 Rheem Drive #B-1, Pleasanton, CA 94588. Phone (925) 600-8110. Web site: www.itaa-net.org.

Relational Theory and Gender

Authors

Belenky, Mary Field, Blythe McVicker Clinchy, Nancy Rule Goldberger, Jill Mattuck Tarule. *Women's Ways of Knowing: The Development of Self, Voice, and Mind.* New York: Basic Books, 1986. Offers a theory of the differences in how women and men understand reality and an analysis of the impact on education and organizations.

Bergman, Stephen J. "Men's Psychological Development: A Relational Perspective," *Work in Progress*, no. 48. Wellesley, MA: Stone Center, Wellesley College, 1991. Posits that men as well as women are motivated by a primary desire for connection and traces where boys become disconnected and, in turn, agents of disconnection.

Bergman, Stephen, and Janet Surrey. *Bill W. and Dr. Bob* (New York: Samuel French, 1987, 2007). This play tells the story of a stockbroker and a surgeon, both alcoholics whose relationship was the genesis of Alcoholics Anonymous. Their relationships with their wives and the wives with one another are also central to the play. The authors are relational theorists.

Butler, Judith. *Gender Trouble: Feminism and the Subversion of Identity.* New York: Routledge Classics, 1990. Questions the categories of "men" and "women" and who decides who is included in them. Asserts gender is culturally "presupposed" and "performed."

Fletcher, Joyce K. *Disappearing Acts: Gender, Power, and Relational Practice at Work.* Cambridge: MIT Press, 1999. Stresses the need organizations have for relational skills and emotional intelligences and how organizations prevent women who exercise these skills from advancing.

Gilligan, Carol. *In a Different Voice.* Cambridge: Harvard University Press, 1982. Challenges traditional universal theories of moral development and posits a relational alternative to decision making.

Jordan, Judith V., Alexandra G. Kaplan, Jean Baker Miller, Irene P. Stiver, Janet L. Surrey. *Women's Growth in Connection: Writings from the Stone Center.* New York: Guilford Press, 1991. Essays on women's development, mutuality, empathy, power, anger, and therapeutic change.

Jordan, Judith V., ed. *Women's Growth in Diversity: More Writings from the Stone Center.* New York: The Guilford Press, 1997. Includes several essays about relational theory and issues of diversity, especially concerning race, gender, and sexuality.

McIntosh, Peggy. "White Privilege and Male Privilege: A Personal Account of Coming to See Correspondences through Work in Women's Studies." Wellesley Centers for Women Working Paper No. 189. Wellesley, MA: Wellesley Centers for Women, 1988. Includes a list of more than forty everyday skin-color privileges from which white people benefit.

Miller, Jean Baker. *Toward a New Psychology of Women*. Boston: Beacon Press, 1976. Analyzes gender and power in society and squarely places relationships at the center of human development.

Miller, Jean Baker, and Irene Pierce Stiver. *The Healing Connection: How Women Form Relationships in Therapy and in Life*. Boston: Beacon Press, 1997. Argues that the value women attach to relationships is not misplaced. Rather relationships lead to successful growth and development.

Robb, Christina. *This Changes Everything: The Relational Revolution in Psychology*. New York: Farrar, Straus, Giroux, 2006. Traces the history of the relational psychology movement from its origins in the civil rights, feminist, and antiwar movements.

Shem, Samuel, and Janet Surrey. *We Have to Talk: Healing Dialogues between Women and Men*. New York: Basic Books, 1998. Based on working with thousands of couples, presents common relational impasses and ways to avoid them.

Walker, Maureen, and Wendy B. Rosen, eds. *How Connections Heal: Stories from Relational-Cultural Therapy*. New York: Guilford Press, 2004. This practice-oriented casebook illustrates how relational-cultural theory translates into therapeutic action.

Organizations, DVDs, and Web Resources

Bergman, Stephen, and Janet Surrey. *Bill W. and Dr. Bob: The Original Off-Broadway Production*. DVD. Produced by Northern Light Productions (Boston, 2007). DVD of the play about the origins of Alcoholics Anonymous, written by two leading relational theorists. Filmed on location at the New World Stage, New York, NY, and available through the Hazelden Foundation. Phone: (800) 328-9000. Web site: www.hazelden.org.

Catalyst. A nonprofit, corporate membership, research and advisory organization working globally with businesses and the professions to build inclusive environments and expand opportunities for women and business. 120 Wall Street, 5th Floor, New York, NY 10005. Phone: (212) 514-7600. Web site: www.catalyst.org.

National Women's Law Center. Works to overcome gender disparity in education, employment, and health care. Good online resources. 11 Dupont Circle, Suite 800, Washington, DC 20036. Phone: (202) 588-5180. Web site: www.nwlc.org.

World Guide to Women in Leadership. A Web resource about women in civil and ecclesiastical leadership. Web site: www.guide2womenleaders.com.

Change Theory

Authors

Farber-Robertson, Anita. *Learning While Leading: Increasing Your Effectiveness in Ministry.* Herndon, VA: Alban Institute, 2000. Adaptation of Chris Argyris's reflective action theory for church leaders.

Heifetz, Ronald A., and Marty Linsky. *Leadership on the Line: Staying Alive through the Dangers of Leading.* Boston: Harvard Business School Press, 2003. Practical advice for bringing about adaptive change in organizations.

Kotter, John P. *Leading Change.* Boston: Harvard Business School Press, 1996. Distinguishes leadership from management. Outlines an eight-stage process for bringing about change in organizations.